STILL HERE

STILL HERE

An Autobiography

HARDY AMIES

WEIDENFELD AND NICOLSON
LONDON

ISBN 0 297 78276 2

Typeset by Deltatype, Ellesmere Port
Printed in Great Britain by
Butler and Tanner Ltd.,
Frome and London

Contents

LIST OF ILLUSTRATIONS vii
ACKNOWLEDGEMENTS ix
PREFACE xi

1 *Early Years* 1
2 *The War* 30
3 *Savile Row* 49
4 *By Appointment* 84
5 *Living Label* 123
6 *Fifty Years of Fashion* 143
7 *Moi* 161

INDEX 187

Illustrations

BETWEEN PAGES 20 AND 21

1 Mary Amies, Hardy's mother (*author's collection*)
2 With sister, Peg (*author's collection*)
3 Aged six, in Miss Gray coat (*author's collection*)
4 At Brentwood School (*author's collection*)
5 The Vernet–Barbarroux family (*author's collection*)
6 The von Claer family (*author's collection*)
7 'Panic' (*by courtesy of Condé Nast*)
8 Early days at Lachasse (*author's collection*)
9 The New Look anticipated (*by courtesy of Condé Nast, photograph: Nepo*)
10 Ramillies Barracks (*author's collection*)
11 After the parachute jump (*author's collection*)
12 Designing the wartime collection (*author's collection*)
13 14 Savile Row in 1945 (*Roland Haupt*)
14 Savile Row restored (*author's collection*)
15 In the workroom at Savile Row (*Keystone Press Agency, photograph: Chris Ware*)
16 The young *couturier* (*Vogue Studio, photograph: Roland Haupt*)

BETWEEN PAGES 52 AND 53

17 Virginia Cherrill (*by courtesy of Sotheby's, London, photograph: Cecil Beaton*)
18 'The New Mayfair Edwardians', outside 14 Savile Row (*Norman Parkinson*)
19 With Alexis ffrench (*author's collection*)
20 Neil 'Bunny' Roger (*Norman Parkinson*)
21 The New Look, outside the National Gallery (*Norman Parkinson*)
22 My first *Vogue* cover (*by courtesy of Condé Nast, photograph: Norman Parkinson*)
23 Setting off for Buckingham Palace (*Keystone Press Agency, photograph: Chris Ware*)
24 'The Queen Dazzles Them' (*by kind permission of the Daily Express*)
25 The Silver Jubilee, the Queen at St Paul's (*BBC Hulton Picture Library, photograph: Serge Lemoine*)
26 The 'official' Silver Jubilee picture (*Camera Press, photograph: Peter Grugeon*)
27 Short evening dress, Erik cartwheel hat (*by courtesy of Condé Nast, photograph: Honeyman*)

BETWEEN PAGES 148 AND 149

28 Dotted tulle evening dress (*by courtesy of Condé Nast, photograph: Norman Parkinson*)

29 Circular skirted dress (*by courtesy of Condé Nast, photograph: Henry Clarke*)

30 Wenda Parkinson at Hyde Park Corner (*Norman Parkinson*)

31 Encrusted evening jacket (*David Bailey*)

32 Rose pink twill cape-coat (*by courtesy of Condé Nast, photograph: Vernier*)

33 Wool check suits with velvet collars (*Hardy Amies Ltd, photograph: Christopher Moore*)

34 Prince and Princess Michael of Kent (*Norman Parkinson*)

35 Miss Jane McNeill marries the Earl of Dalkeith, 1953 (*by courtesy of the Duchess of Buccleuch, photograph: Lenare*)

36 Lady Elizabeth Kerr marries the Earl of Dalkeith, 1981 (*by courtesy of the Marchioness of Lothian, photograph: Norman Parkinson*)

BETWEEN PAGES 180 AND 181

37 The classic man's blazer (*Hardy Amies Ltd, photograph: Christopher Moore*)

38 The Queen in yellow coat and spotted turban (*Fox Photos*)

39 The Queen and Mrs Ronald Reagan, Hollywood (*Anwar Hussein*)

40 Two trouser suits (*Hardy Amies Ltd, photograph: Christopher Moore*)

41 White silk coat (*Hardy Amies Ltd, photograph: Christopher Moore*)

42 Pont Street (*author's collection*)

43 22 Eldon Road (*author's collection*)

44 Chesham Place (*author's collection*)

45 The garden at Langford (*Georges Lévêque*)

46 17b Eldon Road (*author's collection*)

47 The Old School, Langford (*Country Life, photograph: Alex Starkey*)

Acknowledgements

The enthusiasm of Lord Weidenfeld started this book off. It was finished because of the patience and pertinacity of Isabella Forbes, my editor.

I am immensely indebted to Norman Parkinson for the photograph that he took especially for the dust-jacket of *Still Here* and for allowing me to make so many reproductions of his photographs. Beatrix Miller was most generous in opening wide the archives of *Vogue*. To her, and to all the photographers, I am deeply grateful for permission to reproduce. I am also grateful to Michael Shea, Press Secretary to the Queen, for his valuable help and advice.

I wish to thank members of my staff and of my family for their forebearance and assistance: in particular my sister, Rosemary, Ken Fleetwood, Roger Whiteman, Sarah Graham and last, but by no means least, Peter Hope Lumley.

Finally I would like to thank all those friends and customers who have helped me to be 'still here'. Some of them are mentioned in the book, many are not – of them I ask one final favour – that they should not feel in any way offended; the editor's scissors were ruthless.

Preface

In 1984 I shall have completed fifty years in the fashion business; I shall also be seventy-five years old. I was twenty-four when, on 1 February 1934 I started work at Lachasse, an *haute couture* dress house, then as now in Farm Street, off Berkeley Square.

'How was it?' asked my mother, when I arrived back that evening. 'It was just like going home,' I answered. Indeed I was completely at ease everywhere in the business. Had not my first grown-up friends been tailors, fitters and dressmakers? Had I not almost been born on the steps of the dress shop where my mother worked?

This deep seated familiarity with the life of a dress house compensated for my lack of technical training. The fluent French and German, learned during my years abroad, when I had had glimpses of the rich in Paris, on the Riviera and in the larger cities of Germany, helped to remove the gaucheries of a suburban boy.

The story of that boy's progress to become, for over thirty years, one of the dressmakers appointed to serve the Queen, of how he became the head of a business designing and distributing men and women's clothes over much of the English speaking world and beyond, is the story of this book.

In 1954 I wrote a first volume of autobiography, *Just So Far* (Collins). Much water has passed under the bridge since then but I hope that I shall be forgiven for repeating the story of my childhood, my education, my early struggles and entry into the *couture* business, and of how I set up shop in the bombed elegance of 14 Savile Row.

One evening during the war I was a guest at a dinner given by Viva King, a much loved hostess. Fellow diners were a mother, her two Etonian sons, and the author Norman Douglas. Wine had flowed. 'Do you think there should be sex education in schools?' someone asked Norman Douglas, who was a little drowsy. 'Of c-course,' he stuttered, 'so long as they tell how much fun it is.'

I hope that this book will tell how much fun there has been in my life.

1

Early Years

I was born in Maida Vale, London, in 1909. The Amies family came from Kent. Grandfather Edwin Amies owned a small works in Maidstone which made dandy-rolls, with which the water marks in paper are printed. His father would appear to have been a farmer from Loose, just outside Maidstone. That is all the authentic information that I can gather about the family.

I can remember Grandfather Amies, who died in the First World War. He kept up a modest establishment in Ashford Road, and I remember the house, a semi-detached early Victorian villa with a pleasant sunny garden running down to the river. My recollection is that the house was run by my unmarried aunts, but I suppose there were also some servants. The claim to the title of carriage folk, in that a vehicle took my grandfather to his work each day in the latter years of his life, is contradicted by my father's assertion that the conveyance was a hired cab and that the coachman was his uncle.

My father and my aunts all declare that the old boy was a 'bit of a dog' in his day. The fact that my grandmother died quite young excuses his frequent trips to London and, on one or two occasions, to Paris. With his family he was rather a tyrant, and particularly with his daughters. It was indeed true that his three sons were all tall and good-looking: my father, the youngest, even verging on handsome. The girls were equally tall with, however, large feet and hands to match. When the old man died there was found to be very much less money in the family than was expected, the establishment at Ashford Road having been kept up more lavishly than he could afford. But my mother always spoke of him with the greatest affection. He was, she said, entranced with stories of the dress establishment in which she worked. He also viewed with both loud-voiced and whispered approval her trim figure and London clothes. This did not make my

I

mother's position in the family any easier.

All three aunts were involved in the snobbery of late Victorian church-going, middle-class provincial society, and in their crueller moments dubbed my mother a 'shop-girl'. After my grandfather's death the business was carried on by my eldest uncle, but he had practically no business sense, and after his death during the last war the dandy-roll business was dissolved.

My own father, the youngest of the three sons, was sent away to be educated at Sutton Vallance School. Because of a certain financial instability at home, as soon as he had finished his schooling he went to London to become an articled architect; but for some reason or other he did not completely finish his studies and soon accepted a salaried post in the valuation department of the London County Council. It was at this stage that he met my mother.

My mother was a Hardy. Her mother came from a family of small shopkeepers in Windsor and her father kept the Griffin Hotel, Kingston. He was a bad lot, and proved so unsatisfactory a landlord that the Griffin Hotel was sold, and with the proceeds my grandmother bought a glass and china shop in Dorking. He was no better a husband than a landlord and quite shortly afterwards was shipped off, with my grandmother's help, to Costa Rica, leaving her sixth child still unborn.

I am not quite clear as to how my mother came into the court dressmaking business in London. As soon as it was possible she was sent to London to earn her living. I think that both my mother and Elsie Chapple, a friend of the family, started working in an establishment run by a Madame Durrant in Bond Street. One evening in 1905 my father saw her looking into the window of Chappell's music shop in Bond Street and followed her to her Bayswater bus which was to bear her home to her lodgings. This apparently straightforward pick-up was made respectable by my father being introduced to my grandmother Hardy soon afterwards.

They were married in 1906 and had a flat in Delaware Mansions, Elgin Avenue, Maida Vale, where I was born. Two or three years afterwards they moved to a small house in Alperton, Middlesex, which still had some aspects of a small country village on the banks of the canal.

My visual memories of the house at Alperton are very happy

indeed. I have never been back to look at it since we left and prefer only to think of the black and white tiled path leading to the front door which seemed always to need one of those black and white striped blinds to protect its white paint from the sunshine. At the back was a minute garden, my father's pride and joy, and where he grew magnificent crimson roses. It was August 1914.

The First World War not unnaturally dimmed some of the happiness of the little home. Lying in bed I so often heard my father's fine baritone voice coming up from the tiny drawing room singing 'I Hear You Calling Me', 'Grey Days', 'The Indian Love Lyrics' and other songs that he liked. He had a fine voice, and was for some time a paid chorister at St Mark's, Hamilton Terrace. He was summoned from a choir practice to be informed of my imminent birth.

My mother continued to work, even though she was married, at a firm called Machinka in Dover Street and with Madame Durrant. The manageress of either one or both of these establishments was a Miss Gray. She left to start her own business and took my mother with her. My mother had started her business life as a junior in the showroom but was by now a fully-fledged saleswoman. Miss Gray's new establishment was in Brook Street, Mayfair. The business quickly prospered and further premises were taken next door. My mother was such an important part of the establishment that, quite contrary to the etiquette of the day, she was kept working until dangerously near the time of my birth. I like to think that I was almost born on the steps of a court dressmaker.

Miss Gray was not a dress designer. She bought some models in Paris and made others to her own design, which she never pretended were anything other than adaptations of Paris models. She did, however, call herself a court dressmaker and did have the patronage of court circles.

As regards the number of personnel employed, the house was, even by modern standards, quite large: five or six workrooms and, of course, an embroidery room.

My mother went to work by Underground from Alperton Station to Bond Street tube. In those days the house was open on a Saturday morning, and when I was old enough to travel as a great treat I was taken with her. I was outrageously spoiled by the staff, many of whom I clearly remember. Miss English was the stock-keeper, and I was often placed in the stockroom and allowed to play with bits of material to keep me quiet. Miss Fowler and Miss Cook were skirt and bodice fitters respectively, and also good friends; but often this friendship could not stand the strain of the battle that inevitably took place at the waistline, where each other's territory would be hotly disputed. Miss Cook left during the First World War, but Miss Fowler continued working until an honourable retirement. Maud Beard, who became a fitter of mine, was an old apprentice of Miss Fowler's. In due course Miss Gray married and became Mrs Fred Shingleton.

In 1915 my father joined up and my sister was born, and the two events were enough to cause my mother to leave business for ever. But she remained in fairly constant contact with the establishment, and had become such a close friend of Miss Gray, or Mrs Shingleton, that the latter had gone so far as to promise to educate me should any mishap befall my father. Members of the staff often visited us still, and I would sometimes persuade my mother to call in at Brook Street if ever we were in London. But these contacts were to become slenderer as the years advanced and often only renewed at Christmas time.

My father, who had been in the Sharp-Shooters of the City of London Yeomanry, soon became captain and adjutant of his regiment, and was before long sent to the front. My mother let the house and carried my sister and me off on a series of visits to relatives or long sojourns in various lodgings.

I have very happy memories of living in vicarages and farmhouses in the vicinity of the camps in Kent: of regimental concerts, of the sweet soapy flavour of stone ginger beer fetched out by mess orderlies; and of once being taken in a dog-cart to Whitstable by a subaltern where I was given three oysters and a grey silk knitted tie.

I was sent to a kindergarten in Wembley, and afterwards to various establishments convenient to where we were then living, but shortly before the end of the war we seem to have settled back in Alperton again because I was sent to Latymer Upper School at Hammersmith, travelling there each day by Underground. It was in the playground of that school that we were called out to cheer the Armistice in November 1918.

My father returned from the Army with the restless ambition natural in a young man who had risen from being a sort of office boy in the London County Council to a position of importance in his regiment. However, things everywhere were expanding with re-markable rapidity, and nowhere so much as with the London County Council which had on hand vast housing schemes. My father was quickly sent down to the Essex marshes and told to negotiate for the purchase of land on which a housing estate was to be built which was ultimately to be known as Becontree. It was considered essential that he should live on the spot and he was given a small early Victorian farmhouse lying bleakly in the midst of acres of rhubarb fields to the north of the old Southend Road. It had the chilly address of Gale Street House, Barking, but neither my sister, aged four, nor I, aged ten, was deterred by the flatness of the countryside, nor the gauntness of the name. The house was four-square and plain, but indeed was a farmhouse, and attached to it was a series of black tarred and thatched barns: a change from the streets of Wembley, which by now had become overcrowded, and where the rural charm of Alperton had completely disappeared. We gladly exchanged the red Richmond roses for the delights of a good half-acre of orchard.

I was promptly sent to Brentwood School, having to go there by train for a term because there was no room in the boarding houses. The school was then just emerging from the grammar school chrysalis to a full-fledged public school.

I cannot say that I was anything but happy at school, although I was bad at both football and cricket and no other form of sport was encouraged.

I did not suffer from my lamentable performance on the playing fields because I was quickly to win a certain renown on the stage of the school theatricals. The Christmas term was always the happiest for me because it was in December that the play was produced, by tradition either Shakespeare or Sheridan.

After having made a successful début as Jessica in *The Merchant of Venice* in which I looked ravishing in a long black wig, I was only allowed various unimportant roles in plays which in themselves seemed at that time unexciting: *Henry IV Part II* or *A Midsummer Night's Dream*. These were all produced in the Tudor Old School by hissing gaslight. The opening of the new Memorial Hall, its stage gloriously professional with its electric light and swishing drop curtain, was celebrated with a superb production of *The Rivals* in which I somewhat deviously obtained the part of Mrs Malaprop. I am proud to say that my performance was very well received.

At Christmas time the housemaster's wife organized parties for the boys. At one of these I remember she asked us to wear fancy dress which we were to make ourselves. I do not think I was surprised at winning the first prize: it seemed to me so natural that I should be the best at that sort of thing. Once a week she received us in her own sitting room to read aloud: Kipling and Rider Haggard being the authors I remember best. My affection and respect for her were not impaired by my being told by a friend in the town that she was heard to order at the bacon counter at Sainsbury's two pounds of best back and five pounds of scraps for the boys.

As regards learning, I just scrambled my way through everything. I bitterly reproach the history master for having taught me history so badly. If only I had known then what toil this lack of knowledge was to cause me in later years as I tried to catch up.

I also showed no interest in modern languages and only discovered in later years that I had quite a talent for them. The only subject I ever made any stir in was English composition and English literature in general. I had also better mention that in art and drawing I was a little below the average.

Howard Hayden arrived straight from Cambridge to become English master. He came 'trailing clouds of glory' of the ADC with him as he had played Bosola in a particularly successful production of *The Duchess of Malfi*. He immediately took over control of the school theatricals and was responsible for a vigorous production of *Twelfth Night* in which I played Malvolio. His tremendous enthusiasm for the English language made a great impact on the Upper Sixth, at which I had then arrived. I know that I desperately wanted his admiration, or at least approval. Sometimes I got it but I also got some very sound criticism. He told me I was enthusiastic and quick-witted but also extremely shallow and insincere in many ways. I remember we were doing Tennyson, and after describing Hallam's death he asked the class what they thought Tennyson's next move should have been. 'Go and look for another Hallam,' I answered promptly without thinking. That was the first time I had ever been called a cynic.

I have the feeling that in those last years at school I had rather been pushed ahead into classes to which I did not properly belong. I may easily have given the impression of being more mature than I was, for certainly I was terribly backward in Latin and all forms of math-

6

ematics: indeed in all subjects where any sort of accuracy was essential. If the school was anxious for honours on the playing field it was equally so for scholarships at the universities. It was quite out of the question for my father to send me to university without some sort of aid. My masters thought that I had quite a good chance of winning a scholarship, and in order to give me experience in sitting for such examinations I was made to try for school certificate, and also to sit for an open scholarship at Cambridge before I was really ready for either. I failed both.

In the meantime, at home, the Becontree estate was growing to alarming proportions and my father had settled down to be a person of some importance in the neighbourhood. He became the principal resident agent for the London County Council, which meant that he would stay on there and manage the housing estate after it had been built. It was not completed until just after the Second World War.

The question of what I was going to do with my life was often discussed at home. There were the usual family arguments and I am sure that I was tiresome and petulant. Howard Hayden, however, put the idea into my head that I ought to become a journalist and, hearing of this, through the good offices of our local MP it was arranged for my father and myself to have an interview with R. D. Blumenfeld, the editor of the *Daily Express*. I can remember very little of the interview except that I noticed that my father was very nervous. Blumenfeld did all the talking and counselled me to read a lot, especially Macaulay. Some comment by Howard Hayden sprang to my mind. 'Oh, I couldn't read Macaulay,' I said. 'He writes journalese.' Passing over my tactlessness he went on to say that he needed new writers, but that he wanted none who had either Oxford or Cambridge degrees. 'Spend the money letting him travel,' he said to my father. 'France and Germany each for at least a year, and then come to see me again, and I will give him a job.'

Now ours was not the sort of family that took even holidays abroad. My father had been to France and Belgium during the First World War. My mother had never been out of England. They had, however, sent me for a two-week tour in Belgium with the school OTC, and the following year for a month to Touraine, it having been thought possible that I would attempt to take a scholarship at Cambridge in French and English.

7

I cannot remember how strongly Howard Hayden approved of the scheme suggested by Blumenfeld, but he certainly arranged for me to go as soon as possible to teach at the English school at Antibes which was run by an acquaintance of his. Here I went in the Easter of 1927.

Looking back over my school years, I can see that I had at an early age acquired the knack of getting on with my fellowmen. I was too critical and sharp-tongued to be really popular, and Howard Hayden's criticism that I was insincere is true in the sense that I never achieved deep or lasting friendships because I always had a feeling that everything was so temporary and that I would move on to something much more interesting.

I cannot move on to the story of my years in France and Germany – years that were to prove so important in my life and in the formation of my character – without going into the question of my relationship with my mother.

It will have been seen that her independent spirit had helped her to climb out of a background of near-poverty to make in a modest way a successful business career which she followed by a successful marriage: successful in the sense that she had married into a family of better standing than her own, a man who was intensely popular owing to his good looks, his pleasant singing voice, and an altogether attractive and high-spirited personality. His greatest faults were that he was easily gullible, too enthusiastic and optimistic. She, on the other hand, had undoubtedly what is called an inferiority complex. She had above the average good looks and figure, indeed a well-cut face on a long neck, and extraordinarily pretty hands, but she had been born with a slight cast in one eye which at moments, in certain lights or when she was particularly tired, became most marked. In childhood a painful operation had failed to correct it. She always remained most self-conscious about this defect, and was shy of meeting strangers.

Intelligent and sensitive, she could appreciate the security and poise of the women she waited on at Brook Street and, measuring them against the dinginess and mediocrity of her circle of acquaintances at Becontree, she was inclined to shut herself off and to centre herself on the family. My father was not a very ambitious man. He had a reasonably comfortable house and was provided with a motorcar and a driver. True, his income was so modest that it strained to the utmost to keep me and my sister at school at the same time, but by now a senior official on the staff of the London County Council, he would – with the passing of years and without much extra effort on his part – succeed automatically to higher posts and could look forward to an honourable retirement with an adequate pension.

By now the farms around Gale Street, and elsewhere, had completely disappeared in a rash of little houses. Our first friends in the neighbourhood, who were nearly all farmers, were gradually disappearing, and there was indeed very little opportunity for my mother, had she sought it, to make a circle of friends there. Looking back, of course, I realize that there was around us a tremendous experiment going on – the lifting up of a vast population, mostly from the East End of London, and planting it down in a new town – an operation of great social significance. To my father, however, it was humdrum bread and butter. He was only occupied with daily problems of collecting rents, seeing that tenants did not move without paying, or leave bugs behind. He was, in truth, the landlord waging an eternal battle with the tenant. On the whole, it is only fair to say that my mother found life very monotonous, as it indeed was. She had no intellectual resources of her own. Also, she was completely unmusical, and I reproach her for not having encouraged my father in his music.

It would be too much to say that there was any feeling of want, but certainly there was ever present a feeling of lack of money. This is surely no different from any such home. But my mother had a great sense of quality, both in clothes and in the decoration of our home. My father was generous and easy-going, so that they were constantly overspending, not to any marked degree but always to such an extent that there was never any margin for special occasions. But always somehow money for holidays was scraped together, and certainly as far as we children were concerned they managed to spare enough to let us go on trips and jaunts. These, of course, were mostly to London.

I wonder if we were even an emotional family. Certainly there was no marked display of affection. Even present-giving was kept to a minimum and a Christmas present was often a new overcoat or a pair of shoes. My sister, six years younger than I was, I seem to have seen very little. Gentle and capable in every possible way, she had no interest whatsoever in clothes, which proved a great disappointment to my mother. So everything was laid on for me to be my mother's favourite child, but I was self-willed enough, and she too intelligent, too sacrificing I would like to say, to allow herself to have anything of the possessive mother about her, and, as will be seen, I quickly left the family circle. If I say escaped that would mean that there was something unpleasant that I wished to avoid. There was really nothing unpleasant: there was much more a nothingness. I think both my mother and father knew this. Certainly my mother was intensely ambitious for me, but that I should become a dress designer was never mentioned, except in a joking way.

Aunt Louie was my family's adopted aunt. Her real name was Mlle Louise Probet-Piolat. I do not know whether she worked at Machinka's or at Madame Durrant's: I know she did not work at Miss Gray's, although she knew her very well indeed. She was a very grand French fitter, and it was she who had persuaded my mother and father to live in Maida Vale, as she already had a flat there. It is from this flat that I have the impression of sunshine and lace curtains: lace indeed was everywhere, for I remember she had innumerable cushions made of this material. She also bred canaries, and the flat, tiny as it was, seemed filled with their golden voices. She visited us constantly after my mother had retired, always bringing an air of luxury and elegance with her. She always seemed to be wearing a beautiful coat of lustrous black Astrakhan. In 1924 she went to live in a flat in Nice. It was from here that she was to keep an eye on me when I was sent to Antibes three years later.

The journey to Antibes seemed altogether very exciting. I remember I left on St George's Day 1927. At first sight the English school seemed pleasant enough. It catered especially for very young children who were mostly brought there by their American and English parents who then continued their journeys on down to Italy or other parts of France. The oldest pupil was the son of the two owners of the school. He was so outrageously spoiled that it had to be arranged that he won all games. My hopes of delicious French food were quickly dashed. The schoolmaster's wife explained that I was not to expect an English breakfast as we were now in France: by noon she was explaining that it was far too hot to eat a French luncheon. The consequence was that I seemed to spend most of the meagre pocket money that my father could spare me on fresh bread and huge bars of *chocolat Menier*. I was miserable in that glorious sunshine having to stay indoors all day and teach little American children barely more than their multiplication tables and how to spell three-letter words; but I was more miserable still when about four o'clock I would be told to take the whole lot on to the beach; for here I would find the laughing crowd of boys and girls, brown from the day's sun, too galling a sight to bear. Once a month, however, when my allowance arrived, I would take myself to the Casino at Juan-les-Pins, trying to imagine that I belonged to the glittering world there; or else I would go into Nice to dance with my friend Mollie David at the Negresco, or negligently to sip Benedictine, which I refused to believe wasn't an elegant drink in the great heat.

Aunt Louie, who had been brought up in a tough school, thought most of my complaints ridiculous, but she did eventually tell me of a French family who, she knew, were seeking a boy to go and teach their sons English. At the interview Madame Vernet-Barbarroux and I got on so well that as soon as it could be honourably arranged I left the school at Antibes and joined her in a dark little flat near the station at Nice. Here she lived with her mother, who took snuff all day, and three sons, the eldest being about my own age. We did not stay in the flat long in the intense July heat, but moved to Le Cannet du Luc in the Var. Here Mme Vernet owned a *propriété* jointly with her brother. The house was a sort of citadel up in Le Vieux Cannet, a village almost totally abandoned by the inhabitants, who had moved down below to be near the railway station. Here I spent three wonderfully happy months. The boys had no more intention of learning English than I had of teaching them. The whole family, in a typical French way, showed each other great kindness which was also extended to me. I shall never forget the long rambles through the vineyards which clothed the sides of the hills, to seek out the best bunches of the Muscat grapes. In this isolated spot I had ample opportunities for reading, and Mme Vernet, who was not ill-read, introduced me to Guy de Maupassant.

By saving my small salary and pocket money from home, I had enough money to take me to Paris. I stopped at Avignon and Marseilles on the way, and met my mother and father in Paris at the end of a two-week holiday which they were taking. Their intention was to see how I could instal myself in Paris in the same way as I had in the south of France. Miss Gray indirectly gave me an introduction to a man who ran a business of carriers and customs agents. It was a very reputable firm, known for the quick delivery of parcels between London and Paris. He engaged me at a salary of one pound a week. I was to help in the filling out of the forms and declarations for these parcels, most of which were from the big French silk houses to the London dressmakers.

Before returning to England my parents saw me installed in a tiny room in an *hôtel meublé* in the Place Henri IV. Mr Stockwell's offices were in the Rue St Denis. I had to be there at eight in the morning, and seldom left before eight at night. My great friend was the man who worked at the desk next to me. In spite of the fact that he had to keep a large family of small children on what must have been very slender earnings, he never stopped laughing and joking. In between delectable narratives he would join me in a little battle we waged against the rather surly head of the department. At noon we would both go across the road to a sort of communal kitchen where we bought a huge plate of *boeuf à la mode* – or whatever was the *plat du jour* – a long roll of bread and a litre of wine each. This, with cheese and fruit, we would eat on the packing cases in one of the warehouses. We would then go to a nearby café and throw dice for coffee laced with liqueurs, or rather spirits, mostly *marc*. By this time, of course, I was ready to fall down; but I never did so except with propriety, when we would both collapse on a friendly bale until the office reopened between 3 and 3.30 p.m.

This life left me little time to see either the sights of Paris or to make friends, but I did have an introduction to the Paris correspondent of the *Sunday Times* – named Barker. He introduced me to a circle of fairly prosperous people who lived in the Etoile neighbourhood, but it seemed to me that a great many of the entertainments given by the younger members of this group consisted of bottle parties, and the cost of a clean white stiff shirt, added to the thirty-five francs required for the bottle of champagne, was often too high for me. Although I enjoyed these peeps into a world which was far more elegant than I had ever seen before, I did prefer to spend my pocket money on seats at the theatre. I regret to say my choice at the Comédie Française was not always wise: I can remember several terrible little domestic tragedies. However, I remember being delighted with the Théâtre de l'Atelier, where Charles Dullin was working. But on the whole I have very much the impression that I could have done more with those three months in Paris. Most of the time I was lonely and discontented, but by the time I had returned to England at Christmas I had learned to speak French fairly fluently, if nothing more.

Now the plan was for me to go to Germany. Here we had no connections whatever, but my eldest Aunt Hardy had heard of a vicarage in a village on the Rhine which took in young boarders and students, such as I was.

At the beginning of February I set off for the Pfarrhaus, Bendorf-am-Rhein. My destination turned out to be a fairly large eighteenth-century house, in the midst of an ugly little village nestling on a dull stretch of the Rhine between Coblenz and Bonn. The house belonged to the local Protestant parson, Pfarrer Ernst von Claer, and his family. There were two sons, about my own age, and a daughter. I cannot say that Ernst von Claer was very generous in his outlook, or that he kept a very hospitable table, but his wife and unmarried sister, who completed the household, were kindness itself. The house was warm in that over-heated German fashion, smelling strongly of the powdered coal dust that they pressed into briquettes with which they fed the iron stove. There was much pleasant old furniture in the high rooms, and across the narrow cobbled street there was a large shady garden entered by large fine iron gates: within, tall trees and a Swiss Family Robinson summerhouse and much fruit, which the family appeared to preserve endlessly.

Spring seemed to come earlier that year and I well remember sitting in that sunny garden in February with some of the other English guests, poring over my German grammar. There was a constant stream of guests over the year, but they would diminish to a trickle, often leaving me alone, during the winter months. I immediately started German lessons because my father had agreed to pay for my lodgings in full for six weeks, but after that I was to return to the old system of merely receiving pocket money from him – I think it was about £2 10s a month – while I was to try to earn enough for my basic keep. The von Claers had, of course, a large circle of friends and acquaintances in the neighbourhood, mostly from the professional and industrial classes. The vicarage, being the old family house of Frau von Claer, was visited by many members of the family, some of whom had married well into powerful and rich families of the Ruhr.

Frau von Claer aunt lived in another house in the village, and, in order to help keep it up on an income which had been greatly diminished by the post-war inflation of the mark, had let off a floor to the manager of a local factory where glazed wall tiles were made. The manager was a bright-eyed, lively little north German from Bremen called Johann Witte, who was a constant visitor to the house, known to all as Jonny. He had come to Bendorf to manage the factory which belonged to a Dutchman who visited it but rarely. Jonny had been trained in a large similar factory where his uncle and father had worked before him. Such a position was a considerable advancement for him and he threw himself into his work with great enthusiasm. On being asked by the von Claers for his assistance in finding me work, he immediately offered me a job, as he wanted someone to try to help him sell his wall tiles in English- and French-speaking countries.

I started off as a sort of glorified office boy but as the months went by I took on more responsibility. One of my particular jobs was to pay the men on Friday, which meant having to master the rather complicated system of deductions for state insurance tax, income tax and so on. I would have liked to design some of the tiles, but the results of my experiments were not only hideous but unsaleable, and we quickly reverted to the policy of making either industrial tiles in a sort of stone colour or the plain white tile.

Germany in the late 1920s was at the peak of its rebuilding programme: there was a feeling of new friendliness with the Allies. The factory was constantly busy. As time went on, I took journeys to Brussels, Paris, Hamburg, Berlin, and to many of the neighbouring towns, such as Cologne, Düsseldorf and Frankfurt. I have the impression of innumerable train journeys which are so much a part of German life. On Sundays, at some of the little local stations, there was a seething mass of people going on their Sunday outings just for the pleasure of travel, or going to visit relatives. During the week the efficient fast trains carried herds of smooth, grey-suited businessmen. I tried my best to look like one of these. If they were dull and heavy-mannered they at least seemed to have time to visit the opera or a concert, and indeed would think nothing of travelling a hundred miles or more to do so.

Living in Germany I had the feeling of being in the very heart of Europe, although I never went further east than Berlin. I suppose living anywhere abroad between the age of eighteen and twenty-one would have enlarged one's horizons. I mixed freely in the little social world of apothecaries, doctors and retired army men that constituted the minor gentility of the neighbourhood. There was in the village a small casino or social club. This was based on a fine cellar of excellent Rhine and Moselle wine. Thursday was skittle evening, which I greatly enjoyed. I think I managed to acquire a fairly good palate for the wine. If it is essential – and I think it is – that any man should learn how to get gloriously and rapturously drunk, there is surely no better place to go to than Germany. An evening's drinking of one sort of wine made from one particular grape means that you will have to pay very lightly for your follies.

Germany, of course, was going through a most peculiar phase. The upper-middle-class world with connections with the higher nobility and retired military hierarchy, as personified in the von Claers, still kept up a pretence of social formality. Visits were made at the correct hour, even complete with silk hat and frock coat, but the younger generation was passionately absorbed in all forms of outdoor sport, and the Rhine in the summer was littered with brown bodies of girls and boys swimming and sun-bathing. Thus a girl and a boy of my age might have been of a startling good physique while their fathers would be the cigar-smoking Germans of the caricatures, complete with two rolls of fat bulging over the backs of high, stiff collars. The Pfarrers at their best, however, and indeed Jonny too, knew and were proud of the classic Germany, the Biedermeier Germany of Schubert, Goethe and Heine. At their worst they were boringly and sentimentally obsessed with anecdotes of the *Almanach de Gotha*. This, however, does not apply to Jonny, who was an ardent supporter of the new Republic.

As time went on I seemed really to become a second-in-command to Jonny in the factory. I became one of the community and spoke such good German that I was quite capable of interviewing local officials who would come to inspect the books or check on the Federal regulations, without giving away my true nationality. I even had my appendix removed at the state's expense. It was, however, in the field of music that I perhaps learned the most. The town of Coblenz supported a municipal theatre and opera house of surprisingly high quality. I learned to appreciate and love all the operas of Mozart, and if the resources at Coblenz were too meagre to do justice to the vaster scale of Wagner and Strauss, I could hear these works at Cologne or Düsseldorf.

I learned also to enjoy travelling; and sight-seeing has always been a German passion. Hitch-hiking is a purely German innovation with its allied youth hostel movement, although the Germans are willing to admit that they got the idea from our boy scouts.

I was two and a half years in Germany, and left the day after I had attended a festival in Coblenz, organized to celebrate the departure of the last French soldier of the army of occupation. We none of us could conceive the possibility that another war and another army of occupation would come in so few years ahead.

How can I sum up my impressions of those years? I certainly feel that I learned a lot although it is difficult to define in what direction. I had learnt how it felt to run a small factory: how to organize its office routine and how to handle the workmen; how to travel so that the booking of tickets and sleeping berths or restaurant cars did not bother me; and how best to use the services of a large hotel.

I also vastly extended my field of reading. If I had neither the inclination nor the time to go deeply into the German classics, I had at least made a slight acquaintance with them. I became familiar with the great symphonies of Beethoven and the delicate mysteries of Mozart. I had climbed the Alps in Switzerland and I had loitered under the green trees in Baden-Baden; I had seen the curious night life of Berlin and the more virile and vigorous junketing in the dives off the Reperbahn in Hamburg. I had been on innumerable excursions to castles on the Rhine and the Moselle by train, steamer and on foot, and had drunk many bottles of wine. However, in this world of industry, bourgeois comfort and simple commerce, my thoughts were far from *haute couture*.

It was well that with the approach of my twenty-first birthday my father began to get agitated about my future. I had returned home each Christmas but I had shown not the slightest desire to renew my acquaintanceship with R. D. Blumenfeld: indeed, I was only anxious to get back to Germany because there was going to be a new presentation of *The Magic Flute* in Cologne, or because Jonny was expecting me to meet him in Paris, or because we had planned a large party for the Cologne Carnival. I realized, however, that I could not go on working in Bendorf for ever, even though now I was earning enough money to be completely independent.

I was, however, most anxious to stay in Germany. I felt happy there. I felt that any hard work which I did would be appreciated and rewarded, and that means of recreation were reasonably available to all: and properly organized. It was an understood thing that the whole population would want to go to the opera or sunbathe or canoe. Somehow, it would not seem possible to have these things in the suburbs of London, where I was terrified I might have to live if I went back to England. If I had no thoughts for *haute couture*, I equally had none for journalism. What I wanted was some English firm – so that my father would not feel that I had become completely German – which had branches in Germany where I would like to remain.

Such a firm materialized in the Karlsruhe factory of the English weighing machine firm of W. & T. Avery. I was very quickly engaged in view of my sound knowledge of the country, but before I started work there it would appear that the firm had already heard strong rumours of what was going to happen to Germany in the immediate future and how insecure a foreign-run factory in Germany was going to become. Events of course proved how right their information was. It was accordingly arranged that I should return to England to the head office of Avery in Birmingham, where I would be trained in all branches of their business so that I could take up a post abroad when the situation had become clearer.

It does not take me long to get interested in the new at the expense of the old, and I must say that it was with more excitement than regret that I left for Birmingham in August 1930. But my feelings were to be reversed when I found myself that winter in lodgings in Birmingham, having to be at the factory at eight o'clock each morning in the chill and dirty atmosphere, and with the only physical recreation some modest tennis at the weekend with a hospitable family in a neighbouring suburb, and the only spiritual refreshment a concert given by the excellent Birmingham Municipal Orchestra. For several months I roamed the large factory from department to department, enjoying the sight of the lusty iron foundries and the robust humour of the workmen from Smethwick and Aston, but hating the din of the machine shops and the petty routine of the large office. However, the latter was more comfortable than the bleak factory, and it was with some relief that I found myself in the continental department which dealt with the Avery factories overseas which at that time were in Italy, Spain, France, Belgium and still Germany. It was about a year after my arrival there that my rather humdrum existence was shattered by the brisk ruthlessness of the newly appointed general manager, Austin Morley.

There were several young men, such as myself, standing about in various departments of the factory, all of whom were known as trainees. We were being trained for what were called executive posts and were accordingly sent to a sales school, where, if we weighed a piece of meat on an old-fashioned scale it would be shown to weigh 2 lbs 4 ozs, but if it were put on an accurate Avery automatic weighing machine – one of those affairs which give the weight in figures on a revolving drum – the same piece of meat would weight 2 lbs 5 ozs. Our weighing machine would therefore save the shopkeeper the price of an ounce of meat, and, even more than this, it would calculate the price correctly. I left the school firmly convinced that every shop-keeper needed one, which was exactly what the school intended me to do, for their slogan was: 'Sell the weighing machine first of all to the salesman'. I often think of these words to this day when I bring down a new dress from the studio to show it to my *vendeuses*. If they do not like it – and, however polite they are, I can usually tell whether they do or whether they don't – I know it won't get sold, however well it is presented in the collection.

It was a little shattering to find that my 'territory' consisted of an area in the eastern suburbs of London of a little more than two square miles, in which at least ninety per cent of the shopkeepers seemed to have such a scale. However, here and there there would be signs of a new shop being built. I would track down the builder and, after having discovered the odd butcher or confectioner amongst the usual drapers, fried fish shops and undertakers, would proceed to long conferences with the cautious new shopkeeper, and his still more cautious wife. Sometimes I would have to make my way into an already established shop through a crowd of customers, and talk a harassed butcher into allowing me to give a demonstration. From the back of my little saloon car I would seize the very heavy cast-iron-covered contraption, stagger with it into the shop, adjust it, only to find that I had done it so badly that my gleaming modern machine registered less than what the butcher calculated on his pair of scales of apparently inadequate design.

The going was so tough that, in spite of the fact that the prices of the new scales were from about thirty to ninety pounds, we were only expected to sell two hundred and fifty pounds' worth of them each month; if we did that we were made a member of the Hundred Per Cent Club. Fortunately, it did not matter how few months you had been working; the average was all that was necessary. I was launched on this adventure in the autumn so that with my enthusiasm and the considerable help of my immediate superior, who would come rushing down from head office to help me to obtain the necessary signature on the dotted line as soon as there was a smell of an order, I was able to be invited to the Hundred Per Cent dinner at the end of the year, where I was presented with a large silver cigarette box, which I still greatly cherish. We were paid no salary, given a very small allowance for petrol for a motorcar, which I had bought and which I rather enjoyed, although its insides were as great a mystery to me then as they are today. But we were paid twenty per cent commission on our sales so that every now and then I would have a cheque for forty or fifty pounds. I do not remember paying any income tax, and as I was able to live at home I seemed to have more money to spend than ever before. But apart from the moment of exaltation caused by the all too infrequent sales, I think I have never been so miserable in my life before or since. Some days I just simply could not drag myself round the dreary streets, or force my way into the unwelcoming shops, and I would slink away to the cinema.

Fortunately, by the middle of the next year, and long before it was necessary to prove that I could be a one hundred percenter for a complete twelve months, I was moved on to new activities. I was now moved to Reading in charge of the selling of industrial weighing machines for an area which extended as far north as Oxford, and roughly the same distance west. I suppose I must have been there about two years, and the work was altogether more pleasant in that I had mostly to call on factories who had written to ask me to do so. I recollect 1933 as being a perfectly beautiful summer. I changed my motor to an open tourer and would career over the Berkshire Downs learning *The Scholar Gypsy* by heart, which I would chant to myself in a loud voice. I also wrote a three-act play and even went so far as to obtain an encouraging interview with a theatrical producer of some standing, who said that the play was dreadful but that it showed some promise.

When I came back to England to join Avery they had hinted at my being sent abroad for them in due course, but there was no sign of any such job being offered me at that moment. I really had worked hard at a job which I disliked intensely. I had certainly come to the end of my probation period and now there was talk of moving me on. Little did I know what other plans were afoot.

There must be thousands of young men and women who are today in jobs even more uncongenial than mine was at Avery's. It is so true that you can only get out of life what you put into it. No one should be content with what they are doing if they are ambitious or frustrated, but I never believe in forcing open fresh doors. All that is required is to keep on your toes, so that the moment a new door is opened for you you can decide in a flash if the adventure in the next room would be good for you, and then leap unhesitatingly.

During all these years my mother had kept in touch with Mr and Mrs Shingleton. Her visits to Miss Gray Limited in Brook Street were extremely infrequent as most of the people she knew there had left. Since I had been a senior boy at school, however, I had always been invited by the Shingletons to join their party at a dance given around Christmas time in aid of the Middlesex Hospital, where there was a Dressmakers' Ward which they supported. I had been to such an entertainment late in 1933, and at Christmas time I had written my usual letter to Aunt Louie in Nice. I had told her how well Mrs Shingleton looked and described her dress, which was a pleated black chiffon with a bodice embroidered in grey and silver, and said how well it suited her white hair and slim, elegant figure. Aunt Louie, in her Christmas letter to Mrs Shingleton, had reported how vivid she found my description. Mrs Shingleton threw the letter across the table to her husband and said, 'You ought to get that boy into the business in Digby Morton's place.'

A few days later my mother reported to me, not without some excitement, what had transpired at the Shingleton dinner table, to which she and my father had been invited. With the progress of the years, Mr Shingleton, who was some years younger than his wife, had become greatly occupied with the management of Miss Gray Limited, and had also bought a French *couture* house called Paulette, which had establishments in the Champs Elysées, Paris, and in Berkeley Square, London. These three businesses were amalgamated into an English company called Gray and Paulette Limited. All catered for a clientele which was elderly and solid rather than young and fashionable. Mr

1 My mother, Mary Amies, wearing a dress made at Miss Gray's, 1906

2 With my sister, Peg, in the garden at Wembley, 1916

3 Aged six in a coat made by a tailor at Miss Gray's

4 At Brentwood School

5 The Vernet–Barbarroux family (*HA fifth from left*), Le Vieux Cannet, France, 1927

6 The von Claer family (*HA right*), Bendorf-am-Rhein, Germany, 1928

7 'Panic', my first full page in *Vogue*, April 1937

8 Early days at Lachasse, 1935

9 The New Look anticipated, *Vogue*, March 1939 (*Nepo*)

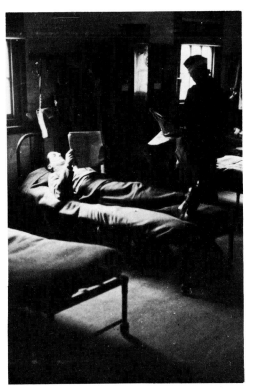

10 Cadet Amies, Ramillies Barracks, 1940
11 After the parachute jump, RAF Ringway,
1942

12 Second Lieutenant Amies designing his
wartime collection

13 14 Savile Row as we found it in 1945 (*Roland Haupt*)

14 Savile Row restored

15 With Maud Beard in the
workroom at Savile Row (*Chris Ware*)

16 The young *couturier*, 1946
(*Roland Haupt*)

Shingleton had also created a business making and selling inexpensive cotton dresses.

The Paulette business was in Lord Northcliffe's old house in Berkeley Square, and an enterprising woman – I believe her name was Mrs Phillips – had in 1929 persuaded the Shingletons to allow her to open a sportswear department in what had been the garages, which opened on to Farm Street. The new shop was called Lachasse, so disguising its connection with Paulette. Shortly after its opening Mrs Phillips brought in as a designer a talented young Irishman called Digby Morton.

The new establishment had an immediate success. The little showroom with its fumed oak furniture and chintzes, into which you stepped straight off the street, was very different from the formality of the usual dress shop, with its liveried doormen, discreet grey salon, and regal *vendeuses*. It specialized in women's suits made to measure, mostly in tweed. It was a tremendous innovation showing a *couture* collection which did not include a single evening dress, and barely one suitable for wearing in the afternoons. This was the heyday of the tweed suit, and the customers belonged mostly to the rich racing set, who wore suits all day long.

Morton's philosophy was to transform the suit from the strict *tailleur*, or the ordinary country tweed fit only for the moors, into an intricately cut and carefully designed garment, so fashionable that it could be worn with confidence at the Ritz. Such clothes have become so much a part of the fashion picture in all parts of the world during more than the last fifty years that it is hard to realize how much they owe to Morton's original ideas. It would appear that Morton did not think Mr Shingleton realized it enough either; for in the autumn of 1933 he left to open his own business in his own name. This made a void which I was to fill.

It was only this last point that my parents, or indeed I, properly understood. None of us had ever heard the name Lachasse, and I rushed up that Sunday to have a look at the outside of the premises which told me precious little. However, I went up to see Mr Shingleton and I knew that I was going to accept the job. My enthusiasm was not even dampened by his offer of a salary which was less than half of what I was then earning.

I suddenly realized how aimless my life had been up until then. Certainly the years in France and Germany had enabled me to learn two languages. I had learned how to look after myself and how to get on with all sorts of people. I had seen the luxuries and riches of the Riviera, and the industry of the inhabitants of the large German towns. I had some idea of how commerce worked, but underneath I had a gnawing sense of frustration, and above all I was deeply discontented with myself because I had seemed always to take the easy line of accepting life as it came to me, making no effort to fulfil myself or to make use of my creative talents. I now see that it was right to be content to do my duty in the best possible way, until luck, which always comes to us some time or other, came to me in this series of coincidences.

I do not remember Shingleton making it clear what I was to do at Lachasse: I do not think he knew himself; he merely had an instinct that another young man ought to be brought in as quickly as possible.

I started work on 1 February 1934. I was put into the showroom, principally because there was nowhere else for me to go, and after a few days began to talk to the customers as they came in for their fittings. It was a comparatively quiet moment as the season had not yet commenced. The spring collection was being made behind the scenes under the supervision of Ann, the only permanent mannequin. All Morton's clothes had been made on her for several seasons, and as she was greatly interested in dress she had managed to think up some twenty or thirty suits and dresses which bore a reasonable likeness to those of Morton's design. She was a particularly striking girl, with the broad shoulders and narrow hips that were then fashionable, and she wore her hair very short and bunched forward into what she called the wind-swept style. She had big, rather prominent blue eyes and very beautiful teeth, and about the sulkiest expression a pretty girl could wear. Fortunately, she was also rather silly, and having been given a position of some importance in the house – indeed almost that of a temporary designer – she gave such a spectacular display of tantrums that after a few months Mr Shingleton dismissed her, but he only did so after he had asked me whether I felt capable of designing the collection in August.

Morton's new business was in Palace Gate, an unusual situation, chosen because his contract with Lachasse restrained him from opening in a nearer neighbourhood; but his reputation and talent had taken a great many customers from Lachasse, in spite of the fact that only one of the Lachasse fitters who had worked for him had followed him into the new business. This was greatly to my advantage. There were also around the house quite a number of copies of models that Morton had designed and these I examined with great care, getting some of the sales girls to show me some of the finer points of their planning and construction.

The management had made a point of only having young people around the showroom so the staff were almost all about my own age, and soon most of them were helping me. Those first six months were, however, not all undiluted pleasure. I see clearly that Mr Shingleton was in a difficult position. He wanted me to be a success, because that would indeed be essential for the business, but on the other hand he did not want me to be so successful that it would be possible for me to go off and do as Morton had done; so it was some time before I had any real authority in the house.

Mr Shingleton only came to London once or twice a week. On those days he had three, often four, businesses to visit, so he would sometimes be at Lachasse for not more than half an hour. Often he would not even see me but would remain closeted with a woman who was really the manageress of Paulette Ltd. I have already tried to explain that the premises of Lachasse and Paulette were in the same building and were often so mixed up inside that you could not tell one from the other. Canteen, counting house, and many other offices were shared by both. Any orders that Mr Shingleton would give to Paulette would often automatically apply to Lachasse, and it was the duty of Paulette's manageress to see that they were executed. By the end of my stay at Lachasse I got to know this woman quite well, and to understand how difficult and delicate were her duties, but for several years I disliked her intensely. She did indeed have a dragon-like quality which aroused the animosity of my own staff. My position was made a little easier when, after a year, Mr Shingleton offered me a contract in which it was necessary for my duties and position to be more clearly defined and I was called in this contract 'Managing Designer'. (When I was planning to open my own business I wondered if he ever wished he had had me called 'Designing Manager'.) By this time I was doing absolutely all the designing in the house, and I was also managing it, although my powers were limited. For instance, I could not engage any staff or increase any wages without Mr Shingleton's consent. I remember getting extremely disappointed, however, when he would not allow me to engage the model girls I wanted because they asked too high a salary.

I learned my business by talking to the customers: the general machinery of the house, the functioning of the stockroom, the way materials were sent from here to the workrooms, the hierarchy of the workrooms, the position of fitters, seconds, first hands, all seemed to me as simple and as natural as if I had known them all my life, which, in a sense, I had. But the customers themselves were something quite new. I knew nothing of the racing world, but as the clientele was in many ways an international one I felt at home talking to them. I would try to chat to them pleasantly while their fittings were going on, at the same time watching the tailor or fitter as carefully as I could.

There were two head tailors, Mr Ernest and Mr Todd. Mr Ernest joined the firm as a very young man, and later joined me at Savile Row. Mr Todd joined Lachasse a little after Mr Ernest, and I think had at one time been a sailor. It is impossible for me to explain how kind the staff was to me. Incidentally, it is rare for a fitter or a tailor to be jealous of a designer. They are usually only too anxious to see anybody with ideas in the business.

I cannot remember a great deal about the first collection that I made, but it was reasonably well received. I seem to have had no real solid success until the following spring.

We were not a successful house, we were not talked about by the rich or fashionable, nor were we visited by the great fashion magazines such as *Vogue* and *Harper's*. I am sure that my designs were not very exciting either; for I had precious little original to say. I made the collection to the best of my ability, but I seem to have been greatly involved in the actual management of the business, day-to-day worries as to whether the customers' fittings were going to be ready on time, and even right if they were ready. My former experience made me most anxious that the business should function efficiently and profitably. I began, however, gradually to produce larger and larger collections, until one season we showed over ninety models.

A great many of the thousand designs I made were extravagant and hideous but all the time I was experimenting and all the time I was learning something. Then suddenly something began to emerge from all this. The suits that Morton had made in his last year with us had a comparatively short, high-waisted jacket, buttoning slightly above

the natural waistline. One day I realized that if you lower the waistline
to its lowest possible point you have a much longer line from under
the armhole to the waist, which gives you much more room to move
when in action and makes the jacket lie almost peacefully on its own
when you are still, avoiding the buttoned-up and restricted look of a
high waist. It took me about two years to find this out. I should add
that at this time the shoulders of suits were also heavily padded. In
order to counteract the top-heavy look I lengthened the jackets. The
effect was to make a more important-looking suit and I had greater
scope to give emphasis to the hips, which was something that had
been quite unheard of for many years. I do not wish to claim in any
way that I started anything new. I merely do claim that I had sensed
what was going on in the fashion world and demonstrated a sort of
summing up of all this in my design. Certainly the general proportions of such suits remained fashionable until after the war, and
some very reputable manufacturers of women's wholesale suits have
told me since that they had been inspired by what they had seen of my
designs and had based their whole production on them.

It was about this time that I thought up my own method of drawing
designs which proved very satisfactory. What I had done was to find
out what sort of clothes the customer wanted. I learned that, although
we were ostensibly a sportswear shop, a customer bought a new suit
to wear not only for luncheon parties in the country, but also on
shopping expeditions to London; and that she would only wear such a
suit for real sporting occasions, such as local race meetings or at
shooting parties, when it began to look slightly old and shabby. The
clothes that sold best were those that were good for town and country.
I realized that the day of the lady's maid was waning, so clothes had to
be easy to look after. It was necessary always to visualize how the
customers lived.

In 1937, Coronation year, many Americans were in London and some
buyers from several great stores, who had probably heard of us
through the fashion newspapers and who now visited us regularly,
bought suits in exactly the same way as they bought models in Paris.
The only difference was that ours were very much cheaper. We were
not organized for this sort of business, and although we knew that
they were taking the suits back to have them copied in America we
charged them no more than if we had been making them for a private

customer. Although the prices were low, we got the name of Lachasse spread throughout the New World, and from that season I have never stopped selling clothes to America. That year naturally stands out from the vague mass of other seasons, none of which I could distinguish from each other.

I do not want to elaborate on the misunderstanding and quarrels which I had with Mr Shingleton. I was longing for the day when I would be my own master and was always wanting to be extravagant. I wanted large rooms in which to work, filled with flowers, and to have only the loveliest and most elegant model girls – three or four or five or six of them constantly parading my models in an unending stream. He wanted no model girls, except on special occasions, and we were to sell the clothes by getting the customers to try them on themselves. He was so right in his estimation that all these frivolities did not help you much to sell the clothes. If the clothes were good the customers would buy them in an attic.

If I was what the world would call lucky, in being offered in the first instance the chance of working at Lachasse, I must have been doubly lucky in that I stumbled across a house which dealt in tailored clothes rather than the variety known as 'soft' or, as the French called it, '*flou*'. A suit has to be planned rather architecturally, whereas a good evening dress flows naturally. Indeed, it is usually made on either a living model or a dressmaker's stand. It so happened that the fitters at Lachasse had themselves had little experience in this type of dress-making, and it was only after I had passed through the House of Worth that I began to make really good evening dresses. While Mr Shingleton's point was an important one, it is, however, true that the decoration of the dress house, if it is to be a genuine one, must express the taste and personality of the designer or head of the business.

I think it must have been some time in 1937 that Miss Gray died. She had been in poor health for some time. When it became clear that the Brook Street business was going to be closed, I asked Mr Shingleton if he would not transfer Lachasse there. I wonder how happy I should have been if he had granted my wish and put the business into those rooms, so full of my first memories, and so closely allied to the memory of my mother; and if he had granted my further wish, which was that my name should be openly and officially quoted. The wise may smile at this desire to see one's name in print. I do not know how seriously he considered all these proposals but certainly they must have been interrupted by the uncertainties and disturbances which culminated in the Munich Crisis in 1938.

For the first month or so after joining Lachasse, I stayed at home and travelled each day on the crowded LNER to Liverpool Street, and thence by tube to Bond Street, exactly as my mother had done years ago. For lunch I would go to Fleming's Restaurant in Oxford Street, but somehow the boiled fish and parsley sauce which I had found so delicious years ago no longer tasted so good – my palate having been educated by my stays in France and Germany; but of course I soon found this way of living too dull and tiring, and after a short stay in furnished rooms I moved to a small flat in Pont Street.

In the late spring of 1937 I got a mysterious message from my father, asking me to meet him in the upholstery department of John Lewis. There he told me that my mother, who had been unwell for some time, was now so ill in bed that she was unable to come to London with him to choose some material for new curtains for her spare bedroom. I was to choose them for her. Whilst turning over the chintzes with me, my father said in a casual voice, 'I have had the doctor's report and it is cancer.' In the same voice he went on in his usual optimistic fashion to say that modern medicine was now so wonderful that such things would easily be cured. The scene is fixed for ever in my mind, and seemed to be so typical in its deliberate avoidance of theatricality.

There followed a year of suffering. Several operations, suggested in good faith by her doctors, seemed to add to her pain and gave little hope of recovery. Only the devotion of the nurses, who knew what good work she had done for the hospital by organizing mending and sewing parties to make and preserve the hospital linens, comforted her.

Visits would be made by my father, my sister and me, in an off-hand family fashion, where any display of emotion would be scrupulously avoided. Only once did my mother manage to take my hand and tell me how pleased she was with the progress I was making in my career: the career she had so ardently wished for me. It has always seemed so sad that she should have seen but the beginning of it. She was not even able to visit my first flat of which I was so proud.

She died very slowly – the end made more fearful by the

diminishing power of the drugs to alleviate the pain and by the incoherent babblings of her brain when the relief of the coma arrived. So it was impossible to take farewell of her: she just slipped away. We noticed, to our shame, that we felt more relief than sorrow; only to be followed by an unbearable remorse, remorse for all the moments I had squandered, and for the times when I had hurried away from her bedside to fulfil some trivial engagement. What would one give for just one of those precious minutes now?

Immediately afterwards, as we had long planned to do, I took my father and my sister away to Austria. We were all in a nervously exhausted state and found little peace, even in the isolated villages, for nearby in Munich momentous things were happening. For it was August 1938. At one time it seemed as though we ought to return at once to England: at another, that my father and sister ought not to travel alone to Bendorf, where I had arranged to meet them, as I was to make the journey there by motor with Jonny. But we made our respective journeys safely, and I remember passionate discussions with Jonny about the international situation. The atmosphere in the Pfarrhaus was perhaps slightly strained. The youngest son, with whom I had been such good friends, was by now an ardent young Nazi officer in the Army. I had been able to watch the processes of the Nazification of the Pfarrhaus, as each year since I left I had always spent about a week of my summer holidays there. The von Claers, of course, were easy prey to the outward attractions of the Nazi creed. They had always disliked the Republican Party. I can remember somewhat bitter discussions as to what flags they should display when it was customary to do so during local or national festivals. The von Claers always wanted to use the old black, white and red German flag rather than the Republican black, red and gold. It would be unkind to imply that they were by any means rabid but, like so many others, they felt a joy and a pride in the recrudescence of a national spirit. Even Jonny, with his strong Republican sentiments stemming from his *petit bourgeois* upbringing, was not untainted. He liked the apparent fairness and order of the new regime.

By the spring of 1939 this international situation was calm enough, or rather we had deliberately allowed ourselves to be lulled into the feeling that it was, for me to take an early holiday in the south of France with two friends, Nina Leclercq and Alexis ffrench. I remember I had just signed another three-year contract with Mr

Shingleton. I went and looked at the outside of the villa which had contained the English school at Antibes where I had worked. I walked boldly into the Casino, feeling that at last I had some right to be there, and the weather fortunately allowed me to spend all day on the beach, without any children to look after. If there were peculiar things going on in Abyssinia we refused to take them seriously. It is so easy to paint a happy picture of past holidays, but this does seem to me to have been a particularly successful one, and I was able to remember it with gratitude during the war years which were about to begin.

2

The War

In spite of the new contract, my relations with Mr Shingleton were undoubtedly deteriorating. Not unnaturally, as each season became more successful than the last, so did my ambition grow. People had begun to discuss me as a designer as distinct from the business of Lachasse.

I no longer had Miss Gray to act as an intermediary in times of extreme distress. At the best of times, Mr Shingleton and I would have had difficulty in getting on, so opposite were we in character. I am only too ready to believe that I also tried his patience to the utmost. The only thing that can have restrained him must have been the fact that the turnover figures were now double what they were when I arrived. By September 1939 I had become extremely restless and, optimistic as I am by nature, once the shock of the calamity of war had worn off I began to accept it philosophically. To me, as I think to many others, it was to be an escape.

Lachasse premises were turned into a fire station. I joined the Fire Brigade, but before I was properly accepted I saw an advertisement in the personal column of *The Times* which said, rather mysteriously to me, that the Corps of Military Police wanted linguists with a knowledge of at least two European languages. I was thirty and would perhaps not be called up for some time, but all around me young and old men were joining the colours and there was too much excitement in the air for me to resist the chance of a change.

I wrote in at once. There followed the inevitable visit to Aldershot, with also the inevitable interview with the man who spoke far worse German than I did. I saw Mr Shingleton who, with rather ungracious alacrity, agreed to release me from my contract. Suddenly I was a private in His Majesty's Army.

We were recruited into the Corps of Military Police and were issued with knee breeches, puttees, and two pairs of white woollen gloves. We all thought these were tremendously smart and wore them on every possible occasion, until Aldershot Command interfered and pointed out that we were not going to be military policemen. I don't think any of us knew exactly what we were going to be; but it turned out that this was to be the beginning of the Field Security Police and, subsequently, the Intelligence Corps. We were at Aldershot only two weeks, in bitterly cold weather, and after walking about a mile – at least it seemed as far as this – from the station with a full kit bag, a tin hat, a heavy overcoat and a rifle, I quickly came to the conclusion that it was all extremely uncomfortable, and it was with some relief that I was told to go back home and await instructions to proceed to an Officers' Training Unit.

No one was more surprised to see me back than Mr Shingleton, but he was quite pleased when I settled down to make the spring collection, as it was by now nearly Christmas and this ought to be launched early in the New Year. May I be forgiven for not having resisted appearing at the first showing of the collection in my private's uniform and hobnailed boots?

The first month of OCTU in another part of Aldershot was the greatest possible fun. It was exactly like going back to school. There were about thirty or forty candidates for the Intelligence Corps, and we were more or less lumped together in barrack rooms on our own. We ranged from university professors to head waiters, and there was a tremendous amount of precious conversation interspersed with the usual gibes at all military institutions. It had, however, been made clear to us that we were at an Infantry Officers' Cadet Training Unit, and unless we could qualify as infantry officers we would not be accepted by the Intelligence Corps. We were also told that we were to keep quiet about our future work – about which we actually knew nothing: I always said that we would end up checking passports on Wigan Pier – a gibe which proved only too unhappily true in some cases. We needed no encouragement in doing this, because we dreaded the tongue of Sergeant Finnie ('Finnie as in 'addick') should he have heard the word Intelligence.

Things got tenser as passing-out day approached, particularly as that was to coincide almost exactly with the dramas at Dunkirk. I scrambled through somehow but felt most inadequately equipped for any command, particularly when my friend Fitz Barrington and I were called to the War Office about a week before we were due to pass out, and it was hinted that we should have to leave forthwith for Dunkirk. I was relieved when the orders were quickly counter-manded, although I trust that my only fear was that of making a fool of myself.

There followed then six weeks' training for the Intelligence Corps proper. This was at Swanage, and during the warm nights we stood and watched the dull glow of bombed Southampton in the distance. Life by then was very earnest, although there was still fresh cream in the buns at the Belgian pastry cook's in Swanage, and excellent lobsters at nearby Corfe. We listened to lectures on the German Army and on the structure of the Nazi Party, given by an officer who seemed to hiss hatred of the enemy in every word. We discovered later the effect of his anger was not caused so much by any deep philosophy as by a set of ill-fitting false teeth.

During the second part of the course I found myself seated next to a tall, ascetic-looking man who seemed rather older than most of us. His face was quite ashen in its concentration, and once, apologizing for his ignorance and explaining that he had only put on uniform the day before his arrival, he leant across and asked me if a corps were bigger than a division. We noticed that he never seemed to go to bed, and by the end of the course he had what is known as 'caught up', and, on the last two or three days, was smiling and relaxed in the knowledge that he had mastered his subject. Never have I seen such concentrated brain work bring forth such quick results. His name was J. C. Masterman.

Naturally, there was a great deal of speculation as to where we would be posted once the course was over. It was, therefore, with some relief that I was told that I had been chosen, with two others, to be sent to Canadian Corps Headquarters as Intelligence Officers on General McNaughton's staff. It was pointed out that we should only hold our posts until Canadian officers had been trained for Intelligence work.

In the early autumn of 1940, I duly settled into pleasant billets near Leatherhead and went daily to work in the nearby Corps head-quarters. The Senior Intelligence Officer was John Tweedsmuir, a shining example of a really good man.

There followed months of boredom, which permeated the whole of the Canadian contingent. General McNaughton commanded the Seventh Corps, but only one division of it was Canadian, the other being the British Armoured Division. The Canadians longed for action, and our officers' mess seemed in a complete state of lethargy, only broken by the violent bouts of drinking which would occur as often as was physically possible. We were equipped with motor bikes and the great game was to leap on them after dinner and go roaring up to London to watch the bombs falling. The nearer they fell to us the more we laughed. I managed my motor bike rather well, although some of my friends complained that I would cut short my visits to them rather hurriedly, with no *adieux*, for the simple reason that once the thing started I had to move off before it stalled.

Just before Christmas 1940 John Tweedsmuir sent for me. 'Your country needs you at last,' he said and solemnly pushed an official-looking letter across to me. 'You are to help open up another front for us: in South America.'

Indeed, the letter, coming from the Board of Trade, said that the Government planned to send a collection of clothes to South America to promote exports. They wanted me to participate and would arrange for my release from military duties for two months, if I could be spared.

'You can be spared,' said John Tweedsmuir.

Very shortly afterwards I therefore found myself back at Lachasse making a collection again, this time with two pips on my shoulders.

Mr Shingleton had arranged to pay me a small sum of money each month whilst I was drawing private's pay at OCTU and until I became an officer. This was generous enough, but I also knew that good business was being done on the collection I had left behind me. However, so happy was I at the thought of being released from the Army and being able to get back to my beloved workrooms, that I did not attempt to discuss financial matters with Mr Shingleton before I began the South American collection. I was now drawing no money from Lachasse and, of course, my Army pay ceased too. I had given up my flat and was forced to stay in an hotel.

The sensible thing would have been to have had a discussion with Mr Shingleton and come to a settlement before I started work. But I was terrified lest any hitch should occur. I had been recognized as a designer by a Government Department: but I knew Mr Shingleton

33

wasn't very pleased about this and would have liked to have conducted the business without my help.

Eventually, of course, I was out of money. There followed a horrible wrangle during which we both lost our tempers and suddenly I heard Mr Shingleton telling me to 'get out and not come back'.

I walked over to the workrooms and announced dramatically that I had been sacked. No one believed that matters would not be patched up again. Nor did I. But I never worked at Lachasse again. Mr Shingleton, in anger, had accused me of being too big for my boots. It was true.

I had tasted blood. I had just been officially recognized by the Board of Trade as an independent designer. Alys Ziegler, the brave, energetic and enterprising representative of the fine New York House of Henri Bendel Inc. – amongst others – got in touch with me and said that she had an open order for some suits if I would design them. The publicity director of Viyella also wanted some dresses made for advertising purposes. I felt there was more such business in the offing, and I knew that I had time to do the designs at night in my billets, and on my days off duty. The problem was where to get the clothes made. Either by accident, or as planned by either one of us, I met Madge Garland, who had recently left *Vogue* and was now Director of Fashion at Bourne & Hollingsworth. She was an old acquaintance of my friend Alexis ffrench and had been particularly encouraging to me in the early days. I remember so well sharing a taxi with her after one of my shows in Coronation year: 'Mark my words, Hardy,' she said, 'you are on the road to going far.' As she was then Fashion Editor of *Vogue*, I felt this to be no mean compliment. She was now to give full proof of her confidence in me, in that she put a dressmaking and tailoring workroom at Bourne & Hollingsworth's at my disposal. I could give them what work I wished free of charge, provided they had full right to copy my designs for their store. As I thought I was only to do exports the arrangement seemed ideal. I distinctly remember spending a leave in one of those pleasant suites at the Hyde Park Hotel overlooking the Park, and writing my signature on a piece of broad white satin ribbon, which I subsequently had embroidered. This became my label.

Some of my friends were horrified at what they thought was a too rapid descent from the world of *haute couture*. But Madge had fired me with the idea that the post-war world would only be interested in mass-produced clothes and that I might as well get my foot in now. I believed her: but I must say I was a little shaken when Alys Ziegler told me that Henri Bendel was disappointed with the suits. 'They were not so well moulded,' she said, but it may well be that he was disappointed in my designs as well. After all, however good a tailor is it takes time to persuade him to do what you want him to do, and I had only been able to pop in at odd moments. I was made very aware how much I missed the Lachasse workrooms. But I certainly enjoyed seeing the cheques go straight into my own banking account.

By April 1941 Canadian officers were ready to take over our jobs at Seventh Corps. I was called to London and on Good Friday taken to lunch at the St James's Club, and on the next day to the Turf Club, by two officers from the War Office. To this day I do not know whether it was their generosity, their love of good living, or their desire to see how I would behave that made them give me two large martinis, my fair share of a heavy Burgundy, two glasses of port and a brandy on each of these occasions. It would seem, however, that I acquitted myself respectably, for shortly afterwards I received instructions to go on a certain train to Brockenhurst in Hampshire, where I would be met at the station.

Here I found a normal-looking Army motor with a normal-looking Army driver who, however, said to me in tones which seemed quite mysterious, 'You are going to the house in the wood, sir.' The house was indeed in the wood at the end of a long drive behind Beaulieu Abbey. It looked as though it had been built by a stockbroker with a Peter Pan complex. This elfin atmosphere was not dispelled by my finding that apparently the only inhabitant was a pleasant hunchback in civilian clothes. He turned out to be an expert on invisible inks, or it may have been codes, or it may have been both. For this was the mess where lived the officers who were running the school for special agents and saboteurs, and part of that by now famous organization called by so many names – some of them impolite – of which that of SOE is perhaps the best known. Later, at dinner, we were joined by another instructor, Kim Philby.

Our colonel – the establishment was run on military lines – was a regular Royal Artillery officer, whose sense of humour must, I fear, have been a sad handicap to his Army career, but was a godsend to us for at most times we were all conscious that we were trying to teach something about which we had none of us any practical experience. My job was to be Liaison Officer between the school and our headquarters in Baker Street, and to give force to this position I was made a captain.

Coming as I did direct from the humdrum round of a Corps headquarters – surely the most 'provincial' of staff centres – I was naturally delighted to find myself in a set-up so unconventional and so romantically hush-hush. The Special Operations Executive was looked on with great distrust by other secret organizations within the services. Its job was to organize sabotage and resistance in the occupied countries in every possible way, but particularly by dropping agents and explosives into those countries by parachute. It was natural that the organizations whose job it was to collect secret information, and whose methods of work, and even network of agents, had been established for as long as there had been a Secret Service, were not exactly pleased to see grow up an army of amateur saboteurs. They dealt in silence: we dealt in noise.

Saboteurs and agents, who were known as organizers because they organized sabotage work, went through a training which lasted about three months, and took place mostly in Scotland. On their way back south they passed through the parachute schools and ended up at Beaulieu for about a month's stay. Here they were to learn the final parts of their business: the principles of which were subversive activities, codes, secret inks, information on German army and secret police, and other refinements which it was hoped would be useful to them. They also had to prepare their 'cover story', which was the recreation of that part of their life which they had spent out of their country of origin, so that they could intelligently answer any questions during interrogation. The greater part of these agents was, of course, recruited from the Allied armies which had escaped to this country.

All this time Bourne & Hollingsworth were making up designs for me and I would spend my leaves and my days off duty working there. The sending of the collection to South America had proved such a success that the Board of Trade decided to organize another such venture, this time to North America, principally New York. They also decided that in order to organize such operations it would be necessary for the dress designers to band themselves together into one body. It was in order to achieve this that the Incorporated Society of London Fashion Designers came into being. There had been in the past some such similar body known as the Fashion Group, and one of its most active supporters was Margaret Havinden, a director of the advertising firm of Crawfords, from which eminence she had a wonderful view over the whole fashion world. I was a founder member of the Society, elected in its very early months.

When I had gone into the Army I had persuaded Mr Shingleton to let me take on Miss Campbell, 'Cammie' to her friends, to run the Lachasse showroom in my absence. She had worked at Paulette until it closed down. In the midst of designing the new collection I was surprised to be telephoned by Cammie who told me that she had received a letter from Lachasse telling her that they did not wish her to return there after her summer holidays. They found that she was voicing her belief too loudly that the business would not prosper unless I returned there to do the designing. I immediately suggested that she should join me at Bourne & Hollingsworth to look after my work there, and such a scheme was discussed with the directors, but she went independently to her old friends at the House of Worth for whom she had once worked. They were apparently willing to engage her as a saleswoman, provided she could persuade me to do designs for her.

By this time the North American scheme had been dropped: there was to be no pressure to obtain exports to the USA now that Lend-Lease had become established. There seemed no point in continuing my little export scheme with Bourne & Hollingsworth. The pressure of my army work was increasing, and it seemed in every way desirable that I should have someone like Cammie behind me to look after my interests.

The arrangements with Worth were as follows: Cammie was to have a small corner of the downstairs showroom where she would show a collection of models designed by me. I was to draw a commission on all sales of my designs. Cammie's salary and all expenses were to be the concern of Worth. Cammie was immediately joined by Violet Allen, a saleswoman who, though small in stature, was great in heart and fidelity. She had originally been trained in the showroom at Miss Gray's, and in the very early days, if not at the beginning, had been moved to Lachasse to work with Digby Morton.

She somehow or other had great confidence in me, and her leaving perhaps the best clientele of all the saleswomen at Lachasse was a gesture which was all the more unselfish in that she did not like Miss Campbell.

An important point in the Worth arrangements was that I was not to attempt to bring in fitters from Lachasse, even if they wanted to follow me. Clothing coupons had not long been introduced, business prospects were most uncertain, and Worth did not want – quite rightly – to saddle themselves with any further expense, the responsibility of running an important house such as Worth in those difficult days being already great enough.

I must explain that the House of Worth had but a slender connection with the original Worth of Paris, and indeed I believe that this was broken during the war by the expiration of a contract which concluded by allowing the London House to have the exclusive right to that name in this country. As the Worth designer's reputation was strongest in softer, feminine clothes, I felt that my models, which were almost entirely suits, would not clash with hers. It was arranged that we would use Mr Leonard as the tailor and Mlle Odette as the fitter. So began a little era in my dress designing career which was to last until the end of the war. It was to prove of immense importance to me.

One of the directors at Worth, Colonel Pay, was himself in the Army, and the house was run by Mrs Charlotte Mortimer who, white-haired and distinguished-looking, carried herself with an elegance she had learned as a model girl under the great Reville. She was never any other than very kind and thoughtful in spite of the fact that when business became good – and it was to become very good – there was often difficulty in getting our orders executed.

During my discussions with Colonel Pay, I had made it quite clear from the outset that I was anxious to have my own business as soon as the war was over. Pay stated that he was interested in the finance of the Paris and London houses of Paquin, and that he might be able to arrange for the finance necessary for my own house. We even went so far as to discuss whether it would not be possible to take a house in Grosvenor Street, adjacent to that of Worth, so that I could pretend to be independent, whereas behind the scenes we might be under the same management, sharing many overheads, exactly as had been done between Paulette and Lachasse. This question of the house next door cropped up on several occasions when both he and I would meet, which later on meant when our leaves or days off duty coincided.

In November 1941 I was called away from Beaulieu and placed in the Belgian Section at Baker Street. There I was given what looked like being a long job to do. In December I moved to Chesham Place.

Now began a regular sort of routine. I would go every day to Baker Street, rather like anyone going to his office. In the evening I could talk on the telephone to Cammie, and very often I could have my lunch in the canteen at Worth.

I think I did some very good designs during the war, principally because I was away from the business most of the time. I always used to say that I had 'jumped the counter'. I had been so wrapped up in my work at Lachasse that I had not been able to see it objectively. I was always experimenting, and was often so pleased with the technical results of the experiments that I was unable to see that they were often artistically hideous. As a young officer I seemed to go out much more, and would judge a dress by whether I would like to go out with a girl wearing it, rather than just see it in my showroom. But poor Cammie and Violet had an awful time at the beginning because the only models they had to show were those I had made for the abortive North American collection. These might have stood a chance of a success in America, but were hopelessly wrong in the new austerity regime.

From the beginning I had established a most happy relationship with Leonard and Odette. Any ideas I could give them they were able to carry through with Cammie's and Violet's cooperation. They also would often make very valuable suggestions based on the many years of experience at their profession.

Customers gradually – rather too gradually for my liking – began to come to us. Although the circumstances were hardly fair, in that I myself was there so little, I began to realise how little power a designer has to keep his customers without the fitters and tailors to whom his clientele is accustomed. I began to wonder where all those customers were who had insisted on seeing me at Lachasse, and whether it had been because I had been empowered to give them special prices. However, each season more and more people went away in clothes bearing my signature, and more and more magazines carried photographs of them.

The members of the Incorporated Society were also commissioned by the Board of Trade to do some designs illustrating their newly created austerity regulations. Curiously enough, I hardly found these regulations irksome. After my first ebullient experiments at Lachasse, I had settled down to an extreme sobriety of design.

The atmosphere in the Belgian sector of the SOE was heavy with intrigue and suspicion. My chief was, I suspect, inclined to be a 'worrier'. His health was suffering. I fear, however, that it was some manoeuvring on the Belgian side which caused his being offered another post.

I had been given my Majority in August 1942, being thus the senior officer left in the section, and was told to carry on at its head. I was given clear instructions that I was to cooperate as much as possible with the Belgians. Whatever their work was going to be in the field, all agents had to be prepared to parachute into Belgium as this was the only sure way of entry. This, with very rare exceptions, excluded the engagement of men over forty. Student agents were put through about a month's rigorous training similar to that undergone by Commandos. This took place on the west coast of Scotland in the Arisaig-Morar area. Here SOE leased a whole series of country houses of various sizes, each one of which would be given over to a different nationality. We were lucky in that ours was run by a very good, keen young officer who understood to a nicety just how great a display of sympathy and understanding could be mixed with the rigidity of his discipline to ensure a happy atmosphere.

The training establishments were, of course, manned by British Army personnel, and in these rather peculiar outposts of the military machine some pretty odd specimens sometimes turned up in the form of batmen and cooks, and it was undoubtedly necessary to enforce strict rules of discipline and cleanliness. But a scene that is indelibly fixed in my mind is that of the Area Commander stumping around a Nissen hut which seemed to me to be glowing with the results of hours of elbow grease, and giving a cry of horror. 'That wastepaper basket,' he yelled, 'look at it – terrible.' 'What's wrong with it, sir?' ventured the poor Camp Commandant. 'Why, it's got waste paper in it,' said the Colonel.

In spite of these delicious little moments, I am quite certain that many hundreds of the Belgians who passed through our hands spent some of the happiest days of their youth tramping over the Scottish hills and coming back to a hefty meal of *pommes frites* – the Belgian national dish – to which we were often able to add, in season, literally mountains of *moules marinières*, which we cooked in buckets over open fires, to the great disgust of the natives, who wouldn't touch such horrid things.

But all this simple fun had a rather fearful object, a physical training to toughen up the men to face the more concentrated rigours of the parachute school at Manchester.

During most of the time when I was working in SOE I was conscious of having an inferiority complex about the whole thing. I was not particularly interested in sabotage, which seemed to me uncosily noisy, and I think I would have fitted better into the subtleties of the Political Warfare Executive. Indeed, I got on very well with the gentlemen in this department, with whom, as acting head of section, I had quite a deal to do. Above all, I know that I had a sneaking sort of feeling that I was having a pretty soft war, a feeling which was to become increasingly guilty as men would return from the continent telling tales of what happened to members of the subversive organizations when they fell into the hands of the enemy.

In the spring of 1943 all officers in SOE were notified that they could volunteer to join a course of parachute training. I sent my name in at once. I knew that I could never become an agent myself: I suppose if I had insisted SOE would have allowed me to go on a mission, although it was always understood that this would be forbidden to headquarters officers for fear that they should disclose, under pressure of torture, too much of the details of central organization. But certain officers had overcome this ban. However, I for one knew very little of Belgium.

Now was the chance of doing something which I hoped would expiate the sins of easy living. We were shipped off to the usual large country house in the home counties, and given four weeks' intensive training, of which the most important part was gymnastics, but as we had to have some rest from this we were made to freshen up our office-bound minds with a series of military exercises, both practical and theoretical, of the Commando type.

It was the last day in May 1943 when we arrived at Ringway Aerodrome, near Manchester. The gymnastics had become more violent, so that we were pretty well in a state of physical exhaustion before the actual jumping commenced. I do not know whether it was my imagination, but there seemed to be just that extra amount of food and comfort and solicitude for us in the mess that gave it the air of a large communal condemned cell. I remember we were shooed out of bed very early in the morning with queasy stomachs, bundled into buses, and after hanging around the aerodrome we were told that the wind was too high, and back we came again. The next day, however, we were luckier, and did a jump from what I believe was a thousand feet. For the non-air-minded reader, this is the sort of height from which you can just see sheep moving like tiny mice.

The aeroplane was completely stripped and covered on floor and ceiling with material that seemed like deeply corrugated paper, made of aluminium, the high ridges of which were unnecessarily sharp. Sitting in rows, we slithered around at the slightest roll and I was always frightened of falling out of the hole before my parachute had been properly hooked up. When the plane flew level I felt that my knees were shaking horribly against my neighbour's but, looking up to see whether he noticed this, I discovered with relief that they were not my knees at all, but his.

At last the time came to move up to sit on the edge of the hole, and at a shout from the despatching sergeant I heaved myself over the edge and let go. This was a vile moment; I was terrified of being clumsy and catching my chin on the corrugated aluminium on the rim. Once through the hole you were caught in the airstream which hit you good and hard and flung you backwards, at the same time opening the parachute. At one thousand feet one then had a few moments to look around the countryside and enjoy the fantastic sensation of floating through the air. But all too soon the earth would be coming up to meet you and you had to try to remember all the things you had been told to do to avoid the heavy shock of landing. This was something like jumping off a very high wall.

Next day the weather was bad again and we were taken to a large hangar, made to climb up to what seemed a fantastic height, hitched on to a parachute attached to the roof, and told to jump off from the end of a long plank. Having acquitted myself fairly well so far, I now got to the top of the tower but firmly refused to leave the hand of Nurse – for fear of finding something worse? – Nurse being the Sergeant Instructor. I really completely lost all my nerve and was only pulled round by the kindness of Henry Threlfall, a fellow officer who was on the tower awaiting his turn with me. Incidentally, Henry did all his jumps with a Boswell's *Johnson* in his pocket. Somehow or other, no one seemed to worry about my little lapse. I think that such static jumps, as they are called, often bring out a fear of height, from which I have always suffered, much more than do the jumps from the moving aircraft.

By Friday, we were so far behind our schedule that we had to do three jumps that day, some from as low as five hundred feet, which meant that you seemed to hit the earth almost as soon as you left the aircraft; and one at night, which was not as bad as it sounded for the simple reason that you had very little idea at all what was going on. As the farewell we did a final jump on the Saturday.

I don't know whether it was because all of us were officers, many of us being like me a major, but certainly the non-commissioned instructional staff gave a display of that gentleness and humour which the British soldier can so often produce. If we jumped before breakfast, one of the sergeants insisted on accompanying us, as he said it made him enjoy that meal so much better, and helped his digestion, if you know what I mean.

Having done these five jumps without mishap – and I don't believe there was a serious casualty amongst us; perhaps this was due to the special care with which we were treated – we were entitled to wear a small parachute on the left sleeve of our uniform. This I did with some pride, feeling, I suppose, that it counteracted the 'softness' of my green Intelligence Corps cap, or better still nullified the effect of the Intelligence Corps badge, of which the rather badly drawn Tudor Rose motif was described by a wag as a 'pansy resting on its laurels'.

By the end of 1943 it seemed fairly clear that D-day would be during the coming year. By this time SOE had come much more into the military picture. In spite of the fact that I was shortly to become a lieutenant-colonel, it had been made quite clear to me that in due course I would be superseded by a more senior and experienced officer.

He arrived late in that year in the person of Commander Philip Johns. Resentment at anyone coming in at this late stage might have been felt by his staff, if he had not been able to arouse in us, as he did, respect and loyalty: for we had all been through years of great frustration and bitter disappointment. Grim moments were experienced when we had news of people we had recruited, trained and grown to like being tortured and shot. Time and again we had seen organizations, little nests of workers with a small network of communications within Belgium, and somewhere in contact with a wireless operator sending back messages to us, discovered and broken up by the Germans. Or, worse still, we had had cases where a captured wireless operator had been forced to send back messages to us. No one will know what damage was caused through such penetration. Fortunately, code experts were able later to invent a system whereby such a situation could be detected almost immediately. One thing was certain, however, and that was that resistance throughout Belgium was kept at a high level of activity.

Very shortly after his arrival in the Belgian Section, Philip Johns was also given the Dutch Section to look after jointly with the Belgian, so that I quickly reverted to being head of the Belgian Section under his close guidance.

It had always been understood that immediately after D-day the Belgian Section would set up its headquarters in Brussels; so as soon as it was feasible an advance party left. A little later in September I joined them. Our advance party had done a good job in procuring for us two large flats and a very small one in a modern building in the rue Belliard. The flats verged on what estate agents call 'luxury', which means that they had two or three well-appointed bathrooms. They had been occupied by the Germans and had been furnished from a store of requisitioned furniture that the Germans kept for such purposes. Everything was heavy and hideous, but quite comfortable, and we were later to find that the building was unique in that it was heated, the lower flat being occupied by a coal magnate. Later on, in that bitter winter when all forms of fuel became so desperately scarce, he very kindly cut off the heating from our portion of the building, and it was my duty to go and argue with him on this matter. In a flat of which the temperature must have been at least eighty degrees, he was seated in front of a large coal fire, as close as he could get. He suffered from some form of arthritis, but he was not at all willing to give up any of his store of coal to heat the liberators of his country. This attitude I must say was very untypical.

There began for us now a most curious existence. We were all caught up at first in the liberation excitement, from which it was difficult to settle down to any sort of work. Ought I to be ashamed to tell of the unending round of parties and dinners to which we were invited? In some cases it was our duty to go, for they were given by people with whom we had been in contact during the occupation. In other cases, we were just suckers, and almost fell victims to the blandishments of astute hostesses, sometimes wives of men who were suspected of being collaborators, who were only trying to ingratiate themselves with us because they thought we belonged to the all-powerful British Secret Service. It took us some time to sort these people out, the situation sometimes being made more complex as Belgians returning from London, where we had known them, would often seem to be quite intimate with such people. I would be more irritated with myself because I allowed such things to affect my Puritan sense of justice than I would with the Belgians, whose affair it was, after all.

Sometimes such pleasures were vinegared with sorrow, when we visited relatives of captured and killed agents, or more often the homes of people who had given them refuge and who had suffered accordingly. Sometimes there would be a reburial service or a Requiem Mass. Always we had to be ready to answer questions: 'Why did you not answer my messages? Why were you such a long time coming, anyway?'

As soon as it became known what we were we had an unending stream of visitors claiming praise or compensation, or both, for the work they had done. Is it cynical of me to say that everyone seemed to have done something? It was so difficult to think of patriotism and self-effacement in what seemed to end up in skirmishes for rewards and decorations.

The biggest trouble was, of course, the inferiority complex of the Belgian temperament. They had none of the *gloire* and *panache* of the French: the Walloon-Flemish problem encouraged a sort of split personality; they were horribly undecided as to what attitude to take up with regard to their King's capitulation. Furthermore, they were uncertain as to what the world would think of the record of the Government which had represented them in England. As regards the Belgians who worked as our opposite numbers, they had been treated in the beginning rather off-handedly by s o e and not as representatives of a sovereign nation. They had had to come to us for assistance in so many matters although, having large dollar resources and the rich Congo behind them, they were one of the wealthiest, if not the wealthiest of the refugee nations.

I think I made a mess of this last part of my relationship with the Belgians. I know I was in a difficult position. SOE was trying quite gently but firmly to hand all the agents who were of Belgian nationality back to the Belgians. We gave decorations wherever we could, but here again thousands were eligible for some sort of recognition, and many had done some very brave work indeed. Some Belgian officers working with us had been parachuted from England by us as many as three times. It was terribly difficult, if not impossible, to estimate exactly what they had achieved, but their courage was indisputable. We were only one fairly unimportant country section at SOE. We managed to get three or four MCs and one DSO, but for the rest it was mostly MBEs.

By April 1945 I was longing to get back to England and was grateful when I was recalled very shortly afterwards.

I must confess that I left Brussels with a tiny touch of bitterness in my heart. I did not think that I had made a success of any of my work there. Seeing sometimes both the British and the Belgian point of view, I had failed to please either, but I tried to console myself with the thought that I had not used my position to encourage or even cover up any Black Market transactions, or white-washing of collaborators, all of which would have been easy for me to do. Nor had I moved from my intention to be scrupulously impartial in my dealings with both the military Deuxième Bureau and the civilian Sûreté. On the other hand, I could but be grateful for the opportunity which had come my way of getting out of England, which all my friends were longing to do. It had been amazing to see how well the Belgians had managed to keep up their standard of living. We were impressed to be asked to dinner parties of twenty-four guests, where the napery and the cooking were of a very high standard. The shops seemed full of wonderful silks and all the best French scents, the existence of which we had almost forgotten.

Above all, of course, I was vastly impressed by the appearance of the women. Many of our hostesses were dressed as soberly as were customers of Worth and Lachasse, but others had made frequent visits to Paris during the war and were dressed in the very height of fashion – and height is the right word – for there were many examples of those very tall, elaborately-trimmed hats, mostly draped turbans, which the

French milliners had invented to irritate the Germans – '*les chapeaux de la Résistance*'.

The shape of clothes was still marked by very broad shoulders, narrow waists and skirts full and short so as only to cover the knee. On the streets one saw many flamboyant and cheaply executed versions of these clothes: the hat heavy in felt and with a bourgeois brim added, the whole topped, or rather 'bottomed', by a pair of platform-soled shoes, made of cork or wood. The costume was completed by an umbrella and often by a short, shaggy fur coat. It was flamboyant, sexy in an abandoned sort of way, and horribly inelegant, but it was provocative. When this fashion appeared in the form of a tailored suit, the jacket was extremely long, imitating the *Zazou* suit invented by the youth of Montparnasse. It was a silhouette that dealt in curves rather than straight lines. To make it graceful it had to turn into the New Look.

I had been back to England for a few weeks' leave at Christmas and had seen Pay and, of course, Cammie. Business was slightly frustrating. It was so good that the workrooms were jammed to capacity, so that it took nine months before an order for a suit could be executed – a very inconvenient period, as many of our customers pointed out – but this suited me very well, because it meant that only one collection a year was necessary. Pay still seemed keen on the idea of financing me, but it was impossible to come to any definite arrangement. I was now determined to lay down some concrete plans.

First of all, I decided to get out of the Army as quickly as possible. Even if I had had any – which I hadn't – I had used no strings either to get into it, or to get on in it, but I was determined to pull everything to get out of it. Above all, I was terrified lest anyone should remember how well I spoke German. Owing to the constant practice I had had during the war, my French had improved to a very marked degree, but German is a far simpler language than French, and I had learnt it more scientifically. Secondly, the whole cry of unconditional surrender had filled me with horror, and quite honestly I could not face up to the thought of being sent to Germany. I felt mentally exhausted by the struggles at S O E and I had a shrewd idea that the administration of the army of occupation in Germany was going to be pretty chaotic. I could envisage the most extraordinary instructions with regard to fraternization, for one thing. So it was easy enough for me to convince myself that I had done my bit.

The powers that be at home were fortunately already laying down their plans for the promotion of exports, and with a minimum of difficulty and only the usual delays I found the project of my early release well advanced. S O E was also beginning to disband, and I think they were not unrelieved to find someone not anxious to cling to his rank and pay appertaining thereto. Very shortly after V E-day I was posted home pending demobilization. I asked to go on leave to Cumberland, where I intended to visit my old friends in the tweedmills. No sooner had my appointments been fixed there than I was told by the War Office to travel to Wentworth Woodhouse in Yorkshire to be formally demobilized at the Intelligence Corps Depot there. I had great pleasure in replying to His Majesty's Minister of War that the date mentioned was inconvenient, but that I would attend on my way back from Cumberland.

So eventually I was presented with a new wardrobe of surprisingly good quality, but most of which I found rather unbecoming, except a cavalry mackintosh of excellent cut.

So ended the war for me.

I refuse to regard those years as anything other than a great training for what was to come.

I had vastly enjoyed the responsibility-free days as a private and as a cadet: the comradeship was warming, the laughter based on the absurdities of Army regulations, the physical exercise was health-giving, and the rhythms of the barrack square exhilarating. As my responsibilities progressed with the years, I had to learn how to control a staff of officers and secretaries. I had had some severe lessons in diplomacy in my dealings with the Belgians.

In my contacts with the more secret departments of the British War Office, I realized that there was no more intriguing, cunning and touchy person than a high-ranking officer in such departments. But the most tiresome thing about the whole boring procedure was that I was not allowed to talk about anything, and I rather like talking.

3

Savile Row

As soon as I got back from Brussels I had several talks with Pay. Finally he made his proposition: I was to join the board of the firm to be created out of the united Worth-Paquin businesses: Worth and Paquin of London, and Paquin of Paris. I never actually got down to discussing what designing I would do – whether, for instance, I would design in London or in Paris – for I immediately saw that I could not accept the condition that I was to give up the use of my own name entirely. This was only going back to Lachasse under a different name.

It is a truth universally acknowledged that a young designer in possession of a good clientele must be in want of capital.

This thought had been constantly in my mind, when, during what were often dark moments in the war, I would lie back and make daydreams of the future. Now the problem was before me in bitter reality. Where *was* I going to get the money? I remembered all the people who had promised to subscribe when we had talked of such things. Some were customers who had sent messages to me through Cammie and Violet – 'If you ever decide to open on your own, do let me know.' Well, I let them know, but now that they have received the little extra bit of attention from Cammie and Violet which such promises evoked – attention which was precious during those war months, when good workers and good clothes were scarce – they became evasive and vague. In point of fact I was not terribly anxious to accept capital from customers. I feared that they would want to interfere in the running of the business, bringing an air of amateurishness and upsetting the staff. But I knew that I needed no such reservations with the three customers I did take as shareholders.

The first was Virginia Jersey. She was an American, a simple girl from Chicago, who had leaped into fame as Virginia Cherrill, the star of Charlie Chaplin's *City Lights*. She had been married to Cary Grant, but was now Countess of Jersey. A stalwart customer at Lachasse and at Worth, she was unwavering in her support. Alas, her heart was bigger than her purse, for by this time her divorce from Lord Jersey was imminent, and her income and free capital limited. But quickly she found someone to help fill the gap – Mrs Dickie Gillson, who hardly knew me, but who subscribed at once 'because Virginia says you're clever and I can see you're nice'. She and Dickie Gillson were quickly followed by Mrs Montague Meyer, an old friend and customer from Lachasse.

My father had by this time re-married and to my stepmother I am indebted, not only for being an original shareholder, before she bought Virginia's shares, but also for a small gift of money during the war, 'so that you have something to come out of the Army with'. I had always hoped to have added to this: but ended up by being thankful I had managed to keep it untouched. For it enabled me to obtain enough shares in the business to get control.

My friend Alexis ffrench also took up some shares, which was generous; for he needed his capital for his own antique business. Once we were well established I was able to arrange for him to sell them.

I was very disappointed in the lack of financial support I got from the cloth merchants and manufacturers. I had always imagined that they would have rushed to support me. They, above all, had seen, both at Worth and Lachasse, exactly how successful my designs could be: the gauge of success of a model being the amount of cloth used in copying it. But now I see their point. They preferred to assist by giving good credit: by supplying cloth without asking for quick payment, rather than tying up their own capital which, they felt so rightly, they might need in the difficulties of post-war trading.

An exception was Miss Agnes Linton, of the famous Linton Tweed Mills in Cumberland. She immediately subscribed the amount suggested by my accountants. I was proud to be associated with this distinguished mill. Old Mr Linton, Miss Linton's father, the founder of the firm, worked in close collaboration with Chanel and, a little later, with Schiaparelli. Together they devised many wonderfully-coloured tweeds, which delighted and startled the world of fashion in the late twenties and early thirties.

Looking back now, I find it hard to remember all the difficulties with which we met. There were days of despair and evenings of triumph. I was only conscious of one thing: I knew that I would get the money somehow.

I had had a few talks with financiers during the war: they had promised support over the dinner table during leaves in the war; but at the subsequent meetings round their imitation Chippendale desks I could see that they wanted to tie me down to impossible terms.

I had the good fortune, however, to be introduced to that essential friend to all businesses, large or small, a good accountant. Dick Hinds-Howell, a wonderfully imaginative accountant, guided me through my first paces and watched the business grow with almost paternal interest.

The first directors of the business were Dick Hinds-Howell, Virginia Jersey and my father: with myself, rather pompously it seemed to me, as chairman. It was nice having my father and I think many things we discussed reminded him of the early days of his life with my mother and the problems at Miss Gray's which she used to discuss with him.

All these financial arrangements took some months to achieve, and during this time both Cammie and I were busy looking for that all-important thing, premises. It was terribly hard. We wanted that impossible thing, something attractive and practical. We knew we wanted a pleasant showroom with plenty of daylight, but at the same time adequate workroom space: for we knew well enough that the business could only be as big as the space was for accommodating the workers. Our capital resources were so small that we could not afford to pay any fantastic sum for a lease or a premium.

I can so well remember the warm late summer evening when Alexis and I were dining in a small restaurant in Soho, and we met an old friend, Geoffrey Houghton-Brown, whose delight it was to spend a great deal of time in the sale rooms, or buying and selling houses. When I told him of my plight he said at once, 'Why, I have just seen a lovely house in Savile Row. It has been terribly bombed, but I could see some wonderful panelling.'

That very evening Alexis and I went off to look at it. I found that it was a house I already knew, for it had contained a good dress shop run before the war by Miss Kay Norton, and which I had noticed bore a plaque over the front door, saying that the dramatist Sheridan had lived there in 1816. I knew that Miss Norton had closed down her business at the beginning of the war, and I cannot think why I had not myself thought of the premises before.

They were, indeed, in a shocking state, for a large land mine had fallen about four doors away, practically opposite the modern police station. No. 14 Savile Row had no windows at all, and so insecurely was the basement door fastened that we were able to walk right in. The fine staircase leading from the ground to the first floor was covered with wet slime, for the skylight over the stairs had long since been blown off and was covered with an inadequate tarpaulin. Not one room on the four floors was habitable. We could see, however, that the one-time drawing-room on the first floor was a beautifully-panelled room of a size to accommodate about one hundred gilt chairs, which was what we wanted. Upstairs, too, the former bedrooms had been completely stripped to make workrooms for Miss Norton, and with their front row of windows on to Savile Row, and their back on the Heddon Street, they were admirably lit. The basement indeed did seem a problem. The former kitchen looked as though it might make a stockroom, and a large room at the back, which I imagine had at one time been the coach house, required constant artificial light. It had, during Miss Norton's regime, been let off to a dancing teacher, for she had not used either this floor or the ground floor, which she had let to a men's tailor.

A discussion the next day with the landlords showed them to be the rather old-fashioned, extremely reliable family sort. They wanted no premium and were willing to take a low rent for the first two years, in order to help me put the place in repair.

Since there was not a single room habitable in Savile Row, we were given temporary shelter by our kind friends Messrs Wain Shiell, the cloth merchants. From this temporary headquarters we began our assault.

There now remained the great problem of staff. For selling I had my ever-faithful Cammie and Violet, but I needed desperately a tailor and a dressmaker. Mr Ernest, the tailor at Lachasse, had left in 1937. His place was taken by Mr Victor, who was the tailor at an old-established firm called Russell & Allen, which Mr Shingleton had bought up and amalgamated with Paulette. Victor, of Czech origin, very quickly proved himself an excellent tailor. We at once got on very well, for he had a magnificent training behind him and was pleased to have some new and up-to-date designs to work on after the rather stuffy

17 Film star Virginia Cherrill, Countess of Jersey, my first backer, 1946 (*Cecil Beaton*)

18 'The New Mayfair Edwardians' (*l–r*) Peter Coats, Bill Ackroyd and Mark Gilbey outside 14 Savile Row, 1950 (*Norman Parkinson*)

19 With Alexis ffrench, Florence, 1952

20 Neil 'Bunny' Roger, 1954 (*Norman Parkinson*)

21 The New Look, 1949, Amies coat (*left*), Molyneux coat (*right*) inside the portico of the National Gallery (*Norman Parkinson*)

22 My first *Vogue* cover, March 1949 (*Norman Parkinson*)

23 (l-r) Betty Reeves, Maud Beard, HA, Mr Leonard, setting off for Buckingham Palace, 1954 (*Chris Ware*)

DAILY EXPRESS

No. 20,205   WEDNESDAY MAY 19 1965   Weather: Rain   Price 4d.

3,000 guests battle to see her at the castle

THE QUEEN DAZZLES THEM

ROYAL TOUR PORTFOLIO
PHOTONEWS
Pages 6 & 7

TV chief Hood is sacked

By MARTIN JACKSON

STUART HOOD, the programme controller who switched from the B.B.C. to commercial TV eight months ago, was sacked yesterday.

He was told at noon by Rediffusion, the London weekday company, that his £160-a-week contract had been terminated.

Immediately he cleared his desk and left his fourth-floor executive suite in Television House, Kingsway.

Mr. Hood, 49 years old and quiet-spoken, left the B.B.C. after two years as a programme controller. There was a disagreement over policy.

'Quicker'

He said at the time: "At ITV I find I do get things done much more quickly. One doesn't have to battle against any sort of mountainous bureaucracy."

But I understand there have been differences at Rediffusion over programme policy which are more important on the profit-conscious commercial television than at the B.B.C.

One of Mr. Hood's jobs as chairman of Rediffusion's programme board has been taken up by the company's general manager, Mr. John Macmillan.

While Mr. Hood was at the B.B.C. he introduced television programmes "That Was The Week That Was," "Compact," "Dr. Finlay's Casebook."

He is married with three children.

From COLIN LAWSON and ARTHUR COXWORTH
Bonn, Tuesday

GERMANY was stunned tonight by a scene it scarcely dreamed of—the Queen at a fairy castle on the Rhine in dazzling array.

TV cameras took the picture into millions of homes, and, illegally, into East Germany.

A PICTURE of the Queen arriving for a state banquet at the Augustusburg Castle wearing a glittering turquoise and white gown with pearl and diamond tiara.

A PICTURE that would have thrilled London. A PICTURE that had the Germans—used to being ruled by dull, if dangerous men—in an ecstasy.

Smiling

The Queen was still smiling gaily too after the long, tough first day of her visit. Before her row was a "political" speech to make at dinner, and a vast reception.

This was no martial affair (Prince Philip had swiftly changed from R.A.F. uniform). It was the Queen's night, a night for every free and fearless to savour, a night for the men to sit back and wonder.

At 100 special guests dined upstairs, there was near-chaos below with 3,000 people arriving for the reception, all pushing and shoving for vantage points along the edges of the royal red carpet.

A "dash" was the signal that dinner was over and the Queen was coming downstairs.

On a long terrace, silk-canopied, people clambered on chairs to peer through the noise windows.

Inside, aisles were cleared by protocol officials. Through the divided ranks a cool, supremely confident and smiling Queen passed slowly, pausing to talk occasionally to peer at a guest.

Down the full 400 yards of carpet she went, turned and came back with Prince Philip following.

Trouble

The Prince's German. It turns out is not so hot. A number of times he opened conversations with German guests and had to lapse into English or call for an interpreter.

His favourite targets were from Cross-beating veterans wearing white tie and tails.

"To one he said "Waren die Engländer ?" "Were you a brave soldier ?" The reaction officer he was speaking to was somewhat surprised and replied "Nein sir, ja." The interpreter had to be recalled.

One of the principal guests who were Prince Georg of Hanover, that the Queen and Prince Philip had asked to be invited was Mr. Albert Speer, first band master at Auschwitz and Grossadmiral Dönitz.

After the reception the Queen and Prince Philip set to watch the German floodlit performance the ceremony of beating the retreat by the castle's gardens, lighted by thousands of candles. It was a grand finale.

The key

Yet the key to this whole evening had been the banquet.

The menu: pâté, consommé, soup, chicken, strawberries. Wines: a 1959 Rhine wine, a 1961 Moselle, a 1961 Rhine, a Fleur Fixin 1959, and German champagne.

Fairly simple fare. The emphasis was much more complicated. This is what the Queen said—

This visit will take us from the northern shore of Germany and from the banks of the Rhine to Berlin, and I look forward to meeting people in all walks of life and in all parts of Germany.

I am also looking forward to seeing historic and other places of historic and personal interest.

The German and British people were very deeply associated for many centuries. For most of their history they have been friends and often allies.

They have gone much in common and much in civilisation and culture. Throughout the centuries there has been a constant traffic in ideas not pointing to all forms of cultural and intellectual...

Robb captures the brilliance of a gown that stunned a nation

Radiant entrance by the Queen

GIRL ARTIST STABBED TO DEATH

Express Staff Reporter

THE night 19-year-old artist Julie Whittaker broke a promise to her father she died—stabbed in a lilac-shrouded lane five yards from her home.

The promise that she would never walk down "Lilac Lane" alone at night.

She always waited at a friend's home for her father to meet her and escort her down "Lilac Lane" where several woman have been attacked. But her fear on Monday night her killer met her instead.

Her warnings were ignored, and red-haired Julie was left dying in her back gate in Oadby, Cheshire. She was found 18 minutes later by a 17 year-old youth.

A senior detective said last night: "This was a particularly brutal murder. There appears to be no motive. There was no struggle and she had not been assaulted."

Julie normally waited for her father at Jennifer Loftus's house 200 yards from her own home. But on Monday, after an evening out, she left Jennifer at 10.30—and started off home.

Nine more than 50 police are trying to fill in the vital minutes after that.

Lady Churchill picks title

Lady Churchill gave a title yesterday to the portrait she chose for the state pension. She will be known as Baroness Spencer-Churchill, of Chartwell in the County of Kent.

Paintings found

The two Turner landscape paintings drawing from Marble School turned up yesterday at Norwich, Middlesex, after two weeks away. Two men found them wrapped in newspaper on a car bonnet.

A-men walk out

Seven men walked out of Austin Benwick Redmayne, stood steel drop forging plant at Dudley yesterday and 250 more were laid off when a lunchtime between the manager and a workman.

Skipper plans an appeal

BEVERLEY Tourley skipper Lome Tourley of the Grimsby trawler Aldershot was sentenced to four months' jail today for defaulting and threatening two members of his crew, intends to appeal against the disqualification.

In Grimsby the trawler's agents said Crosby had been refused booking an agency and would travel back to England.

Furniture Blaze

Furniture worth £6,000 was destroyed in a fire at Kirby St. Wheeler, Buckinghamshire, yesterday.

Springtime now ...

... fall in high gear at Kent's Mest Railway yesterday.

COST OF LIVING JUMP IS HIGHEST FOR TEN YEARS

By TREVOR EVANS

THE cost of living index rose higher in April than in any month for nearly 10 years. And most of the increase was due to the Budget.

This will affect the pay claims of more than 3,000,000 people and is bound to dominate acceptance of Mr. George Brown's incomes policy by other unions.

Last night, Mr. Ray Gunter, the Labour Minister announced that the Index of Retail Prices on April 13—a new index for the Budget—was 113 (100-9 on March 16).

This rising has not been equalled since October-November 1955.

Of the increase, 1.4 was accounted for by Mr. Callaghan's dearer drinking, driving, and car licences. The rest was shared by local rates and variations in domestic foodstuffs. A rise in food prices was only partly offset by seasonal reductions in the price of coal.

H.P. squeeze

The big hire-purchase firms yesterday decided to fall in with the call from Bank of England Governor Lord Cromer to keep lending down.

Car buyers will face bigger down-payments and have to repay faster.

£13 million exit

Dr. Richard Beeching, in his report outlining the future of Britain's railways, says the cost can be cut by £13 or £20 million a year.

Full details—Page Thirteen

No point

German currency will not be declared in Britain this year—Commons Answers yesterday.

LATEST

AMMONIA ATTACK
Matthew Hayton Pinkton, aged 23, of Willesden Lane, London, called to hospital after gunshot officers ammonia over at junction of Harlesden Road and Fortune Road. Gunders Green stopped Pinkton's car and three gunmen in his door.

BUS CRASH
LEEDS: Rain was fire and students killed and about 20 injured when a bus and lorry plunged 100ft. down embankment near Leeds today.

RADIO, TV Page 18

No other weedkiller does)

FLEet Street 8000

BEING beautifully dressed means being perfectly dressed for the occasion. The Queen is always just that. Last night, for her first evening reception, the Queen paid her German hosts the delicate compliment of wearing a gown in the blue and white of the family colours of the creator of Augustusburg Castle. The dress is shaped like a hack glass, with narrow stem bodice and belling skirt. It glitters like a chandelier. The bodice, of turquoise blue organza is entirely encrusted with bead embroidery—tiny white china beads and lozenge and rose cut diamante. Mr. Hardy Amies, the London couturier, was inspired by this embroidery motif by the lavish Rococo decorations by Cuvilliés at Augustusburg Castle. The shining skirt gleams in pale turquoise blue satin with a tiered stitched hemline.

---

24 'a gown that stunned a nation': the *Daily Express* reacts to the rococo-inspired dress worn by the Queen at Schloss Brühl, Germany, 19 May 1965

25 The Silver Jubilee, the Queen at St Paul's, 1977 (*Serge Lemoine*)

26 The photograph of the Queen that adorned a thousand biscuit tins at the time of the Silver Jubilee (*Peter Grugeon*)

27 Short evening dress, bodice in guipire lace, Erik cartwheel hat, *Vogue*, March 1950 (*Honeyman*)

atmosphere of Russell & Allen. He left Lachasse shortly after I did, but was now unhappy in his present employment and agreed to join me. I needed him desperately, and I could never say that I paid dearly for his services, for he was a beautiful tailor and all those first models that he made for me were wonderful.

Cammie had always told me that, if I left Worth, Odette and Leonard would follow me. I did not want to disturb the House of Worth by taking either of them, particularly as Pay, and especially Mrs Mortimer, had been so kind to us. I tried hard to get Miss Sutherland to come to me as a fitter; she had been at Lachasse before the war and had left because of ill health, but she felt she was not strong enough to help build up a new business . I felt I had to speak to Odette, and she said straight out that she would have been most hurt if I had not taken her. I think she felt that as she was not one of the head fitters at Worth, which meant that she was not entrusted with the most important models, she would have missed not working for me; or it may just have been that we both liked each other very much, and respected each other's work. What was fine for me, but rather wretched for Worth, was that practically all of Odette's workroom wanted to move with her: such moves are traditional in our business.

But all this did not take place at once. On Monday 12 November 1945 we officially moved into 14 Savile Row. We were a party of about eight or nine. Only two rooms on the very top floor were habitable, or even watertight. We had no stocks of material, or indeed of anything except several rolls of brown paper. It was from this that we immediately started to cut out patterns. I had, of course, prepared a whole bundle of sketches beforehand, having worked on them in the country.

I was in one room with Cammie and Violet. In another there was Victor with a few workers. The following week Odette joined us from Worth. I had engaged as house manager a very reliable administrator, Ted Fothergill, who had been in charge of the SOE mess and office in Brussels.

So we started working, chased from one room to the other by the workmen. We were desperately short of workroom hands both for the dressmaking and the tailoring. There were simply none to be had for so many had gone into the services and were not yet released. Furthermore, in our business, employing as it does so many young girls, there has to be a constant stream of apprentices to replace those who go off to get married. We found ourselves, therefore, with just a handful of middle-aged workers and a lot of youngsters whom we had to train. We took on all sorts of strange bodies, refugees and complete beginners.

There were a million things to see to, and a million battles to be fought. The Board of Trade was as helpful as could be, but of course its benevolence took a long time to warm up the frigidity of the Ministry of Works. I just went blithely ahead, but I could not afford to do more than the necessities.

No sooner were models finished than we seemed to have visitors who wanted to order clothes. I would only see overseas buyers who could not come back again when we were better established. Many of the important American stores had sent over representatives on this, their first trip since the war. Many came for the very first time, and whilst they seemed to appreciate intelligently the models, some of them simply had no idea as to how we worked, and seemed to think of us in the same terms as they would of the big wholesale houses on Seventh Avenue in New York. We had booked quite a quantity of orders for firms like Marshall Field of Chicago, and I. Magnin of California, before we actually had our opening show on 28 January 1946.

It was only a few hours before this opening that the showroom was ready for occupation. The last pieces of felt were being tacked down as the customers came up the stairs. I say felt, because in those days we simply could not get enough carpet, which was a good thing, because I could not have afforded it anyway. I was glad, however, that I made the mistake of choosing a very dark purple felt, which looked almost black. It showed up every thread and every dusty footprint. Never, dear readers, have a dark carpet. Besides it makes the room look terribly small. I was glad to cover it up a year or so later with beige carpet.

The panelling in the showroom was certainly beautiful. Miss Norton had had it stripped, which pleased everybody except the purists and connoisseurs of Georgian architecture, who never ceased to tell me that I must have it repainted and that such panelling was designed for painting and gilding. I eventually gave in and it is now painted white. The house was quite difficult to furnish cheaply. I had had no experience of George II architecture, and furniture of that period had always been way beyond my purse, so of course I easily made the mistake of buying Victorian and Regency things, which looked hopelessly wrong. To make the purple felt carpet worse, I added sour yellow curtains, which were absurd. However, nobody seemed to mind all these things and I had great fun, as the months went by, months going into years, in getting rid of my mistakes and buying afresh, particularly when I had completely absorbed the atmosphere of the house and understood its proportions.

'Child,' said John Fowler, who always talked as if he were one's grandfather, 'child, you must remember this house needs weight. You must give up all attempts to make these beautifully proportioned rooms look like a dress shop.' He then proceeded to decorate my office as if it were that of a solicitor: a rather unreliable, smart solicitor, I may add, which was just the effect I wanted.

Alexis ffrench helped, mostly by telling me not to be extravagant, as it was only a shop. He rather spoilt the effect by producing a handsome bookcase and looking-glass which were exactly right and which he knew I would find irresistible.

In those early days, however, our thoughts were on more vital things. It was the clothes that mattered. It is a most wonderful feeling when you know exactly what you want to do, and then do it. I have never been more single-minded than in making that first collection. I knew that I wanted to make tailored clothes, curved more strongly than ever before. We did not think of narrowing the shoulders, which had remained wide through the whole of the war. Victor, indeed, had made them in my opinion too wide, whilst he had been working away from me. He had a technique of draping the material from this width over the bust, which was particularly becoming to stout women. I wanted all attention to be centred on the hipline, and the only way to achieve the effect I desired was to put in tiny pads covered with canvas. Our first attempts were not always successful: even on the models we sometimes got them in the wrong place, but we were saying something, and the Americans, who had never seen anything like that before, were most impressed. Of course it took a long time for our fatter customers to get used to the idea. Later we achieved the same effect with shaped canvas rather than with any actual padding.

There was an enormous amount of tiresome and difficult work to be done behind the scenes. The weather was also most unhelpful, for it was cold and damp that winter. The eighteenth-century house was riddled with draughts and we only had central heating on the first floor. The workrooms were heated with a mixture of electric and gas stoves. Owing to the high pressure of business, tempers became frayed and Cammie, never very lenient to the inexperienced, continually complained of Fothergill's shortcomings. He, poor man, tried to enforce an Orderly Room routine on a pack of slightly temperamental and excitable women, and only succeeded, excessively conscientious as he was, in worrying himself into an illness. He was away with double pneumonia most of all those critical early months. However everybody worked with great good will and dresses were sometimes delivered by one of the builders' workmen who, of course, were with us for months.

It all settled down somehow, for on 30 April I went over to the United States where I was received with enthusiasm and where I showed the first British model clothes since before the war.

I came back to find business so good that I had to devise a scheme whereby each saleswoman had a quota. We tried to work out what would be the output during the season of each workroom, and this was divided equally amongst the saleswomen, otherwise it would be found that a saleswoman had taken a lot of orders which simply could not be executed.

We were still desperately short of workroom hands, and I visited several technical schools and art schools, and indeed anywhere it seemed likely that we could recruit labour.

Before I settled down to designing the autumn collection, I snatched two weeks' holiday with Alexis and some friends in a villa near Cannes. All of us had known and loved France before the war and this was a most exciting return to well-loved sights, smells and flavours. I was able to go over to Nice and visit Aunt Louie and tell her all my exciting news. She was still living in her little flat, doing her own chores, happy in her few wants, and proud of her independence.

Working near our little corner at Worth there had been a Worth *vendeuse* named Marthe. She was a Frenchwoman, married to an Englishman, and had lived over here for many years. I believe even before her marriage she had started to work at Worth. She was thus an old friend of Cammie's. She had always used Odette as a fitter, and she was naturally considerably upset when Odette came to me. Furthermore, Leonard the tailor was also getting restless. Any scruples that Marthe may have had at leaving a fine old well-established house like Worth for a new one such as mine, not to mention the loyalty that she owed to that house, were overcome when she saw that if she moved Leonard would come too. It all seems so natural now, but it was an important move then. Marthe as a saleswoman and Leonard as a tailor, complete with a good workroom of experienced hands and both with a very good clientele, joined me in the autumn. This operation, I must say, did produce a protest from Pay: quite naturally. But I can honestly say that I never persuaded them in any way to make the change by offering them any more money or any other form of inducement. I merely told them that I should be delighted to have them. Such changes are very typical of our business. People have often moved on from me, to better themselves financially or to express themselves artistically, or just because they are restless and want a change; it is as inevitable as the acorn falling from the tree to bring forth the sapling of next spring.

After the initial shock, which was barely more than an inconvenience, both Lachasse and Worth continued to flourish.

About this time, too, little Violet Allen, my faithful friend from Lachasse, decided that she would retire and devote herself to being a wife to her husband, whom she had married before the war. She had said that she would not leave me until she saw me comfortably settled, and now she thought this time had come. Her place was taken smoothly and silently by Betty Reeves, who had joined Paulette as a junior in the millinery showroom exactly at the same time as I started work at Lachasse. From there she had moved on to join me as a salesgirl at Lachasse, which she left in due course to join the Forces.

I now had two tailors, Mr Victor and Mr Leonard, but I had only one dressmaker, Odette. Apart from the pressure of work it seemed imperative to have another dressmaker in case Odette should ever fall ill. Curiously enough, fitters and tailors never do fall ill: they drag themselves in to fittings even though they feel extremely unwell; and if they take to their beds you can be sure they really are sick. There is nothing like a crowded appointment book for keeping you from worrying about your health.

With my usual luck, fate had let it be known to Miss Maud Beard that I was in business and needed her help. She, with her sister Mabel, had been apprenticed in the dressmaking workroom with Miss Gray during my mother's time. She had moved with our old friend Miss Fowler, the skirt fitter, when she joined Lilian Moon at her newly-opened business in Conduit Street. There she had remained until it was closed down at the outbreak of war, and she went to supervise the making of parachutes. Although she had known me since I was two, I knew very little of her work, but no sooner had she started with us than we saw what a genius she had for the handling of all fabrics. She had practically no workers, and we had quite a struggle mustering a workroom for her. However, eventually she collected a skilled little band around her.

Following another, successful trip to America I returned to find all well, except that it was perfectly evident that we were sadly in need of a really good manager, preferably a male with a good knowledge of the business. Not for the last time Marthe came to the rescue. She suggested I should see young Stanley Cox. His mother and his father had both worked with Marthe at Worth, and as a young boy he had been put into the stockroom at Molyneux. He had now gone back there after his war service, but was fairly unhappy. I could tell at our first interview that he was just the person I was looking for. I went straight round to Molyneux and asked if they would release him. Kathleen Molyneux, who managed the business while her brother was in Paris, seemed to think that I was placing too much responsibility on inexperienced shoulders. I suppose she still saw Stanley as the young boy who had joined them years ago. However, he joined me and became a highly respected addition to the staff.

From the beginning we had done as good business with the great stores of Canada as we had with those of America, and it had been hinted that the Canadians were a little piqued that I had already been twice to the United States, without apparently bothering to visit them. It was absolutely necessary for me to go to the States again that autumn, because Marshall Field's had commissioned me to design a wedding scene for the St Luke's show in Chicago for which they wanted a European design. It was very flattering that they should have chosen me from the whole of Paris and London *couture*.

I had gone to America this time by sea, on the *Mauritania*. I had stayed a few days in New York and in Boston on my way to Montreal. Although the Canadian invitations had been most cordial, I had not gone to Montreal sponsored by any store in particular, but I had received great encouragement from Henry Morgan's.

As in the USA, my days were crowded with press conferences and visits to all the various departments in the labyrinthine stores.

From Toronto I went to Detroit again, and on to Chicago. I returned to New York on the *Twentieth Century*, but this time I had graduated from an ordinary sleeping berth to a drawing-room, which means that I sat solemnly all by myself in quite a large compartment, to which my meals were brought. I would far rather have gone along to the dining car. I suppose it is one of those things that one ought to do once in one's life.

Back in New York, I was happy to find Nina Leclerq. At the end of the war Nina had left Fortnum's and had gone back to *Vogue*, but this time to work in Paris as fashion editor of the *Vogue* published there. She was paying an official visit to New York in that capacity. We had a happy luncheon together at Voisins, which was my favourite New York restaurant, but now alas, is no more.

About this time Peter Hope Lumley joined us as public relations consultant. He was a nephew of Captain Edward Molyneux; his mother was Kathleen Lumley, who for so long ran the London House of Molyneux. He had worked with his uncle but had not got on with him, which so often happens amongst relations. By this time, my House had settled down to be one of some importance. In the old days, as she had done for me at Worth, Cammie had looked after the press, but now she was too busy with her customers to attend to this important matter. At this stage, however, I realized how necessary it was for us to give the press good services, even if only as a matter of mere politeness. Having the new premises next door, I was able to lease Peter a small office. He was to work representing all sorts of other firms, but of course no one else in *haute couture*. This was the beginning of a most happy relationship. Peter interprets to me the point of view of the man in the street. As the years go by and I am able to afford things like a motorcar and chauffeur, so can I get more and more isolated from the everyday facts of life. Peter can bring me back with a jolt.

So another year drew to its close, ending up at it always did with a Christmas party. In 1945 we held this in the attic workrooms, with iced cakes that I had coaxed Mme Floris into making. The next year we all had roast turkey in the canteen, but 1947 was noted for the terrible discomfort and overcrowding, so big had our party become.

In the spring of 1948 I went over, as I so often did, to spend a few days in Paris. Nina had her own little flat in the Place du Palais Bourbon, and it was wonderful to have her as a guide to all the restaurants and theatres, but the highlight of my trip was a visit to Christian Dior's establishment. He himself was not there, but through Nina's good offices he had left instructions for me to be shown anything I wanted to see. I was, of course, vastly impressed with the collection, but what interested me most was to see behind the scenes. For the house, open only a little more than a year, now held between six and seven hundred employees. Some of the workrooms were so crowded that the girls sat on the stairs, with the long trains of some of the more important dresses hanging over the balustrades. I think all the girls were happy to work under any conditions for that great man.

In the late summer I received a visit from my old friend Mr Ernest, the tailor from Lachasse. He had been in the Army during the war and was now tailoring again, but was most unhappy in his present position. Would I not take him on? Now, as it happened, the pressure of work on both Leonard's and Victor's room was quite considerable. Victor above all seemed to be suffering from overwork. With a little juggling I felt that we could arrange for the space to open a third tailoring room. So Ernest came to me for the opening of the autumn season.

In the spring of 1949 I was off again to the States; this time I went there and back on the *Queen Elizabeth*. I planned this journey very carefully and, having managed to obtain the comfortable cabins I wanted, thoroughly enjoyed the trip both ways, although I was shocked at the banality of the décor and the pretentiousness of the food, however much I admired the magnificent organization and the excellently disciplined services. I had long since given up hopes of seeing all those beautifully dressed, witty people one saw in the advertisements. The return trip I remember as being one during which we hardly left the card tables, as I had learnt canasta in New York and was by now an addict.

When I got back I found Victor in a very unhappy state. Ever since we had opened we had never been anything other than extremely busy. There was simply no slack season at all. Indeed, I had had to give instructions that no orders would be accepted from customers for about a month before the end of the season, in order that there should be space in the workrooms available to make the new collection. Victor was by no means an old man, but I think his health had been impaired greatly by the sorrow he had suffered from the loss of his only and much-loved daughter during the war. Cammie's character also, never the sweetest, was beginning to show itself most difficult. She used to nag Victor mercilessly. A customer had only to hint that she wanted her suit by such-and-such a date for her to magnify this into a matter of life and death. I was not only aware of this state of affairs, but I also had a suspicion that Victor really wanted to go off and start a little business of his own. He had often hinted this. When he formally and correctly gave his notice, I had a long talk with him but I could see that his mind was clearly made up, and in these circumstances I have always felt that it is better not to persuade people to change it.

Cammie, however, during the next season did nothing but bemoan the loss of Victor. In a curious way she was one of the most unadaptable women I can think of; she did nothing to help Ernest: and it was so essential that he should be built up to gain the customers' confidence, as quickly as possible. The hostility between Cammie and Ernest became so bad that in the end Ernest came to me and said that he would have to leave, unless it could be arranged that he did not have to work for Miss Campbell.

The time had come for me to do some very serious thinking. I had no idea how old Cammie really was, but I suspected that she was over seventy although she didn't look it. Usually dressed in black, with very high-heeled shoes, I have never seen her with anything other than four rows of pearls and a large imitation *cabochon* emerald ring. She wore her clothes with a certain distinction, and she was always of an immense neatness, but no matter where she was, if you thought twice about such things, you would have said at once, 'A dress shop': and why shouldn't she look like this, for the dress shop was her life?

In the true court dressmaker tradition, she knew the lineage of anybody who was anybody. She was a great reader of newspapers, particularly of the type that are full of gossip, but she would also delight in talking politics, and when I asked her one day why she did not read *The Times* she said, 'Oh, I can't bear it: it never has any news in it.'

I cannot describe how much I owe to her in the formation of my business; she also knew a great deal about dressmaking, and herself sewed beautifully. She was one of the most competent and experienced saleswomen in London.

Although she was never away ill for one day during the whole time of our acquaintance – indeed, I can only remember one instance when she left the business early because she was feeling unwell – it was quite evident to all of us that her health was deteriorating: she looked thin and drawn, even under her heavy make-up.

I would consult her, as always, about many matters, and if I gave her time to reflect her opinion was usually of great value. As in the old Army days, she would often telephone my flat in the evening and we would have a long chat, which we often did not have time to do at business.

I cannot remember that I had any particular reason for being nervous or rundown that winter. Although the loss of Victor was of importance to the house, I had had such confidence in Ernest that I had not changed my plans to spend a month in Venice that summer. This is not the place to describe my feelings for that beautiful city, which I was to visit for two further years. But Ernest's attitude, when he came to tell me he was going, suddenly made me realize how difficult and impossible Cammie was becoming.

Throughout the whole of January, when I was making the collection, I kept on wondering how it was going to end. There was a horrible atmosphere in the house, which I knew could not go on. About two days before the shows which open the season, we always have what is called a 'Costing Conference'. The price of each new dress which has been seen at the dress rehearsal is discussed, the *vendeuses* are told what it has cost, why it cost so much, or, less frequently, why it is so cheap; the stock-keeper reports where the material has come from and what chance there is of getting any more of it and for how long. It is always rather a nerve-racking business. If a black lace dress is being discussed, you may be sure that someone will say it is not as pretty or as cheap or as becoming as 'Spider's Web' of last season. I suddenly looked up and saw Cammie shaking her head in the way that only obstinate old women can do. In a flash I realized that she was a very sick, obstinate old woman, and that the time had come for me to do something about it.

Although she scrupulously kept herself apart from my private life, Cammie was as near a mother to me as anyone has been since my own mother died. That is to say she took the part my mother would have played, in so far as the business was concerned. She felt I was 'her baby': as indeed I was. It was a terrible moment and I suppose I felt as a son might when asking his own mother to leave a family business. It was all over in fifteen minutes. Ten minutes later she was out of the house, and I never saw her again.

A year later I was suddenly telephoned by someone who said that she was the wife of a doctor who was an old friend of Miss Campbell's. This doctor had attended her husband in his illness, but since that time neither she nor the doctor had seen Cammie. 'She rang up and asked my husband to go to her, and when he arrived he was shocked at her appearance. He quickly examined her and found that she had five open cancerous wounds, some of which she must have known about and had tended for several years. We got her immediately to hospital, but she was dead within three days.'

She left instructions with these friends that she was to be cremated. At the funeral there was no one except the doctor and his wife, Marthe, Odette and me. She left no will and it took a year for her solicitor to discover about a dozen Campbell cousins, amongst whom her little estate was divided.

I know I did the right thing in making her leave then: but I still think I did the right thing badly; I hope I never again have the opportunity of doing it better.

In the weeks that followed my dismissal of Cammie, I felt pretty low. The whole business seemed to weigh heavily on my shoulders and I got no pleasure from the fact that we were still extremely busy. Kind as all my staff were to me – and at moments they were very kind – I felt extraordinarily lonely. I did not want to make any particular member of the staff my confidant: I did not want another Cammie.

The business continued to prosper, and by 1950 I felt sure that we were a success. Also in that year we were commanded by Princess Elizabeth, as she was then, to make clothes for the state visit to Canada. The results of this were to have far-reaching implications for the future of my business.

Although Hardy Amies Ltd was thriving and all the workrooms

63

were busy, I sensed at about this time a feeling of change in the air. Up till then all our business had been conducted along the strict lines of *haute couture* manufacture; that is to say, bespoke tailoring. But some of the French fashion houses had begun to experiment with an alternative method of manufacture, that of ready-to-wear clothing. The idea was to have a department within the house making clothes of simpler construction involving perhaps only one fitting, and which, therefore, could be sold far more cheaply. This was designed to bridge the gap between the swelling prices of *haute couture* clothes and the shrinking incomes of the regular customers. This department became known as the 'boutique'.

Since all the intelligently run fashion houses had their boutiques, the idea of opening one in my own house intrigued me, and I set about making space for this new department at the back of the showrooms in Savile Row. From the outset I had determined that this boutique would not be a prop to the couture business but merely a healthy offshoot from it. It had to be totally independent, therefore. The all-important question that arose from this decision was who was actually going to run it. Only one name came immediately to mind: Nina Leclercq.

Nina Leclercq had been a friend of mine from the early days of Lachasse. Totally English on her mother's side and educated at English schools, she had nonetheless quite a lot of foreign blood in her. One of her French cousins, Michel de Brunhoff, was the then editor of French *Vogue*. Another cousin, Lucien Vogel, was the proprietor of a famous fashion magazine, *Le Jardin des Modes*. She was thus steeped in the fashion world, and moreover, through her subsequent work on French *Vogue*, had an intimate knowledge of the fashion scene in Paris as well as in London. I had doubted whether she would accept my offer of returning to England to run the boutique, but to my great delight she did.

To begin with the boutique offered ready-to-wear suits and overcoats but soon expanded to include such items as fine gloves, cashmere sweaters and scarves, linen blouses, and silk and wool dresses. Throughout we made strenuous efforts to ensure that what we offered was unmistakably English and unlike the *frivolités* to be found then in the French boutiques. Naturally, we had worried from the outset whether the sales of these items at their reduced prices would have any impact on the sales of our *couture* clothes. In fact the worry proved groundless and the *couture* side of the business continued to expand of its own accord. The boutique also increased its sales and within two years had become half as big as the *couture* business.

The boutique business as it was then is very different from what we know of it today and not everyone at the time thought it was a good idea. Marthe had been particularly wary of the venture. Although married to an Englishman, she had deep-rooted connections with the *couture* business in France where her mother owned the important fashion newspaper *L'Officiel*. Marthe had thought the advent of the boutique meant the death-knell of *couture*. So strong had been her feelings on this that she persuaded other saleswomen at Savile Row to follow her in her anti-boutique campaign. The result of this was that, to begin with, we had to have separate showings of the boutique collections. It was some years before we were able to show these clothes with the main collection, a practice which eventually became the accepted norm in all fashion houses.

In the boutique we started to sell men's ties. I had had these made by the celebrated firm of Michelsons. The head was a charming man born in Cologne, with an English wife. I loved them both and still do. Hans Wallach had noticed the beginning of the use in Paris of women's designers tastes and names on men's ties. It was 1959. Jacques Fath had started ties in Paris: Cardin was to follow. Hans Wallach's foresight made my entry in the men's field, mostly with ties, amongst some of the first. They have been successful ever since. Our visits to the tie silk weavers of Como, to lay down plans for the coming year, to watch Hans Wallach's successor, Harry Bonser, fold neatly a piece of tie silk into a knot, are delights of which I never tire. Ties are designed by merchants like Harry Bonser with a designer like me at his side, in rooms literally adjoining the looms. Alternatives to designs and to colours can be discussed in the morning and new samples woven during luncheon in a lake side *albergo*, ready for further examination during the afternoon.

Meanwhile back home we were doing more and more business with customers abroad, particularly in the United States and Canada, largely as a result of the work I had done for the Board of Trade during the war. One of the results of this expansion into the foreign markets was that during this period in the fifties I had to go abroad more and more often to promote and sell our clothes. This meant, of course, leaving the team at Savile Row to cope with the London end of my business. They were all expert people and I had no hesitation in leaving everything in their care. But as the business expanded so the running of it became increasingly complicated and burdensome. We needed extra managerial help. Without hesitation I thought of Eric Crabtree. He was to play a very important part in the development of my busienss. I had known Eric for some time but not very well, and it was only after the war, when he had decided to give up practising law to go into business instead, that we became closer.

Naturally, Eric's first advice had been to get more capital into the business. We went to the head office of our bank and showed all the figures. Eric was very persuasive in such moments. The bank official listened for a while and then excused himself from the room. When he returned he said simply, 'You can have the money. I'll go and get the papers for you to sign,' and left the room. Eric, who was always a great embracer of people, leapt up and embraced me before we both started on a graceful Viennese waltz around the office, which was only interrupted by the return of a very surprised banker.

Shortly after this it was arranged that Bill Aykroyd (now Sir William Aykroyd) should join my team, bringing with him some more capital. A very distinguished accountant, Campbell-Nelson, joined my board of directors at the request of Bill's father. A little later Bunny Roger, who had had a small dressmaking business of his own, brought to Savile Row his little team of workers and some further capital.

Both Bunny and Bill brought a lot of verve to the house, and they were of immense help in building up our reputation. They were to show the true strength of their friendship to me by quickly agreeing to sell their shares to Hepworths and Debenhams when asked to do so.

Both the *couture* and boutique sides of the business continued to prosper throughout the fifties, and by the end of the decade our reputation couldn't have been higher. By then we were well established as one of the Queen's dressmakers, and as a result of this work we were also holders of the Royal Warrant, a seal which gave us extra prestige. Our export business had increased not only in volume but also in the number of new retail outlets in the United States and Canada interested in selling our clothes. We were therefore secure and all that was needed was a steady hand in ensuring that the business continued to flourish along the lines we had so carefully established. I had no ambitions at the time other than to see that this was the case. But a chance telephone call was to change all that and to steer my business in a direction that I hadn't foreseen.

In 1959 I was telephoned by Prince Yurka Galitzine, who handled public relations for Hepworths. He said he had a business proposition to make and he asked me to lunch with him at Brooks's in such a charming way that, although he was a stranger, I remember having no hesitation in accepting. He wanted to interest me in the idea of designing men's clothes for Hepworths which was at the time a powerful clothing business with retail outlets throughout the country. He felt that I could help them. If I was interested I was to go to Leeds to meet the directors to discuss the possibilities. I agreed, but only on the understanding that I would be accompanied by my financial adviser, Eric Crabtree. The first thing Eric did when he heard of the offer was to check out Hepworths' Stock Exchange card, something which, quite frankly, I never knew existed. He came back to me with the words: 'It isn't a card, it's a poem!' Armed with this information we set forth for Leeds.

There was an air of mystery and subterfuge about the arrangements for the visit. Eric and I were to go straight from the station in Leeds to a private room in the Queens Hotel. The project we were to discuss was considered too revolutionary and too full of potential disturbance to the staff of Hepworths for it to be done any other way. If we reached agreement then I could visit the factory. We came to an agreement very quickly, a fact which at first surprised the directors. They were even more surprised when I told them that I could have a collection prepared for them within about two months. They seemed delighted and it was arranged that the collection, when ready, would be shown to their managers. A fee was arranged and we set to work at once.

There followed another one of those exciting times in the life of a designer. I knew exactly what I wanted to do: I wanted to make about thirty outfits showing how I thought a man should be dressed. I gave no thought to the fact that Hepworths' clientele were not rich and that the greater part of their chain of over three hundred shops was situated out of London, mainly in the midlands and in the north. The style of their clothes could be described as more middle-of-the-road than fashionable. It has never been my policy to play down; in clothes you must make men and women look up. In those days fashion's job was to make a man or a woman look and feel richer and younger than they were, and more attractive. I went straight to my old friend Mr Wyser, of the tailors Wyser & Bryant, the man who had made me my first London suit in 1934, and told him what I was going to do.

When the suits were ready there arose the problem of how to promote them. The directors of Hepworths were uneasy on this, and they were even more worried when I told them that I planned to give a show, just as we did with our women's collection, only using male models. They thought the sight of a group of male models parading up and down would make them a laughing stock, but I managed to persuade them that this would not be the case. The first showing was in a house owned by Yurka Galitzine. At the end of it there was a stunned silence. Then one of Hepworths' managers said in an amazed voice, 'By gum, we could sell these!' Within weeks the suits were on sale in all the Hepworths' stores.

The second show was held in the Savoy Hotel and three hundred guests were invited. Among them were many members of the press, not all of them by any means fashion journalists; there were city editors as well as other staff reporters. A dozen male models paraded up and down with umbrellas in the military shoulder-arms position and to the accompaniment of the tune of the *British Grenadiers*. The show was an immediate success and was the first of a series of September shows that were to be a feature during the following seven years. More important to us was the fact that the show attracted attention from overseas. At one showing was the director of Genesco, the American corporation. 'Boy, just what I need in the States!' he said. As a result of this encounter I was invited by Genesco to go to the United States to show some of these men's suits and to discuss arrangements whereby they could be made and sold under licence. It proved to be the beginnings of what was to be a major diversification of my business.

It may be asked why it was necessary for an established firm like Hepworths to have approached a women's fashion designer, like myself, to be involved in designing men's suits. The answer is that in men's fashion there were no designers. There had been none of the traditions found in women's fashion. More to the point, there was no time to train designers and so it was natural that they should have come to someone like me for help. Also, it was useful for them to be able to market a product bearing a name, and preferably a name based on a solid reputation. From Hepworths' point of view the use of my name gave the suits a semi-*couture* status. In time this use-of-designer-names, as it became known, was to have a dramatic effect in the development of the whole field of men's fashion.

This venture into men's fashion proved a great success, and after a time we became so built into Hepworths and so much a part of their image to the world and the Stock Exchange that Eric Crabtree persuaded them to put money into my business. This they did and one of their directors joined my board at Savile Row. Eric, meanwhile, had become a director of Hepworths. He had also by then sold his firm Cresta to another clothing firm, Debenhams, in a deal which had allowed him to continue in the running of the company. Thus by 1965 I was able to brush shoulders with the leaders of two very powerful companies trading in men's and women's clothes. The link with Debenhams particularly was to play an important part in the history of my business in the following years.

Eric had also enlarged the scope of the women's side of my business by making an arrangement with Selincourt, another large clothing company, the head of which was an absolutely charming man called Louis Mintz. Mintz, a Jew of the strictest and most orthodox kind, also had businesses in Israel, and one day he insisted that Eric and I go with him on a trip there. He thought we could help him with some of the problems he was having in certain areas of his clothing business. We waived the matter of a fee for this and asked only that he pay for our travel and lodgings. We also stipulated that we would only be available to him every other day, thus leaving us free days in which to travel and see the sights in Israel. Eric was a friend of the British Ambassador in Israel and with him as our guide we could not have spent our days more profitably.

I mention this episode because as a result of having to make this trip there occurred a chance meeting which, yet again, had a dramatic influence on my future and the future of my business. In the waiting room at the start of our journey I saw a tall and elegant lady whose face seemed familiar. She seemed to recognize me too, and was the first to approach. 'You're Hardy Amies, aren't you. Do you remember me? I'm Tom Parr's mother. I was Mrs Parr, now I'm Lady Burney. That's my husband over there.' After introductions all round, our little group fell into lengthy and animated conversation. As Mrs Parr she had been a favourite customer at Lachasse and there was much to talk about. I had a seat next to her on the plane while Eric sat next to her husband, Sir Anthony Burney. Anthony Burney had just retired from the very eminent firm of accountants Binder Hamlyn. Eric was now quite a power behind the managerial scene at Debenhams and the two of them had a lot in common in the world of business. They quickly appreciated each other's qualities and seemed to talk non-stop throughout the journey.

After this chance meeting Sir Anthony Burney became chairman of Debenhams. Eric became a director of the company and, subsequently, vice-chairman. In 1973 Debenhams bought the whole of my company and in the process Hepworths were paid off, as were all the remaining shareholders, who behaved very generously in not doing anything to hinder the sale. Thus I added still a little bit more to my own capital.

Debenhams had originated as the famous dress shop Debenham & Freebody, housed in a magnificent building in Wigmore Street. In the post-war years it had succumbed to the craze – I can describe it as nothing else – of acquiring businesses. The bigger you were the better you were.

I will try to view my years working within the Debenhams group as objectively as possible. They were not unhappy years and it was regrettable that our final parting was tinged with a little bitterness. There were many faults on my side. Debenhams themselves had, I feel, not quite been able to decide what sort of image they wanted for their shops. They tended to think that the best way to ensure healthy profits was through a very high turnover of goods.

When Sir Anthony Burney took the helm he saw that this approach was not necessarily incompatible with *haute couture*. He thought it would be a good idea to purchase Hardy Amies Ltd, which held the Royal Warrant as dressmaker to the Queen, and H. & M. Rayne Ltd, shoemakers to the Queen. It seemed a splendid idea. We had made a good name for ourselves; we had a successful 'high-class' dressmaking business in Savile Row, *haute couture* and boutique, and we had been involved for fourteen years with Hepworths in the men's field. Above all we had established a licensee business abroad for men's and women's clothes bringing in revenue each year of quite interesting proportions. The moment seemed right for the development of our skill and experience and the exploitation of our name.

With the wisdom of hindsight it is easy to see now that one of our biggest mistakes in our association with Debenhams was in not insisting that a proper plan of campaign be set up. Both of us were very busy. A very serious obstacle was the sudden decline following the earlier boom years. The recession had already started and money was getting scarcer. When I think of the problems of my own little business I am overwhelmed by the thought of the magnitude of the difficulties that confronted a group like Debenhams.

The establishments of independent dress designers, whether *haute couture* or wholesale businesses, have been bought up by large consortiums all over the world. Some of the results have been happy, some not. I had learned of the need for independence when working for Lachasse in the thirties. Debenhams had promised that they would not interfere and that the standard and style of my life and my business would be unchanged. In this latter respect they behaved more than correctly. I was, however, encouraged to take but a little part in the running of the financial side of the business. This was not an uncomfortable arrangement for our licensee business overseas was growing rapidly and required a great deal of my time. With my newly appointed licensee director, Roger Whiteman, we were constantly visiting the flat in New York which we had taken in 1969. Ken Fleetwood, in the meantime, saw to it that the customers at Savile Row were well looked after.

With this newly formed association there came a strong desire to burst out into a scheme of manufacturing women's ready-to-wear clothes, particularly in the field of sporting and casual wear. We opened a boutique in Harvey Nichols and an independent shop in Hans Crescent, opposite the side of Harrods. These were successful in the sense that they were busy and the clothes sold well, but there was not a proper organization of manufacture. Two such shops, combined with the boutique at Savile Row, made a total of three. It is very difficult to organize successfully and profitably the manufacture of clothes of your own design to service only three shops. The cost of employing skilled cutters and graders to size are high and should be spread over a quantity of clothes far greater than the amount that can be absorbed by only three shops.

Even greater difficulties arose with the men's shop we opened only a few doors away from the women's. It proved quite impossible to find manufacturers of men's suits to execute our ideas of style and quality and who were willing to accept an order for only one shop. If it was ill-advised to open the shop in the first place I must take the blame because I badgered Debenhams to let me do so. But there was interference and in practice there was not much clothing in the shop which pleased me. None of it was bad but too much of it was indistinguishable from what could be bought in other shops. The poor manager had no choice but to buy overseas, either from France or Italy. I had wanted to put over a modern and athletic British look.

An important part of the purchase agreement with Debenhams was my signing a contract of service. This was generous in its terms and more than correct in its execution. It was, however, to be reviewed in 1979 on my seventieth birthday. In the spring of that year the manager of Hardy Amies Ltd, who was of course appointed by Debenhams, told me that he was instructed to negotiate with me a contract for life. At that time all the Hardy Amies shops gave the appearance of prospering.

The necessary contracts were therefore drawn up. There were the usual legal quibbles with solicitors, but eventually agreement was reached without much difficulty. By August the documents were in the hands of my solicitor who, quite innocently, went on holiday. The signing, I had thought, would be a mere formality.

A few days later I was called to the offices of Debenhams by the chairman, Robert Thornton, Sir Anthony Burney having by then retired. There had been some disagreement with my own board and particularly with those who represented Debenhams. They had lost money on a scheme to put Hardy Amies clothes into Debenhams' shops and we were unhappy that the money we had so carefully earned overseas with our licensee businesses and from the nurturing of our business in Savile Row was being wasted. Bob Thornton for his part explained that Debenhams was suffering a decline in retail trading. 'We are closing down everything which isn't directly to do with Debenhams,' he said. 'You must close the men's shop in Hans Crescent. We will see about the boutique in Harvey Nichols and the women's shop in Hans Crescent in the near future.' There followed more argument. Eric Crabtree was present, but uneasy and silent. 'Bob,' I said, 'it was Tony Burney's idea to buy me; that was before you had joined Debenhams. When you did I was already there. You inherited me. We have made money for you overseas and our business there is likely to increase. You have opened thirty Hardy Amies/ Hepworths shops in Debenhams stores. Our association with Hepworths has therefore been useful to you. But I think you feel that development of the dressmaking side of the business has not been a great success. We feel this is because Debenhams have created Hardy Amies ready-to-wear operations on their own. They have been ill-planned from the outset. They have lost money; money hard earned from our foreign business. I don't think you are pleased with us any longer. Don't you think it would be a good idea if I found someone to buy back Hardy Amies Ltd from you?' 'It would be a wonderful idea,' said Bob Thornton.

I went straight to see Lord Chelsea. I knew that he had bought the tie firm Michelson which had held our licence and that he was happy with this purchase. I knew also that he wanted to be further involved in the men's clothing field and that it represented a chance to diversify away from the real estate business. He was interested in the idea of buying my company and a series of meetings were set up between the Cadogan Estate and Debenhams' accountants. I shall always be grateful to Charles Chelsea for his interest in my affairs during this critical moment.

There were, however, difficulties which I had not foreseen at the time. The activities and finances of Hardy Amies Ltd were so intricately bound up with those of Debenhams that it was difficult to settle on a price satisfactory to both parties for the buying back of the original business.

During the course of these negotiations I discovered that the only real asset that the company possessed was me. Licensee contracts, the revenue from which amounted to many hundreds of thousands of pounds, were all in my name. Some specified my personal attention and some had a clause annulling the agreement should I die or retire. From the outset I had given an assurance to Lord Chelsea that I would sign any contract with him that he thought was desirable. But since discovering that I was the only real asset of the company the idea came to me that perhaps I should buy back the company myself.

I spent a sleepless night pondering this move. I thought of the state of our licensee business in the USA, Japan, Canada, Australia and New Zealand. I thought of our happy relationship with Hepworths; I knew I had contracts of many years' standing to fall back on and hence the good name I had in the market; I thought of the fine reputation we had established with our dressmaking in Savile Row and of the Royal Warrant as dressmaker to the Queen; I thought of the cvo awarded me by Her Majesty in Jubilee Year and the fact that she had worn a dress of ours during the celebrations. These and many other thoughts accumulated in my mind, and by morning I realized that I ought to be able to stand on my own feet.

I went to the bank. My approach to them was greatly helped by my accountant and tax adviser. The bank granted us a loan for a ten-year period and an overdraft was arranged.

Thus in Februrary 1980 I bought back the business which I had sold to Debenhams in 1973. In the event the price was modest because I had realized by then that what was for sale was really only the shell of my business. They had been unable to touch the overseas business and the flat in New York. Nor had they been able to touch the customers in Savile Row and the dressmaking business we had established there. More important than all of this, though, had been the realization that they could not sell the business without me.

We disengaged ourselves quickly from any association with the shops in Hans Crescent and also the boutique in Harvey Nichols on the sound advice that the rents involved were rising steeply and profits would be endangered. Arrangements were also made whereby Debenhams were forbidden from trading under the Hardy Amies name.

Sole ownership of my company has been tough going. We have all been sustained by the success of the licensee business at home and abroad. Very little has to be deducted from this licensee revenue: the cost of the flat in New York and a tailoring workroom in London for making prototypes; also, some travelling expenses, although very often these are paid for by the licensees.

I had, however, no idea how expensive it was going to be to run the establishment at 14 Savile Row. Debenhams, during the years they had owned and run my business, had operated the counting house. I had presumed in all innocence that our old method of costing and book-keeping was still used. In fact, everything had changed radically and modern computers now handled it all. It came as a rude shock to us all when we began the process of rethinking our methods of operation. We had no idea, for instance, how expensive it had become to borrow money from the bank and the interest rates that this involved. Nor had we appreciated fully how much the basic costs of overheads had swollen. Although we had had nearly ten years of inflation, we had been protected from the facts of business life throughout most of this period our financial structuring had been controlled and looked after by Debenhams.

More important still from our point of view was the realization that the whole costing system involved in a dress house had become completely out-dated. It has always been difficult to put an accurate figure on the cost of a hand-made dress. Out of sixty models in a collection no two would be alike. Of the seamstresses involved in the stitching together of a dress one might be fast and one slow; the slower one may in the end be the more accurate. And no sooner had we got somewhere near to working out a proper costing system concerning the pricing of individual dresses than the problem of reassessing wages would arise. This was an area in which we had to be particularly sympathetic. Our workrooms are only a minute's walk from Piccadilly Circus in the heart of the West End, yet some of our workforce live as far away as mid-Essex. Everyone knows how the cost of travel has risen in recent years and it is only their devotion to their trade which has kept many of these skilled hands working for me today. With these problems and many more besides to contend with, it is no surprise that the results of this first year were worrying.

It became apparent very quickly that what I needed was modernization and, even more important still, the goodwill of the banks. This I have had. A sound piece of their advice was to revise the whole system of submitting bills. Cloth is chosen for the models in a collection in October. It is woven for us abroad (in Lyons, for example) and delivered to our workrooms at the end of October ready to be made up into the clothes for the collection which we show in mid-January. A customer orders a copy of one of the outfits at the end of February, has the fittings in March, and the dress is then delivered at the end of April. Traditionally the accounts would be sent out at the end of April but in the almost sure knowledge that the customer was going to be away or abroad throughout the Easter holiday. Such a customer would, without in any way being ill-mannered or thoughtless, then settle the bill in May. Throughout this time the dress house would be expected to support itself without any revenue coming in from the customers. This procedure is obviously unsatisfactory and we revised it completely. Now bills are sent out with the dress or, at the latest, the day after. Fortunately, all our customers seem to understand, and indeed some of the newer customers, who are used to the way things are done in the United States and France, even offer to pay a deposit with their order.

Honesty forces me to say that I did not want to listen to planning schemes when I bought back Hardy Amies Ltd any more than I did when I started my business in 1945. I then just knew it had to be a success and that self-belief and will-power were enough to see me through. But in those days, of course, there was the added advantage of a general mood of optimism brought about by the relief of a hideous war having just ended. In 1980, however, we were sliding into a terrible depression of world trade which was made worse by the feeling of political gloom. High interest rates created a shortage of money, and over-production in many industries, such as steel and the motorcar, added to the picture. And there was stiff competition nearer to home with the appearance of a whole new school of enthusiastic and alert young designers.

But it was not all a tale of gloom. Our licensee income benefited suddenly from the rise in the value of the dollar and the yen. Since our foreign earnings were paid in these currencies our financial position was a great deal healthier than it might otherwise have been. Well over half our income today comes from abroad, and I suppose over the past twenty years our foreign operations have earned this country several millions of pounds. The banks who support us obviously respect us for this and with their help and understanding we have managed to keep up the volume of business done at Savile Row. We still have two tailoring workrooms and four dress workrooms making clothes to measure.

However, part of this restructuring of my business has meant that we now have to charge more for our clothes. An overcoat in good quality cloth, for instance, now costs a little over £1,000. To this we have to add fifteen per cent value add tax. VAT was introduced in 1973 in the days when we were still owned by Debenhams.

I may be considered indiscreet for mentioning these figures, but one cannot hide from the realities of modern business. A thousand pounds for a coat is not thought excessive in Italy or France, but an

Englishwoman thinks it is a high price indeed. I do not think it is; it is half, and sometimes a third, what can be asked in Paris or New York. I feel very strongly that to pay for a garment made in an establishment such as mine is a very good investment if you can afford it. Moreover, customers say that our clothes never wear out.

I have always believed passionately in the *haute couture* method of making women's clothes. There are still a few women who cannot bear to wear clothes that are otherwise made. They are a diminishing number but their bodies need to be flattered and constantly revitalized with new clothes so there is always enough work to be done. For the price of an *haute couture* dress or overcoat a customer is getting the undivided attention and advice of a very experienced saleswoman which is backed up, if necessary, by the extra guidance of myself, Ken Fleetwood or one of his assistants. It is then put together by a team of expert tailors and dressmakers with what I can only describe as loving care. There are few places left in the world, let alone England, where this kind of service can be provided.

To maintain this service these days is not easy, not least because of the difficulties in obtaining quality materials. By tradition *couturiers* only buy enough cloth to make a model. They then wait until customers place their orders before buying in what are called 'repeats'. These materials are supplied by cloth merchants who have always understood the workings of our trade. But as the *haute couture* industry has dwindled over the years so too have these cloth merchants had to cut back on their range of stock, and in some cases they have had to close down altogether. We are able to offer the customer, therefore, less and less variety. Some of the ancillary crafts associated with the dress trade are becoming rarer. Belt-makers, for instance, are hard to find, and we can no longer find the firms who used the dye buttons specially for each order. There are still a few craftsmen left, however, to whom we can turn, such as Mr Lock and his nimble-fingered team of embroiderers. Often, to maintain the quality that our customers have grown to expect, Ken Fleetwood might have to fly over to Paris for the day to bring back the lengths of cloths and the accessories needed.

All of this has to be watched very carefully, particularly since buying back my own business has meant that I am now very much the master of my own destiny. In my blackest moments I had thought of selling off my Savile Row establishment and moving to New York.

Even now I think I could make a very good living there. But I realized very quickly that I would not be able to exist for very long without my Savile Row base. Here I have a band of people not only of great loyalty to their craft, as well as to me, but also a group of highly skilled and experienced artisans. Savile Row is a place where we make things of beauty and of use. A dress is only beautiful when in use, it is then alive; hanging in a cupboard it is merely a sort of shroud. With such a team around me, I know I can make the best overcoats and dresses in London. I can also produce equally good prototypes of men's suits. These resources must be treasured; for it is here, on the tree of a dressmaking establishment, that the fruits of our licensee operations abroad are borne.

Today this tree isn't too unhealthy. It is nearly forty years old. I have been helped in the caring and tending of it by close friends. The first is Ken Fleetwood, who came to Savile Row in 1950 to help me with the sketches. He is not only able to do good drawings but he has a true feeling for romantic clothes. We started working on the collections together. He knows my mind better than any other. It is our custom to walk across Kensington Gardens on our way to work every morning and it is while doing so that we discuss the day's business.

Ken Fleetwood is in essence an artist. At Savile Row his studio is next to my office so there is plenty of opportunity for me to see the dresses being fitted. He is in charge of all the women's operations and to help him in this he has a studio staff plus, of course, the whole team of tailors and cutters in the workrooms who carry out the studio designs. As the volume of our licensee business abroad is more concerned with designing for men than for women, I need to be out of the country for months at a time and have to leave the women's business entirely in Ken's hands. To help him in this he was given complete control and a free hand to plan collections and to buy cloths in my absence. I have never found fault with his choice.

Ken and his studio never stop designing. His taste and flair for romantic dress goes into his designs for ballgowns and wedding dresses. As a house however we are fascinated by modern day clothes – clothes to live in, travel in, work in. Ken even designs what are called 'work clothes' for our flourishing overall licencing operation in Bristol.

His chief assistant is Jon Moore who can cut a toile and sew it with his own very nimble fingers. His considerable charm is of great value in dealing with the customers.

The second close friend who has been of great help is Roger Whiteman. He has been with me for the past fourteen years, and during that time he has been responsible with me for keeping an eye on our licensee operations at home and abroad. In this he is a very good administrator. An important aspect of his job when he started was to travel abroad with me and oversee some of our operations and to keep in touch with our foreign buyers. Fortunately we are both very good and tidy travellers. Roger can read a complicated timetable better than some experienced travel agents. Remembering how carefully we had to nurse our resources in our youth when we had little money, it is a great relief and pleasure for us both these days to enjoy the comforts of good hotels and first-class travel. If this extra expense seems excessive, it is excused by the necessity to keep up good appearances.

Roger's other task is to see that the licensees get the service that we have contracted to give them. When new designs are requested he is responsible for seeing that the studio provides them. He knows that our reputation rests not only on the designs we provide for these licensees but on the general aura of taste and modern thinking which we have come to symbolize at Savile Row.

Ken Fleetwood and Roger Whiteman are my most loyal supporters at Savile Row. They could not be more different in personality. Ken is by nature a dreamer though with his feet kept on the ground by a strong streak of northern common sense. He is a musician with perfect pitch and has the power of total recall. Roger, by contrast, is tidy-minded and keeps immaculate books showing how and when licensee money is due to be paid to us. He has a good relationship with the managers of the licensee firms with whom we deal; they are pleased to be able to work with someone who has a strict business mind. While it is Ken who wins over the respect and admiration of the designers, it is Roger who ties up the loose ends on the business side. He has to deal with the legal documents of the contracts; our trade mark has to be protected carefully.

In a fashion business there are always conflicts. These are caused by the struggle between the desire to achieve perfection in the clothes and a wish to make a profit. It is sometimes impossible to do both. I have to see that neither side is too predominant for too long. I said once that our motto could be: 'Less than Art, and more than Trade.' I had this, perhaps rather pompously, translated into Latin as: *Impar arte, negocio superior*. Ken strives to improve and maintain our reputation as designers of originality and taste. His Lancashire blood makes him a shrewd shopkeeper. Roger, with his Scottish blood and a Birmingham upbringing, helps to see to it that this talent is promoted successfully.

Sarah Graham, my secretary, has been with me for five years. She is small and pretty and exceptionally wise. I have had many secretaries in my time but never one with such a soothing manner, a wonderful memory, and an ability to look fresh and lively all the time. She possesses the most exquisite tact and feeds me, when necessary, information concerning the goings-on in the House. She can tell me about the joys and despairs of the members of the staff without in any way being a gossip or a troublemaker. She brings harmony to the trio of Fleetwood, Whiteman and Amies.

Another vital member of the team is Derek Cattel, chief accountant and company secretary. He knows the drawbacks of computerized accounting and as a result he has mercifully taken us back to the old method of doing it by hand. He has some extremely important book-keepers under him.

Kim has been in charge of the sales ledger for ten years. She has to keep track of customers changing addresses and, what is more difficult, changing names. (Mrs Gerald Legge became Lady Lewisham: Lady Lewisham became the Countess of Dartmouth: and the Countess of Dartmouth has now become the Countess Spencer.) Kim is also aware of the paying habits of faithful customers and she knows how, with tact, to persuade these customers to improve their habits if they become outmoded in the modern world of high interest rates.

Anne struggles loyally with British Rail to bring her up from mid-Kent each day to man the telephone and at the same time organizes the 'bought ledger'. This deals with all our purchases and supplies. When the flow of money slows down because customers don't pay – in holiday time, for instance – or when overseas cheques are delayed, she has to be very tactful with our suppliers when payment to them is overdue.

Then there is the team of tailors and dressmakers, the people who really bind the loyalties of our customers together. Lilian, who makes for the Queen, has been with me for twenty-five years, as has Roy the tailor. Roy started as an apprentice with Mr Ernest who was at Lachasse when I was there. Rita the dressmaker was trained by Victor Stiebel and joined me when he retired. Mr Michael, the Queen's tailor, came to me twelve years ago from Michael of Carlos Place, but was previously at Lachasse. Raymonde came to me from Dior, having had a career of great distinction going back to the great Madame Vionnet herself. Rudi Newton is one of those Germans who have lived and worked in London so long that they have literally stitched themselves into the fabric of England. He runs at Savile Row a little department of his own which organizes the making of clothes for customers, each individually cut and sewn, but which require no fittings. This is immensely successful and, of course, much less costly to the customer. His great gift is his skill in pattern-making, which he learned in the best houses in Italy, France and Germany. Finally there is Torcy, who is so much part of the house that I am not surprised to discover that she has been with me for twenty years. She came to me as a dresser in the 'cabine', the mannequins' changing-room, but was already an experienced machinist. She is now in charge of a group of very clever machinists who make clothes for the boutique.

A pillar of any dresshouse is the stock-keeper. She is, in many instances, the buyer; certainly the buyer of linings, buttons and zips. The choice of cloth for models is, of course, the duty of the designer. The stock-keeper must however be aware of all sources and be able to make recommendations. She must maintain happy relations with all the suppliers; it is her job to cajole them or bully them into making exceptionally fast deliveries. The pillar of Hardy Amies Ltd is Dora who has been with me for sixteen years after her ten years with Worth of London.

Pino is the tailor for the men's clothes. He is from Puglia. Not only is he an immaculate stitcher, but he is a cutter of great skill. He helps me to make the collection of men's clothes each year which demonstrate to the licensee holders our thoughts for the future.

We like to have new blood entering the studio. Ken Fleetwood was a star pupil at St Martin's College of Art and returned there for many years to lecture. He is now too busy to do this but keeps track of promising young students of fashion design. One has just joined us to help with menswear designing. Skilled and experienced sketchers are hired when required. Ken holds the studio team together and encourages them to remember and respect the traditions of the house and to realize that their first duty is to the customer. The young designers are always bursting with new ideas. I need this new blood, this new energy, to sustain the inventiveness so essential to a fashion house.

I am a great believer in junior designers joining with the saleswomen in serving and advising the customers. This gives them the chance to see realities face to face and to learn what the customers seek from us.

I have left till the last the saleswomen, or *vendeuses*; it is they who are in the front line. This sounds as if it were all a battle, which it isn't; there are more kisses than blows. A good *vendeuse* will know the family history of her client, her lifestyle and the size of her fortune. She will anticipate the customer's requirements. The *vendeuse* will also know the potential of the house for which she is working. She will be aware of the idiosyncrasies of·the fitters and tailors; that one dressmaker, for instance, has the lightness of touch required for romantic evening and wedding dresses, whereas another has the precise eye needed for the tailored lines of a day dress. She must know every dress that is hanging on the rails ready to be sold as a ready-to-wear garment. She must know all the sizes that are in stock and what cloths are currently available in Paris, Rome or Lake Como and how long it will take for them to be ordered. She must be aware of the state of the customer's account and be prepared, if necessary, to ask tactfully for payment. She must be prepared to ring up a customer during a cold February when the workrooms are short of work and persuade her that spring is bound to come and that a wise woman of fashion should be prepared for it.

Every customer has the right to be exacting; indeed, it is the fastidiousness of customers that helps to perpetuate the traditions of good workmanship. But there is often a neurosis which creeps into a fitting room. This has sometimes more to do with the customer's private life than that of the dress house. Very early in my career a wise old *vendeuse* said to me, 'Hardy, when a woman cries in a fitting room about a dress, it's not the dress that's wrong, it's her love life.'

Several times in this book I have pointed out that no dress designer can exist without a clientele and that the relationship between client and *vendeuse* is crucial to our business. The *vendeuses*, then, are the real guardians of a dress house.

To return to the tree of Savile Row, and continuing with this useful metaphor, Ken Fleetwood, Roger Whiteman and myself are therefore the chief gardeners. We are by no means alone in this task of cultivating and nurturing successful growth. There is no room for old people in the dress trade. Some members are mature in years, but all have to be young in heart. We are all reborn twice a year with the showings of our collections: in January for the spring and summer clothes, and in July for the autumn and winter selections. As the winter orders get finished in November and December, so we have to gear ourselves to work and plan ahead for the following spring and summer designs. Life never stops.

The desire for new clothes is as old as Adam and Eve and the fig leaf. From the day of that famous coupling there has never ceased the tradition of love and marriage. Marriage is important to us dress-makers and at 14 Savile Row we can make the most beautiful wedding dresses in London. But it is love that really sustains us. The urge to make love is perhaps the biggest incentive to dress well. Even the wish to be liked, which is only a minor form of wishing to be loved, arouses in everyone a pride in appearance. Love, birth, marriage and death – these are all a part of the spectrum of life, and the desire for clothes for these events cannot, and never will, be repressed by either taxes or laws.

4

By Appointment

People often ask me how I became dressmaker to the Queen. The answer is that it was purely the result of having a good clientele. It is the job of a designer and his saleswomen to build up the clientele of a dress house and, through the excellence of the service provided, to attract business from their relatives or friends. When I opened my own shop in 1946 I was lucky to have three such expert saleswomen working for me: Cammie, Violet Allen and, later, Betty Reeves. Their loyalty to me, for which I will always be grateful, was such that they left Lachasse, where we had all worked together before the war, to join me in my business at 14 Savile Row. The good relations Violet and Betty had established with several of their customers during the pre-war years meant that many of the customers followed them over to our shop in Savile Row.

One of these clients was very grand: the Countess of Ellesmere. She was tall, slightly forbidding, but very charming in manner once she began to speak. She brought her two daughters to us to have their suits made. They were the Lady Susan Egerton and the Lady Alice Egerton. Once or twice Betty had whispered in my ear that Lady Alice Egerton had recently become lady-in-waiting to Princess Elizabeth.

I remember vividly the day Betty came up to me and in a state of great excitement said, 'It's happened!' We were aware for some time that Princess Elizabeth had let it be known on several occasions how much she admired Lady Alice Egerton's clothes. Now her approval was official: she was soon to embark on the first tour since her marriage and wanted to order some clothes from us. This was to be the tour to Canada. The year was 1950.

Shortly after this we were notified that Princess Elizabeth was coming to see us at Savile Row. She was to be accompanied by Princess Margaret. The collection was shown privately in my office with only Betty and myself present from the Savile Row staff. I remember the princesses greeting us with smiles and handshakes, like any of the well-born English ladies on whom I had previously waited. Everything was relaxed but also totally business-like.

A few days later we were summoned to Clarence House. Sufficient warning of this had been given to allow us to prepare some sketches of the wardrobe we intended to submit.

I had already a good idea of what kind of clothes I thought would be appropriate for a royal princess. In this respect it is interesting to reflect exactly what stage fashion had reached. We were only three years on from the New Look of 1947. I had felt then, like so many designers, elated by Dior's famous collections. It had shocked some people, but not us. All I could say at the time was, 'Of course, that's how it should be.' For in the collection I had launched at Lachasse in the spring of 1939, inappropriate as it seemed for a season which was but the prologue to a terrible war, I had sent the girls out to start the collection in tiny corsets. There was to me a feeling in the fashion world of a romantic revival around the corner. All this exuberance was quickly smothered by the dullness of the phoney war and the damp snuffer of the restrictions of the utility laws and regulations.

In my first post-war collection in the spring of 1946 I had taken up matters where they had been left in 1939. I had not dared to narrow the shoulders, nor had I thought of lengthening skirts. In fact, I am sure that without the authority of a French house like Dior, with a massive display of some three hundred models instead of the modest sixty of London, it would not have been possible to change so much in one collection. By 1950 things had settled down. There was still the small waist, but the long, almost ankle-length skirts were shortened to just below the knee or certainly just above the calf. It was this look that I wanted to give to Princess Elizabeth.

I was particularly known for my tailoring; so there was no trouble with the coats. I already had the idea that royalty should be dressed like royalty, so I used rich materials. I also wanted to get away from the cliché of the pale-blue dress; at the same time blue was obviously going to be the Princess's great colour, dictated by those oversized blue eyes. So our first success with Her Royal Highness was a dress and coat in heavy silk, dull and with a slightly crinkled surface. (This helps to keep the seams straight; thin, plain-surfaced silk is liable to pucker.) The colour was truly thunder-blue; neither pale nor dark, and the coat was cut on what is appropriately known as a 'princess' line: that is to say, there is no seam at the waist, the seams flowing from the shoulder to the bottom of the skirt. There were several seams with a little bit taken out of each to give shape at the waist, then the line released gradually over the hips so as to flow into the skirt which then moved exceptionally gracefully. To balance the line of the skirt the line of the hat should have been wide and flowing. However, we already knew instinctively that a wide-brimmed hat would be undesirable for royalty. Hands must not be used to hold hats in a wind: they are for waving or holding bouquets. Nor must the face be obscured from the onlookers. Far more acceptable was the fashionable small hat, almost nothing more than a feather wrapped around a piece of tulle and shaped to the head.

This first order consisted of two overcoats, two day dresses and two evening dresses. If this order seems modest by modern standards, I can only say that at the time we were all immensely proud to have been asked at all. It was a new experience for us all and none of us could have imagined then that it was but the prelude to thirty years' service in designing clothes for Her Majesty the Queen. I was reminded of this first wardrobe when, at a recent fitting of an evening dress in gold lace, the Queen remarked that it was like the first evening dress we ever made for her.

A short time after the Princess's return from the Canadian tour, we were commanded to prepare another collection. This time it was for the forthcoming tour of Kenya and South Africa. Once again Betty Reeves and I made several visits to Clarence House, first with sketches and then to supervise the fitting of the clothes.

Looking back I do not think the clothes in this collection were as successful as were those we made for the Canadian tour. Because the clothes were designed for wear in a hot climate they involved the use of thin materials. It is more difficult to make regal clothes out of thin materials than it is with thicker, richer ones. If a lack of experience was responsible in part for this collection being less successful, I am glad to say now that it was a fault we managed to correct on subsequent lightweight designs for the Queen.

This second tour was curtailed in Kenya by the tragic news of the death of King George VI. It was February 1952, and instead of continuing her journey to South Africa Princess Elizabeth returned at once to England. We were, of course, greatly saddened by the news of this untimely death, though we realized that our feelings were trivial compared to those of the Princess and her entourage. The burden of responsibility, however, that awaited her on her return as Queen of England was something with which the whole world sympathized.

The Coronation followed in June 1953. On that June morning Betty Reeves and I took our seats on a stand facing the Victoria Memorial outside Buckingham Palace, waiting to catch a glimpse of the Queen as she set out for the Coronation Service at Westminster Abbey. We had been given these seats by Miss MacDonald, the Queen's dresser. It was a moment of great excitement and also great pride for both of us. There we were, comparative newcomers, and yet able to view the proceedings from a special platform and as a guest of Her Majesty the Queen. I did not know who the other guests were but I imagined them to be members of the Royal Household. The rain that followed was but a minor distraction from the sight of the Queen, with that unforgettable smile, as the royal procession set out for the Abbey.

I had seen the sketch of the Coronation dress in the paper that morning and had admired it. I am not given to praising my colleagues, but I do think that Norman Hartnell had done an absolutely superb job and I can think of no one who could have done it better. I have to this day a clear picture of the dress as being very pearly in appearance, made up of muted pale colours, each blending into the other, giving an effect of immense iridescence. What I also admired when I saw pictures of the service later on television was the cut of the skirt which moved so gracefully as the Queen walked in her procession.

Throughout that Coronation Day I remember thinking: 'This is Norman Hartnell's day.' He was, of course, in the Abbey. But a further thought began to settle on me as the day progressed, and that was the realization that I, too, could call myself dressmaker to the Queen. For, with a tour of Australia scheduled for later that year, we had been commanded once again to prepare a wardrobe. I was therefore by now firmly established as the Queen's number two dressmaker. I did not know it then, but if I continued to serve the Queen for three years I could apply for the Royal Warrant. When I did so I found that the years of serving Princess Elizabeth counted in my favour.

I was very happy to have Betty Reeves with me on that Coronation

Day. She was more than just an employee or a colleague: she was the link with my mother. Betty had met my mother when she had visited Lachasse. She knew how deeply embedded was the influence of my mother's background on my present career. My mother had died in 1938, four years after my start at Lachasse in 1934. I would bring to her deathbed stories of my little successes at Lachasse which made her happy. Betty shared with me the wish that it would have been possible for my mother to have known that we were sitting there outside Buckingham Palace as guests of the Queen.

A new reign is as exciting as a new year: it is a time to feel that all the old mistakes can be wiped out and there is hope for the future. When the Queen is a young girl and beautiful, when she is a reigning Queen in the tradition of her great forebear Queen Elizabeth I, and when the memory of our last reigning Queen, Queen Victoria, is still very much alive, the excitement knows no bounds. If my feelings towards the Queen amounted to a deep-rooted sense of chivalry, what, I wondered, were the feelings of the statesmen and members of the household who served her?

The gala performance of Benjamin Britten's opera *Gloriana*, commissioned as part of the Coronation celebrations and given six days after the Coronation, was for many their first sight of the Queen as crowned head of state. The whole audience was much moved by the sight of this woman who had so much responsibility thrust on her so quickly. There was a tremendous ovation on her arrival. The Queen, wearing a Norman Hartnell dress, looked quite splendid. I had been lucky enough to be present at the occasion because David Webster, the General Administrator of the Royal Opera House, Covent Garden, was an old friend and had given me tickets. I had also been fortunate in being allowed to sit in on some of the rehearsals, and was therefore probably one of the few people privileged to know in advance the nature of the opera.

At the time I had been intrigued by the innovative style and texture of the music which seemed to shimmer and sparkle in what appeared to be a very Elizabethan idiom. But the gala performance itself, it must be said, was little short of a disaster and the opera had few fans by the end of the evening. It had seemed such a good idea to tell a story woven around the life of Elizabeth I, but the tale of the jealous love of an ageing virgin queen for a young courtier proved to be terribly inappropriate for the occasion. In particular, the great scene where Essex discovers the Queen without her wig and make-up seemed, in a backhanded way, to be even discourteous to the new Queen.

As regards dress, however, the evening was a glittering occasion and was a pointer to many such evenings in the future. We soon learned that nobody can surpass the Queen at night and that nobody can wear jewels so well. The Queen's jewels are of unparalleled splendour and they have played an important part in our thinking when designing clothes for the evening. (It is sometimes asked whether we design dresses for a special piece of jewellery. The answer is no. We make as pretty a dress as we can, knowing full well that the Queen will have some suitable piece of jewellery to go with it.) The Queen wears a tiara with insouciance. The Queen's dresser was to tell me on a later occasion that the Queen was the only person who could put on a tiara going downstairs.

On gala evenings at Covent Garden, staged to entertain visiting heads of state, the clothes of the English ladies would be compared unfavourably with those made in Paris and worn by the visitors. It was always the British, however, who wore the most important jewellery. As a wag once put it (it might have been me): 'The frogs may have the frocks, but we've got the rocks.'

With the clothes commanded of us for the tour to Australia we were now working on our third wardrobe for the Queen. In the days when she was Princess Elizabeth we went to Clarence House; now, for the first time, it was to Buckingham Palace. In the normal course of events a customer wishing to order clothes from us at this time would have been invited to see the collection. This would have consisted of sixty to seventy outfits. A collection is made by a *couturier* to demonstrate his idea of what a customer should wear in the coming season. If he is wise he takes care never to forget what sort of life his customers lead: dresses must be an integral part of that life. But what is more important is that the designer must be sure that the ideas he puts forward for that season will have authority and standing the following year. He must persuade his customers to move forward in the cool, inexorable way that good fashion does. A fashionable dressmaker cannot be a dictator unless he is so rich that he can ignore the fact that he is a shopkeeper.

Contrary to what is thought by the general public, special designs are very rarely done, with the important exception of wedding dresses. For a collection is also a series of experiments and when an experiment is successful it turns into a 'best-seller'; that is to say, there are always dresses which are more copied than others. The stories of ladies being affronted at a party by the sight of another lady in the same dress are almost always untrue. It might happen with a grand ball dress but then the *vendeuses* should take care to see that two customers do not order the same dress for the same grand occasion. When it comes to day dresses intelligent and sophisticated customers are amused and flattered to find that the dress they have chosen is a best-seller and seen often around the town. They pride themselves that they have chosen wisely.

With a customer as important as the Queen, however, the routine and the approach to the business of designing clothes are completely different. For one, the duties involved in being the head of state make it impossible for the Queen to visit us at Savile Row. Her days are too full for her to give up time to see anything so frivolous as a collection of clothes. The only time when it has happened was when the Queen was expecting a baby and therefore not expected to fulfil her normal routine. It is only natural, then, that we should go to Buckingham Palace. Even there time is precious for the Queen, and from early on we learned not to waste any of it. In this respect the routine has hardly changed over the years. Fittings are prepared in the workroom on stands, but it is impossible to judge the effect until it has been put on a body. So intent are we all on our work that there is very little time for chat. However, there is no strain during this silence; the atmosphere is relaxed and it is fair to say that we look forward to our visits.

On our first visit to Buckingham Palace Miss MacDonald told me that I could myself always use the Privy Purse entrance if I wanted but that my staff should use the side entrance. When I go with sketches I make use of the privilege of the Privy Purse entrance, but if I have any bolts of material with me or, of course, if I am with any member of my staff, I go in through the side entrance with pride. We are shown up to our waiting room, which is a small room near the Queen's fitting room. I think this latter was instituted by Queen Mary and it is a large dressing room with good light and space for the Queen to walk up and down to try the effect of a skirt in motion. I sit in the corridor outside the Queen's bedroom waiting to be called in after the Queen has been clothed by the fitter and the *vendeuse*.

I have sat many times outside the Queen's door over the past thirty years listening to the light murmur from within, interrupted quite often by the Queen's silvery laugh. Sometimes there is an ominous silence but this does not always mean that there is any trouble afoot. It is merely an indication of concentration. If it is a first fitting I may in spirit be concentrating on that also. But if it is a second or final fitting, about which I have reason to be happy, I have time to look around me.

One part of our work that has changed over the years is the way we work with the milliner. During the early days we had to work with the Queen's milliner, Miss Kate Day. This lady made it very clear to us that we were not going to be allowed to forget that she was well established in the Queen's confidence and that we, as newcomers, would not be in the room when fittings of the hats took place. This attitude, though friendly and polite on the surface, was of little help to us, especially after Miss Day received a warrant appointing her the Queen's milliner in her own right. Discussions took place over sketches once the Queen had made her choice, but it meant that there were no fittings in which hats were matched with dresses or coats. This practice continued with the Queen's second milliner, Aage Thaarup, though it was much easier working with him since he was an old friend.

Death eventually released Miss Day from a painful illness and Aage Thaarup retired. The Queen asked me to suggest a milliner with whom I could work. My first and obvious choice was Freddie Fox, a clever Australian who had taken over the millinery business of Rose Vernier. I am pleased to say that since Freddie Fox's appointment in 1968 the fittings of the hats have always been incorporated into the fittings of the Queen's day clothes.

Betty Reeves also retired and was replaced by Mrs Sheila Ogden whom I had known for many years, first as a customer and then as a saleswoman. Sheila Ogden is a woman of great taste and worldly experience and it is she who now accompanies me on my visits to Buckingham Palace. Christian Dior, a far cleverer man than I will ever be, always said that a male designer very often needed a woman's guidance. Sheila Ogden is only one of many women who work with me whose advice I have found admirable.

In those first years of waiting on the Queen we were always anxious that Her Majesty should have exclusive designs only. In time we found this practice to be unfair in that it deprived the Queen of the chance of wearing some of our most successful dresses, so now we often bring dresses from our collection to show her and the Queen appears to enjoy trying them on. We explain the good points of a particular dress which we intend to keep, show a sketch of the dress with the proposed alterations, and take bolts of materials with us which we intend to use and which will be used only for the Queen. In this way the Queen has the advantage of using a cut which has proved to be successful but made up in a material that will not be seen on our other customers.

Above all I have felt from the beginning that the Queen needs clothes that help her in what I can only describe as her work. The Queen once spoke of this to me as 'going about my business'. I would deem myself a very disloyal subject, not to mention a thoroughly incompetent designer, if I offered the Queen any clothes that were difficult to wear. The Queen's clothes are not only those in which she works, they are those in which she lives. It is for this reason that the Queen is known to appreciate her wardrobe as much as does any customer of a *couture* house.

I have to say, however, that the task of making clothes for the Queen is not an easy one. Not that the Queen has been anything other than totally cooperative and professional in every respect. In some ways I often wish that the Queen had been more difficult and demanding. I can count the garments on the fingers of one hand that have been rejected as unsuccessful, and more than half of these were withdrawn at my request. No, the reason for the difficulty is that the lines of modern clothes, especially day clothes, are not those which you would choose if you were given a free hand to use for a queen's robes. It is by modern fashion standards that the Queen is often judged. Queen Mary, however, was able to depart from the day's fashion and achieved a magnificent presence by continuing to wear long skirts when very short ones were fashionable. Furthermore, she did not hesitate to wear metallic brocades by day, and I remember as a teenager seeing Queen Mary driving through the East End of London in the morning in pale-green lamé, wearing emeralds. The Queen today is too much in the public eye and her wardrobe too much the subject of fashion comment for her to be able to do this.

My work in designing clothes for the Queen enabled me early on to apply for a Royal Warrant. This warrant states quite simply that my work for the Queen is 'By Appointment to Her Majesty the Queen'. I am therefore, and have been now for nearly thirty years, the Queen's dressmaker 'by appointment'. The holder of a Royal Warrant is automatically a member of the Royal Warrant Holders Association. This body has, with the help of the household, drawn up some sixty-odd rules concerning correct procedures and practices. Most of these relate to the use of the royal coat of arms and where it can be placed. This is important since the honour of holding a Royal Warrant is a privilege that must never be abused.

I am only one of three designers who supply clothes to the Queen. Even my third of the wardrobe takes so much time to fit that there is often great difficulty in finding time to squeeze the fittings into the Queen's busy diary. There is no reason, therefore, for any jealousy to exist between the designers, and when I first started my work with the Queen Norman Hartnell wrote me a very kind letter which, in a nutshell, said just this. Virtually all the clothes I have made for the Queen over the past thirty years have been for the royal tours abroad. It will be seen, however, that many of the outfits are worn on more than one or two occasions and that some of these take place nearer to home.

Looking back to that night in Covent Garden when the Queen made her first public appearance after the Coronation, I could have had no idea then that some twenty-five years later the Queen would stand on the balcony at Buckingham Palace during the Jubilee celebrations wearing a dress designed by me. Nor could I have known that when such an important dignitary as the Pope visited the Queen in 1982 she would again be seen wearing an outfit of ours and that photographs of the occasion would be circulated worldwide. The Queen wore a day dress of ours made in bright turquoise wool. The cloth was closely but beautifully woven so that the material was light yet draped well. The dress is what is called 'plain tailored', i.e. the skirt is short but covers the knees. The neckline was plain – an admirable background for the conventional row of pearls which the Queen loves to wear. What marks the dress as being fashionable are the full soft sleeves. (Volume in sleeves will be a fashion sign of the eighties to the future historians of dress.) Such a dress is useful to the Queen; it has a matching overcoat. The Queen will be kept warm for an outside ceremony. Her Majesty is *frileuse*. In spite of its plainness the dress could be considered suitable for the morning yet it would be chic enough to wear at an investiture. The Queen holds fourteen of these per annum. Dress has to be considered: it is morning and yet it is a festive occasion, and of course one memorable to the recipients and their families. 'Good for investitures' is often the final seal of approval of the Queen when choosing new designs.

My first sight of the Queen that day in 1950, when as the young Princess Elizabeth she came to my office in Savile Row, aroused in me a deep feeling of chivalry which has never subsided. Elevated as the Queen is, anointed by an ancient church, and confirmed and greeted by her people, I think I can allow myself a grain of pride in having been permitted over these past thirty years to contribute one tiny spot to the superb panorama of her successful reign.

If I am pleased to have given good service to the Queen in supplying clothes for the royal tours over the past thirty years, I must share this pleasure with the team of craftsmen and women who actually made the clothes. These are the people who are in close contact with the Queen in every way. I was always there in the background to see that everything went smoothly but I wish to dispel here any impression that I was the all-important person. Throughout I was only the leader of the team. It is only fitting, therefore, that I should comment on the people involved and the parts they have played in helping to shape the Queen's wardrobe. In particular I am thinking of the roles of the tailor, the fitter, the *vendeuse* and, of course, the designer.

The Queen has had to suffer three changes of tailor over the past thirty years. The first was Mr Leonard with whom I had worked at Worth during the war. He had been one of the first people I had recruited when I opened my own shop in 1945. He retired in 1965 and his place in the team serving the Queen was taken by Mr Ernest. My association with Ernest went back further to the days when I worked at Lachasse and where he was one of the two head tailors employed by Mr Shingleton. When the time came for him to retire my staff had already been strengthened by the addition of Michael, and it was he who took over the duties as the Queen's tailor. Michael was a very talented tailor who had originally learnt his craft working for Michael of Lachasse, later Michael of Carlos Place. These, then, are the tailors.

They are responsible for the important job of cutting the cloth and supervising the actual making of the clothes by the working tailors and tailoresses under them. The *vendeuse* responsible for the Queen's wardrobe was, as I have said, for a long time Betty Reeves. Betty was exactly the same height as the Queen and equally neat of figure. She had the perfect style of a professional *vendeuse*: a mixture of bossiness and servility. ('You can't have that, Your Grace: it isn't you!') She was also a fusser and got into a stew at the very thought of going to the Palace. As a Christmas present she had been given by the Queen a brooch in the shape of the royal cipher and she was careful always to wear it on what the house called 'Palace days'. She surprised us all one day by announcing that she was leaving the firm to go and get married to Teddy Knox, a member of the Crazy Gang. We never saw her again.

The natural successor to Betty Reeves as the Queen's *vendeuse* was Mrs Sheila Ogden. No one could have been more different from Betty than Mrs Ogden. She takes the visits to the Palace calmly and in her stride, as you would expect of someone who has once glided across a throne room as a debutante in full evening dress with the traditional three feathers in her hair. She married, had a child, divorced, and, seeking independence, became a *vendeuse*. She gathered around her a distinguished clientele culled from her friends in the social and racing world. It has been most useful having her in the team when we are working out our choice of cloth and sketches to present to the Queen.

Probably the most important person in the team is the fitter. The relationship between a fitter and a customer is a very intimate one. There must be sympathy between them. In the case of such an important customer as the Queen this is crucial. By tradition it is the right of the *vendeuse* to choose which fitter would be the most suitable for a new customer. Naturally, in the case of the Queen, I was consulted. We were all agreed that the first fitter the Queen would have was Maud Beard. She had been an apprentice in the workrooms at the time my mother was a *vendeuse*. She had progressed considerably, however, and by the time she joined me when I opened my shop was highly skilled in handling cloths, making models, and fitting copies on customers. When the toll of years forced her eventually to retire we had already taken on a new, talented and very painstaking fitter in the form of Miss Lilian.

The design studio has been headed throughout this thirty-year period by Ken Fleetwood. He has been of enormous help in preparing designs for the Queen. He has also been responsible for the running of the women's side of the business throughout most of this time; a responsibility made just that much more onerous by my frequent absences abroad. It is only in the last two years that it has been possible for him to join the team that visits the Palace.

This, then, is the team that serves the Queen when preparing wardrobes for the royal tours. Some of the personalities have changed over the years, those retiring being replaced when necessary by newer ones, but the roles have remained essentially the same. During this thirty-year period we have been responsible for designing and supplying wardrobes for over fifty-eight tours or state visits. It is a tribute to the hard work and quality of craftsmanship of my staff at Savile Row that we are still commanded from time to time to make clothes for Her Majesty.

The Queen's approach to the business of preparing a wardrobe for a tour is a straightforward one. Throughout the reign it has been the Queen's practice to call her dressmakers to the Palace to discuss the clothes needed for a particular tour. This message is usually relayed to us via the Queen's devoted dresser requesting us initially to go to the Palace with sketches of clothes we intend to propose. A series of fittings at the Palace follow and eventually the wardrobe is delivered to the care of the Queen's dresser, who is then responsible for its packaging and transport on tour.

With so many tours spread over such a long time it would be impossible for me to comment on, or even remember, all the episodes that took place and all the occasions when the Queen was seen wearing one of our outfits. For the most part we had to wait on the reports in the press or on television and sometimes these were slow in coming. Also, it has to be said, I was not present on these visits and therefore in no position to comment directly on events. There were, however, some occasions when I was present, but only through the coincidence of my being in the same country as the Queen on matters of business. And here I have to make it clear that on these occasions, which have been great moments in my life, I was always present as a private person. Nevertheless, the Queen has often been aware that I was in the audience. My comments on these tours are by necessity bound to be selective.

If I begin with the tour to Australia in 1953 it is as much because it was the first tour made by Her Majesty after her Coronation as because we, her *couturiers*, learned a great deal about some of the problems of preparing clothes for a long tour. I think it had always been understood that this first state visit would be to Australia since it was there that the Queen had been going before her journey was curtailed in Kenya by news of the King's death. There were several duties for the Queen to perform after the Coronation, so it was not until 24 November of that year that the tour got under way.

The Queen flew first to Canada and then on to Australia. It proved to be a tremendously long tour and it was not until 10 May 1954 that the royal party set foot in England again, having travelled 44,000 miles. More startling than the number of miles travelled, however, was the fact that the Queen had been abroad for nearly six months. My impression was that this tour was too long and fatigued the Queen to an unnecessary extent. Those responsible for arranging tours and state visits must have thought so too, because the Queen has never since been expected to undertake such an arduous tour.

From a dressmaking point of view we learned much from the tour. At the outset of our visits to the Palace to discuss the wardrobe the Queen had warned us that the tour involved visiting hot countries such as Fiji, Tonga and, on the return journey, Aden. I have spoken already of the difficulty of making the Queen look regal in modern day clothes; this task is even more exacting when making dresses to be worn in very hot and humid climates. The choice of material is critical. Even when we were preparing the wardrobe, long before the tour had begun, there had been a clamour of voices from the experts offering us conflicting advice. 'Nylon!' said the pundits; 'Polyester!' cried the textile traders; '*Infroissable!*' advised the French. We tried them all. Many were uncrushable, but too heavy. In the end we settled on pure silk and lightweight wool. In retrospect we discovered that even these materials were too heavy for the Far East. Today, some thirty years later, there are some stunning cloths in man-made fibres resembling pure silk which are also extremely light in weight. But at the time they were unheard of and therefore unavailable.

My recollections of the clothes we made for this first tour are often clouded by the sight of a photograph of the royal party at the moment of their return to Portsmouth on the royal yacht *Britannia*. The photograph hangs over the oyster bar at Wilton's in Bury Street, and the sight of it has often threatened to spoil my lunch. For the Queen's taffeta coat which we had made for her is not a happy one. It is very difficult to tailor taffeta and I have not proposed it since then.

The first royal tour to have any personal significance for me was the first state visit to France in 1957. It was a very brief visit, lasting only from 8–11 April, but it was the first time I had felt able to ask the Queen if I might design an outfit with a specific occasion in mind. It was the Queen's practice then, and still is today, never to make too decided a choice as to when a particular dress is to be worn. There are always too many imponderables to consider, such as the weather. Paris in the spring wasn't so much of a problem in this respect, but some of the other places on the itinerary were more remote and less familiar. However, with this visit we were lucky enough to have been allowed to see the programme before it was officially published. This was tremendously useful to me because I learned that the itinerary included a visit by the Queen to attend a matinée given on her behalf at the opera house in Versailles. I asked Her Majesty, therefore, if I could submit designs of dresses especially for this occasion.

I had been to Versailles previously on several occasions and knew a little of its history. I knew, for instance, that the opera house, built originally by Louis xv in 1770 for the marriage of Marie Antoinette to the Dauphin, had been used since the mid-nineteenth century for parliamentary purposes and that the gay pastel-coloured marble walls had been covered in a serious dull brown. Since the French Government had gone to great lengths to restore it to its former glory, and as the Queen's visit was going to be the inaugural function, it seemed reasonable to presume that the interior would have been repainted. I surmised, quite rightly as it turned out, that the predominant colour of the whole opera house would be blue. I suggested to the Queen, therefore, that a dress and coat in palest blue ribbed silk might be appropriate and, to add a touch of richness to the outfit, cuffs in mink. I was then bold enough to suggest that the bodice of the dress should be lightly embroidered, remembering how magnificently Queen Mary could glitter at any time of the day. In the event, it is fair to say that we didn't put enough embroidery on the dress but this was, in any case, hidden as the Queen was allowed to keep her coat on.

The spectacle offered the Queen at this afternoon gala performance was that of several scenes from the ballet *Les Indes Galantes*, with music by Rameau. The costumes and the scenery were magnificent reproductions of those of the period, but the choreography was a little boring. It was not a great success and the audience fidgeted throughout.

I was delighted to have been allowed to do the dress for this occasion: above all it appealed to my sense of history, and I believe that Queen Elizabeth II was the first Queen to visit Versailles since Queen Victoria. My outfit, however, was quite modest, and although it was right to use gold thread and diamanté embroidery on a dress we had not used it with any great authority or chic.

What made the afternoon quite memorable for me was that with me was Norman Hartnell, the Queen's number one dressmaker. The French Government had kindly sent us invitations and had given us seats together in a box. Norman was flattering about how well the Queen looked on her arrival at the opera house, and I was able to return the compliment by praising the magnificent dress he had made for the state banquet at the Elysée Palace. Even more splendid was the very slim evening dress he had made for the Queen to wear on the river trip up the Seine. It was a dress embroidered entirely in silver and worn with a white fox cape. It was an outfit of great chic and much admired by the watching crowds. Overall it was Norman Hartnell's clothes which were the most spectacular and which had the greatest success on this trip to Paris. Nonetheless, it was a very pleasant experience for me to have shared the visit with him.

My turn had come with a message from the Elysée Palace to the Ritz, where I was staying, asking me to go and see the Queen before she left for a reception at the Louvre. For this occasion the Queen had chosen a dress of ours; it was a full-skirted evening dress in peacock blue faille. (Faille is a thick form of taffeta with a rich dull surface.) It was the first time we had offered anything so brightly coloured and the Queen remarked when accepting it that it was time to make a change from the usual soft pastel colours that had been used up till then. The Queen received us in full glory with all her jewellery on and said that she hoped that the dress would glow in what she thought would be the rather gloomy decor of the Louvre. And she was right.

The visit to Germany in 1965 had a great fascination for me, not least because the programme showed that there was to be a banquet and reception given by the President of Germany in the Queen's honour at Schloss Brühl. This was the extraordinarily lavish and elegantly decorated summer palace of the Archbishop and Elector of Cologne, Prince Clemenz August. I knew the palace and its magnificent interiors, built around 1740, from earlier visits and during my two and a half years spent on the Rhine as a young man, when I had visited the place often. Schloss Brühl was not lived in but kept for official entertainments given by the President, who himself lived in a fairly modest villa in nearby Bonn.

The German state had already begun the painstaking process of restoring the Schloss to its former splendour. It must be as little as one tenth the size of Versailles yet it is no less impressive for all that. What I remembered most about the building was the splendid stucco work and, above all, the beautiful blue and white tiles that decorate the summer dining rooms and kitchens. Blue and white, I was soon to discover, were the official colours of the Wittelsbach family and of Prince Clemenz August. It was with these colours in mind, therefore, that I submitted to the Queen suggestions for the dress to be worn and we were all delighted when she kindly accepted. We chose a pale-blue soft satin, in no way stiff, for the skirt. The bodice was embroidered in white beads and pearls in a rococo design which reflected the influence of the stucco decoration. My pleasure at the Queen's acceptance of our design was equalled only by the delight I felt when a card arrived inviting me to attend the reception.

The excitement of seeing our Queen on that particular evening was intense. My sister was there to share it with me only because she had very nobly asked if she might be my chauffeur on the trip. We were joined by a further companion, Peter Hope Lumley, my public relations consultant. No one more than Peter knew how personally involved I felt about this trip to Germany with all the memories of my earlier time there, and no one worked more enthusiastically at making it such a memorable occasion.

There is very often a great deal of interest shown by the press in the Queen's wardrobe on state visits such as this. To accommodate this interest the Queen had given permission for sketches to be issued in advance but with the expressly stated proviso that no sketch could appear before the Queen had worn the dress in question. Peter, more than anyone, knew this yet his ingenuity on this occasion was to come to the fore. He had arranged with the artist Robb, who was on the staff of the *Daily Express*, to have sent over to his office his copy of our sketch of the Queen's dress as soon as we were certain that the Queen was wearing it. This we were able to know from getting a glimpse of the Queen as she set off on the drive through Bonn to the banquet. Peter, who was there to see this for himself, telephoned Robb with the confirmation before the three of us drove off to the reception which was to be held after the dinner. The result of this careful planning was shown the next day in full glory on the front page of the *Daily Express*. Our sketch of the dress filled over half the front page while next to it the headlines read: 'The Queen Dazzles Them!' I can only say that the *Daily Express* certainly dazzled me.

For the reception itself more than a thousand people had gathered. All the notables from the world of diplomacy were there as were those from the world of the arts and industry. Some of them I knew; indeed, some of them I had known from the days I had spent there before the war. They were able to understand how moved I was by the thought that the young trainee working in the factory making ceramic tiles in the nearby village of Bendorf all those years ago had now become one of the dressmakers to the Queen and was about to see her appear in one of his dresses. After about an hour of excited chat and fidgeting, during which time we had edged slowly towards the landing at the top of the astounding stuccoed staircase of Balthazar Neumann, the royal party duly appeared and inexorably wound its ways upwards and towards us. It was a stunning and unforgettable sight.

In the course of the evening there was a torchlight procession, an event which by old tradition in Germany is reserved for the entertainment of royalty. It was a splendid occasion and made all the more enjoyable by the fact that the number of guests present was just right for the size of the rooms. Thus the Queen was able to move around comfortably and talk to people.

There was only one black spot on the evening: the calling-up system for the cars after the reception was over. It did not function very efficiently. Knowing that my sister and Peter Hope Lumley had been waiting for nearly two hours in the car park, I left the reception early and was perhaps the second or third person to join the queue for the calling-up of the cars. To my dismay my car did not appear for a further two hours. The first names given over the wire had not reached the car park. But my distress was nothing compared with that of elderly German princesses in *décolleté* dresses, inadequate furs and family jewels, frantically waiting in the rain which, during the course of the evening, had increased to a steady downpour. In spite of this episode and sorry as I was at the time for the unnecessary delay suffered by my loyal attendants as they waited in the car park, I can record that my pleasure went undimmed.

The ceremony next day at Coblenz was even more moving. Coblenz is a town built at the confluence of the Moselle and the Rhine. There is a triangular spit of land at the place of joining known as the 'Deutscher Eck'. On the neighbouring bank there was an hotel, the Riesenfurstenhof. This was the grandest hotel in the area and it was here in August 1930, just after my twenty-first birthday, that I had been given a farewell party by my German friends. It was an end to my two and a half years in Germany. It was also a farewell to the French army of occupation. That same day they left the fortress of Ehrenbreitstein on the opposite bank of the Rhine. I never thought, on that day in August 1930, that I would one day be back in a seat given me by the mayor of Coblenz, and on a stand of honour, ready to welcome the Queen of England on her first visit to Germany and the Rhineland. Still less did I imagine that the Queen would be wearing an outfit designed by me and made in a dress-house bearing my name. It was a cherry-red wool overcoat over a white and cherry-red printed silk dress, suitable for wearing on the river trip up the Rhine. It was a much simpler outfit than the blue and white Wittelsbach evening dress from the previous night, but the Queen's wearing of it moved me almost more.

Norman Hartnell had already made his mark on the tour by providing a brilliant yellow ensemble for the Queen's arrival in Bonn on the first day. A further contribution from him was a very beautiful off-white silk coat and dress for the triumphant tour in an open car through the streets of Munich. My sister and I were there to see this.

That night the Queen went to the opera to hear a performance of *Rosenkavalier*. It was with delight and surprise that we saw a photograph of the Queen wearing a dress of ours in the newspapers the next day. We had not even known that that particular dress had been included in Her Majesty's wardrobe for the tour of Germany.

One of the highlights of the second state visit to France, in 1972, was to be a reception in the Galeries des Glaces, at Versailles. Once again my knowledge of the Palace of Versailles was of use. I am sad to say that the choice of cloth available for a dress to be worn at a reception by the Queen in the august surroundings of the Galeries des Glaces has shrunk to uninspiring proportions since then. Even in 1972 I wasn't satisfied with the cloths offered by the silk merchants of Paris. I had wanted something quite exceptional. By what now seems to be chance I was discussing my problem with Michael Szell, a distinguished Hungarian who had recently opened his own cloth business in London. Although he specialized in furnishing fabrics, he had connections with silk weavers in Italy and he put me in touch with one. He showed me some of the most beautiful satin that I have ever seen. One of the samples, known in the profession as 'double face', was a material with a satin shine on both sides. Ordinary satin only has a shiny surface on one side while the reverse is just dull and does not reflect the light. Very often cotton threads are introduced in the material to give it stiffness and, in some ways, a kind of richness. But 'double face' satin, on the other hand, is all silk and this particular one was so cleverly woven that it was immensely supple and fell in what I can only describe as 'caressing folds'. Delighted by this discovery, we ordered it to be made in the very palest mauve imaginable. It is a shade of colour I have only seen elsewhere on the petals of very rare alpine violas.

The bodice was embroidered in imitation pearls and diamonds. Here I must pay tribute to Mr Lock, who has run an embroidery business for as long as I can remember and who holds the Royal Warrant as embroiderer to the Queen. We give Mr Lock the clearest indications possible as to what we want and together we choose the stones required, but it is his skill which brings the whole operation together. Embroidery in my view must always blend in with the cloth used for the rest of the dress; it should add another texture, as do pebbles in a garden path of gravel. There was a shimmering iridescent quality in the satin of the skirt which was reflected in the bodice. Above all we had got the shape right: just enough volume at the hem for the Queen to be able to walk comfortably without in any way disturbing the silhouette of the dress. The Queen is happiest when her evening dresses have sleeves; in this case her commands were fulfilled without any stuffiness.

I had gone to Paris in a happy and confident mood. Ken Fleetwood and Peter Hope Lumley were with me at the Ritz to share in the fun of the occasion. We were, as they say, glued to the television for any coverage of the Queen's tour. Surprise, surprise! – almost the first picture we saw was of the Queen walking off the plane on her arrival wearing one of our outfits. It was a quite new-looking outfit for her as it was a dark-brown coat trimmed with a black and white print which repeated the pattern of the dress worn underneath. Freddie Fox had made a hat which was larger than anything the Queen had worn to date. It was an immensely photogenic ensemble.

The Queen has never discussed the effect of photography – and in particular of television – with me. I consider that the Queen chooses with impeccable taste and a wonderful sense of appropriateness outfits which are always totally suitable for the occasion. It is as if the Queen knows her audience. I have never heard a criticism of the Queen's appearance from anyone present at a particular occasion. It is how she looks in photographs that has often been subject to criticism, particularly by the press in America who do not, in the first instance, understand the standards which the Queen sets herself. They are those of a well-bred lady who would hate flouting convention.

As a designer I was not happy with the mini-skirt era. We succeeded in persuading the Queen to wear quite short dresses but the Queen always made the final decision after she had seen the effect of the skirt sitting down, knowing that she would often be seen on platforms, getting in and out of motorcars, not to mention aeroplanes and yachts. The very short skirt looked best worn without a hat. Mrs Jackie Kennedy was a stunning exponent of the style of this time. Journalists abroad would compare her appearance with that of the Queen's, forgetting totally that Mrs Kennedy was a president's wife and that the Queen was a reigning queen. For the Queen almost any appearance is an official one; and for an official occasion the Queen would be unhappy not wearing a hat, gloves, and carrying a handbag.

The sight of the Queen's arrival in Paris had been a happy beginning to the day. More was to come. I was invited to dinner that night by Lillian de Rothschild who had become a much-loved friend. I had by now learnt how cosy it was to go to a dinner before a ball and to move on with a group of friends. We drove off to the reception at Versailles together.

There was an immense crowd at Versailles but everything was very well arranged. When the Queen moved slowly through the throng I could see amongst the people gathered Marc Bohan (the head of

Christian Dior), Pierre Balmain and Pierre Cardin. The Queen looked truly magnificent and I felt very proud. We had made an evening coat plainly tailored in the same satin as that of the dress. This was for wearing on the journey from the Petit Trianon, where the Queen was staying, to the reception at the Palace of Versailles. Marc Bohan came over to congratulate me on the dress and I was able to return the compliment by praising the red dress he had made for Madame Pompidou.

For the second evening the Queen quite definitely needed a coat. Norman Hartnell made her a magnificent one, heavily embroidered and trimmed with white mink. The Queen entertained the French President to dinner at the British Embassy and then went on to a military revue at the Champs de Mars where she saw a display of military riding.

The next few days were taken up by what the official programme called 'Départ en Province'. (This description could only have been penned by a Parisian, one presumes.) We were thankful that although it was May the weather was not too hot so the Queen was able to appear chicly and fashionably dressed in a variety of woollen suits of our design.

Returning to Paris on the last night of the visit, the Queen gave a dinner at the British Embassy followed by a reception. To this the ever-thoughtful and kind Lady Soames had invited me. The Queen wore a dress of ours in gold gauze, very much plainer than anything worn previously. It was correctly understated, as befitted an outfit worn by the hostess.

The success of the earlier visit to France by Queen Elizabeth the Queen Mother, when Norman Hartnell made her an all-white wardrobe, has become a fashion legend. I don't think we achieved anything like that this time, but the French papers did give us some praise, even if at times inaccurately. This is my translation of what *Paris Match* said after first reproaching Prince Philip for wearing a camel overcoat at the very dressed-up evening at the Champs de Mars:

> Everybody has been favourably impressed by the elegance of Her Majesty Queen Elizabeth II, except as regards the millinery where, on occasions, there seem to be certain difficulties. The viewer in the street as well as the viewer of colour television has been well pleased with the colours and the cloths of her dresses and suits. A young English couturier of the new generation, Hardy Amies, is gradually taking the place of the celebrated

Norman Hartnell, principal dressmaker to the Queen since the start of her reign. Here you have the reason: Norman Hartnell, now seventy-one years old, is retiring with a certain Victorian glory and with the satisfaction of knowing in his lifetime, from reports in the French press these past few days, that the Queen of England is the best dressed woman in Paris.

As I was already in my sixty-third year, *'jeune couturier'* was not exactly accurate! They had muddled me up with Ian Thomas, a comparative newcomer, but one who was to go on to do very good work for the Queen.

Hats are a problem and one with which Freddie Fox, the Queen's milliner, copes valiantly. Paris has always been a milliners' city and it is reasonable therefore to understand their feelings of chauvinistic pride in this one area. It was always very hard, even in the heyday of the hat, to find good working milliners in London. Today, after a no-hat era of some twenty years, it is even harder.

Before going on the state visit to Mexico in March 1975 the Queen explained that there would be several evening parties held on the summit of those historic mountains, Monte Alban and Mitla. I had been in Mexico a year or two before and knew the decor. The Queen stated that she had been requested in advance to wear full evening dress and jewellery for these occasions, but that the men would only be expected to wear lounge suits. We thought it correct to provide the Queen with rather rich, dark clothes and found a beautiful thin soft silk, in dark blue, into which was woven a large pattern of gold, bright green, and red flowers. We made a simple flowing dress which was very easy to wear and provided a shawl made of the same material with a heavy silk fringe. I knew that the tops of those mountains could be draughty. As always we waited with impatience to see pictures of the Queen, either on the television or in the newspapers. It was in the newspapers that we saw the picture: the Queen huddled under somebody's mackintosh hastily thrown across her shoulders and under an umbrella. It was pouring with rain. Such was the fate of our carefully thought-out outfit! We subsequently learnt that the entertainment offered to the Queen had been a Mexican dance invoking the rain god to open the heavens.

The Queen's visit to Japan later in the same year of 1975 was of special importance to me as it coincided with negotiations for the extension of a licence arrangement we had there whereby men's and women's clothes of our design were reproduced and sold in Japan. Licensee arrangements are usually for terms of either three or five years. In the case of Diatobo, the firm with whom we did business, it was five years. In 1975 this arrangement was up for renewal and it corresponded with the Queen's visit to Japan. A visit by me was due. The Japanese insisted that I be there at the same time as the Queen.

I vividly remember being in a boardroom with my Japanese colleagues discussing our work when we were interrupted by a request to view the Queen's arrival in Tokyo on television. Once again I had no idea what the Queen would be wearing, and it was therefore with surprise and delight that I saw her looking young, fashionable and regal in a pretty mauve silk coat of ours and with a clever hat made by Freddie Fox out of tightly woven-together flowers of lilac. 'Imperial colours,' said the Japanese. 'How flattering to us!' I kept 'stumm', as they say in New York; I had no idea that mauve was an imperial colour, but I shouldn't be surprised if the Queen had known.

It was in Tokyo that I saw the Queen wearing a dress by Ian Thomas for the first time. He is the third dressmaker that the Queen patronizes and he has been making clothes for her ever since that tour. It was an evening dress in green, embroidered in cherry blossom. It was a nice gesture to the Japanese and, consequently, much applauded.

My turn came on the next night at the British Embassy where the Queen was hostess. She wore a long-sleeved dinner dress in bright green silk with gold embroidery. There was nothing wrong with this except that the shape of the design of the embroidery did not harmonize well with the ribbon of the Order of the Garter – we should have thought of this. What is most memorable to me about the occasion was the scene in the garden of the Embassy after dinner where the Queen and Prince Philip were going to *cercler*; Prince Philip to the right and the Queen to the left. We automatically made three rows of guests in a circle. In the front were the Japanese and Indonesians. Behind them members of the European diplomatic corps, and at the back the tall British, including some members of the Queen's suite and her dressmaker. Readers will realize that this was not the first time that I had waited to see the Queen at a function of some formality and even solemnity. With no disrespect I wish to say that the Queen has a marvellous way of looking at you and winking without moving any portion of her eyes and eyebrows. Such a look was accorded me that evening and I responded, of course, with the sharp inclination of the head which I knew to be correct.

I was slightly crestfallen when I heard that the Queen was due to go on a state visit to the USA in July 1976. I know New York well enough to be aware that the months of July and August can be exceptionally hot and humid. I have already described the difficulty of making royal clothes for such a climate because of the problems involved in using thin materials. Washington can be even hotter than New York and the Queen was due to visit both places.

The visit started in Philadelphia, and I was relieved to see that the Queen chose one of our outfits to wear on that occasion. I think it is one of our most successful designs. Freddie Fox had made a very beautiful plain hat to go with the outfit. The material was blue and white striped voile which photographed well. The day must have been cool enough for the Queen to wear the coat as well as the dress. Both were, of course, gossamer light. I have always thought that a dress alone, without a coat, never has enough 'presence'.

The visit to New York was intentionally planned to be an informal occasion. The Queen came ashore wearing an off-white linen dress of ours for which Freddie Fox had made a hat out of natural coloured straw. My experience is that the Queen can wear almost any colour provided it is a colour; beige is not strictly a proper colour in this sense. More successful, perhaps, was the outfit she wore for the afternoon. It was green and white spotted chiffon with a neatly draped turban of the same material. This way of using the cloth gave a harmony to the outfit.

I was nothing short of disappointed that the Queen did not wear what I thought was going to be our star number: a dress and coat in very bright pink silk. I fully understood, however, that it was perhaps too hot to wear in New York. It was not forgotten, I am glad to say, for after the five-day visit to the USA the Queen moved on to Canada. The highlight of this visit was the opening by the Queen of the Olympic Games in Montreal. Once again the Queen had shown her infallible good sense and taste in choosing this occasion to wear the dress. The very bright pink was the ideal colour to wear in a stadium holding 68,000 spectators.

At no time throughout her reign has the Queen been busier than in the Jubilee Year of 1977. It is amazing to see the list of places overseas visited by her during that year. In between engagements we had many fitting sessions with her. The Queen had ordered quite a number of clothes, mostly in very thin fabrics. We were fitting even up to the week before Jubilee Day, Tuesday 7 June. The weather was already unpredictable. One particular dress we had been working on was in a very pretty pale green chiffon, and Mrs Ogden had told me that in her opinion the Queen intended to wear it on Jubilee Day if the weather allowed. In the event the weather was anything but accommodating; it got colder and colder during the weekend, and by Tuesday morning I knew that the chances of the Queen wearing one of our dresses were very slight indeed. At the time I reproached myself for not having proposed something outstanding in wool. We had made some wool outfits but they really were not sufficiently exceptional or suitable for a jubilee celebration.

I think it was one of the biggest surprises in my life as a dress designer when I saw the gold coach coming out from under the arches of Buckingham Palace and we suddenly caught a glimpse of the Queen wearing a bright pink silk dress. 'Goodness me!' we all cried. 'It's our dress from Montreal'. To the best of our knowledge the Queen had not worn it since the Olympic Games the previous year. It was, of course, the perfect outfit for the Jubilee celebrations. It stood up well to the buffeting of the winds on the steps of St Paul's Cathedral. I gave myself a pat on the back for having insisted that the loose coat be lined with the same material as that of the dress. This was extravagant because the heavy silk crêpe was very expensive but the weight of the two materials enabled the coat to hang well, even in the high winds.

Perhaps the most moving moment of the day for me was when I saw the Queen as she sat down in her open carriage to make the return journey to Buckingham Palace put a little scarf around her shoulders. The Queen had been carrying this all through the ceremony in the Cathedral. As I have explained, the outfit was originally made for the visit to New York the previous year, and I had made the scarf for the Queen to keep her shoulders warm if she had been required to abandon the coat. I had known on that occasion how treacherous the air conditioning could be in American buildings. Now my little scarf was being used for quite a different purpose. There is no doubt from our point of view that this pink outfit is the most important that we have ever made for the Queen.

All my staff and I were immensely pleased to see a photograph of the Queen wearing the satin dress that we had made for the visit to Versailles in 1972 widely used at the time of the Jubilee. Our work is, therefore, immortalized on thousands of biscuit tins to become antiques of the future.

The visit to Saudi Arabia and the Gulf States in February 1979 was of great interest to us because of the Queen's commands regarding the styles of the clothes Her Majesty thought expedient to wear. The orders were for no bare necks or arms and skirts to the ground.

One of the most important functions on the itinerary was to be what the Queen described as a picnic in the desert. The Queen said she intended to wear boots, which she did. It turned out that the picnic took place in a series of large tents with carpeted floors and that the most delicate and flimsy clothes could have been worn. The Queen had hinted that the most acceptable designs would be those which showed possibilities of being converted into dinner dresses for wearing back in England. The Queen accepted our suggestions that we should make soft dinner dresses which could be *décolleté* but with long-sleeved and high-necked jackets to go over them. We added in one case a turban with flowing ends. (I think our idea was to contrive something like the outfit worn by Marlene Dietrich in a desert film she made with Gary Cooper.) The colour chosen was a beautiful sapphire blue in heavy chiffon crêpe. What we had totally overlooked, however – indeed, nobody had even spoken of it – were the very strong winds that could suddenly come up in this part of the world. These winds hit the Queen as she came off the aeroplane and seemed to wrap her in yards of cloth. This effect did not make Her Majesty look very elegant in the photographs. The more tailored outfits we made in crêpe de chine were more successful and, indeed, once the skirts had been shortened to normal day length on her return to London, were worn by the Queen at Ascot.

When it was announced that the Queen was going to pay a state visit to Italy in October 1980, which would include an audience with the Pope, my thoughts immediately went back to the Queen's first visit to the Vatican in May 1961. There had appeared then stunning photographs of the Queen in black lace with tiara and veil. It was, of course, what is called a 'gift'; you couldn't fail with such material. I thought I would be very clever and use neither black velvet nor heavy black lace but something much more diaphanous. I found a very fine lace of a type which is known as 'chantilly' and achieved, by putting it over layers of white and grey tulle, an effect which I can only describe as a cloud of very dark charcoal grey. We went through the routine fittings and the Queen seemed perfectly satisfied. It was even mooted at the time that the outfit could serve as a good dark dinner dress for another occasion, an idea which the Queen accepted readily. I was, however, unable to attend the final fitting. Both Mrs Ogden and Lilian had assured me that all was well and that they could manage perfectly in my absence. I had received a call from our American business colleagues in New York requesting that I attend an important conference to discuss the planning for the next year. It was impossible for them to change the date. Such situations have often occurred. Ought I to put the Queen's commands first or should I give preference to work overseas which made the money to help me keep the business going in London, and thus be able to support an organization which was of use to Her Majesty?

Mrs Ogden and Lilian reported that the final fitting had gone well. It was therefore a great disappointment to us that when we saw the photographs of the Queen being greeted by the Pope Her Majesty was not wearing our dress but another one instead, but looking, I may say, very splendid indeed. Matters were not made any better by television and radio announcers stating that the Queen was wearing a Hardy Amies dress. Mr Ian Thomas, the designer of the dress worn, quite rightly complained to Peter Hope Lumley, who had to explain how innocent we were in this misunderstanding.

We realized that our dress was not conventionally black enough for a church occasion but that it would be perfect for wearing at private dinners whenever the Palace was in mourning.

In the spring of 1981 the Queen ordered some new clothes, some of which were to be in very light materials suitable for the forthcoming state visit to Sri Lanka in October. There were to be visits also to Australia and New Zealand. The Queen had given us a date on which to submit suggestions on designs and cloths but this was not to be until my return from a business visit to Australia in February.

It was during that Australian visit, while I was in Sydney, that the announcement was made of the Prince of Wales's engagement to Lady Diana Spencer. When the wedding date was announced subsequently we began to hope that the Queen might choose something of ours to wear at the ceremony, and I started to turn my mind to the possible materials that would be suitable for the occasion. The search for materials suitable for the Queen's dresses gets more difficult year by year; there are fewer weavers and still fewer merchants who can depend for their livelihood on the whims of the rich. But there are still enough men and women who cannot bear to lower their standards and, in the end, we invariably manage to find cloths which can excite and inspire us.

We waited on the Queen many times during that spring but the wedding was never mentioned. We took this to be a sure sign that the Queen was not going to wear one of our dresses. However, we have had too many pleasures and small triumphs over the past thirty years for us to grumble. I mention it because it is a good example of how completely the Queen is mistress of her own wardrobe.

In that summer of 1981 we did indeed make some stunning dresses for the Queen. We even had a fitting with Her Majesty lasting some hours on the day following the wedding. When I thanked the Queen for giving us this time so soon after what must have been a very hectic schedule, the Queen replied that she was pleased to have something to do as life seemed rather flat now that the wedding was over.

The weather on the visit to Sri Lanka turned out to be colder and wetter than we had expected. ('Weather is always exceptionable,' as the Queen is fond of saying.) So it was not until some months afterwards that we saw the Queen wearing a few of the outfits that we had planned and fitted in the summer. One outfit in particular which I had always hoped that the Queen might have chosen as being suitable for the wedding was in a heavy soft cloqué silk in bright Chinese yellow. The material was so beautiful that we had made the very plainest day dress and a neat tailored coat in the same material, the sole decorations of which were looped buttons and buttonholes in the same silk down the front. Freddie Fox had made a very successful hat to go with it. But, once again, the Queen was to show perfect judgement in deciding which dress to wear on a particular occasion.

In the following year, 1982, I was once again in Australia on business at the same time as the Queen was making a state visit. One of the important acts to be performed by the Queen was the official opening of the new art gallery in Canberra. But by far the most spectacular event of the visit was the duty of the Queen, as head of the Commonwealth, to officiate at the closing ceremony of the Commonwealth Games in Brisbane. This event has enormous popularity and is one of the high points of the Commonwealth calendar. Not only does it attract tremendous television coverage throughout the world, but it is followed with great pride by the peoples of the host country. It was at this ceremony that the Queen appeared in our bright yellow outfit. The Queen looked absolutely splendid in the outfit as her car made several circuits of the stadium, surrounded on all sides by a milling mass of cheering competitors and spectators.

In the early autumn of 1982 we learned that the Queen was going to visit the west coast of the United States in the spring of 1983. There had been no visits there on previous tours of North America. The Queen was first to visit Jamaica and the Cayman Islands and to spend a few days in Mexico before arriving in San Diego. The next stops were going to be Los Angeles and San Francisco; the Queen would then go on to the west coast of Canada.

Just before leaving England on one of my trips abroad, I was relieved to receive a message from Buckingham Palace in which I was asked to be ready with sketches for this Caribbean and North American trip on 1 November 1982. I say relieved because I knew that by that date I would be back in England. However, no sooner had I arrived in New York than there was a telephone message from London saying that there had been a mistake and that the Queen wanted to see the sketches on 1 October instead. I was in a quandary. When I was asked if Ken Fleetwood could go in my place I readily agreed. I had always intended that one day I would ask permission to take him with me to the Palace. It all turned out happily and the Queen sent a message saying that she had spent a very happy afternoon; the number of outfits ordered – the best sign of approval – had showed that we had satisfied our most important customer.

An essential part of these visits when showing sketches is that the choice of materials should be made so that they can be ordered in good time. Ken went to the Palace with the idea that the Queen should be persuaded to have clothes in colours rather darker than those we had used over past years. I knew that the Queen likes to have bright colours so as to stand out in a crowd. However, on this occasion Ken was persuasive and the darker-coloured clothes have turned out very well. I had to point out that some light-coloured clothing would be necessary for the bright Californian sunshine and these were added to the wardrobe.

It gave me immense pleasure and pride to be able to introduce my protégé and, I hope, my successor to the Queen. But the greatest pleasure of all has been to see how Ken Fleetwood had become completely beguiled by the Queen's personality. Being extremely percipient, he has not missed any of the tiny shafts of humour which the Queen never fails to throw out. Above all, I am happy that there seems to be no strain put on the Queen by our presence together. There is room for us all in the Queen's large fitting room at Buckingham Palace.

My absence abroad on business during this time proved to be fortuitous in one respect which was to be of great use to me on my return. Part of my trip required me to be in San Francisco to pay a courtesy visit to Grodin's, a firm with a chain of shops on the west coast which sells our clothes under licence. They gave a large cocktail party at which I was the guest of honour. Also present at the party was the British Consul and various members of the consulate staff. I was able to press him for details of the Queen's visit to California. He told me that nothing had been finally settled but that it was almost certain that there was going to be a formal state dinner given on Her Majesty's behalf in San Francisco, and also what he called a 'jolly party' in Hollywood. He requested my discretion on this since the American aides had not finally settled on the arrangements with the Queen's advisers. Nevertheless, even this unconfirmed information was enough to give me some idea of what sort of time the Queen could expect in America and what kind of wardrobe would be most suitable. The consul also told me that if I happened to be in San Francisco at the same time I would be more than welcome to attend a cocktail party at the Consulate.

By the time I returned to England in November the time available to prepare and fit the various outfits for this wardrobe was short. The

Queen's engagement book was particularly crowded during this period. Not only were there the normal duties of state to be carried out, but there were the routine breaks of Christmas at Windsor and New Year at Sandringham to be considered. It seemed that there would never be enough time to visit the Palace to work on the collection. But such was the urgency to have the wardrobe ready for the visit that Her Majesty very kindly arranged for us to go to Sandringham where we could complete the fittings. Once or twice in the past the Queen had commanded us to go to Windsor or Balmoral to carry out similar work, but never to Sandringham. It was with a feeling of excitement, then, that we set out on our visit to Sandringham on 28 January 1983. It would have been nice if Ken Fleetwood had been able to go with us but since this date was a Wednesday, and Wednesdays are the day we have dress shows at Savile Row in the spring and autumn, he felt quite rightly that it was his duty to stay and help in ensuring a successful season in the House.

Sandringham House is described in some biographies as a very ugly house. I can only report that I did not find it so. The day was helped by a display of magnificent winter sunshine. We were given a warm welcome by the Queen's servants, and in the suite put at our disposal a splendid luncheon was served during a pause between the morning and afternoon fitting sessions.

On the train going back to London that evening I reflected on the totally English charm of Sandringham. Style is so much more satisfactory than chic. Style has heart and respects the past; chic, on the other hand, is ruthless and lives entirely for the present.

It was necessary to have the final fittings of the evening dresses on 8 February. The Queen then left for Jamaica on the 13th. I mention these dates to give the reader an idea of how crowded is the Queen's schedule and how rushed things can be for all concerned when preparing a wardrobe. It has to be borne in mind also that I am only one of three dressmakers to the Queen, so if this period seems to be a busy time for me and my staff I can only say that the burden on the Queen must be trebled. It is a tribute to Her Majesty's marvellous gift of using her time so well that she manages it all with the minimum of fuss.

We were very pleased with the wardrobe we had prepared and we all looked forward to seeing the photographs of the Queen wearing our outfits on her visit. The dark colours suggested by Ken Fleetwood looked very new and smart. There was an olive green overcoat with two matching dresses: one in wool for cool days and the other in silk suitable for wearing at a luncheon party. Another dress and coat was in a fairly strong blue, a cross between turquoise and peacock; again a woollen coat and a silk dress. These were the sort of outfits we knew were most useful to the Queen, especially on those days when she would be expected to leave her residence (in this case the royal yacht *Britannia*) at ten in the morning and not return until six o'clock in the evening, having perhaps fulfilled five appointments ranging from civic luncheons to visits to power stations and children's hospitals.

While preparing this collection I had always had in mind the need to design an outfit for the Queen which would be suitable for a special occasion in California. I had remembered a dress designed by Norman Hartnell for an earlier visit to Canada based on the design of the maple leaf and which had been greatly appreciated by the Canadians. I had remembered also the dress designed by Ian Thomas for the state visit to Japan, which had been equally well received. What could I do to make a similar impact in California? The idea of the Californian poppy came to mind. I had learned also that at the party to be given in Hollywood dress for the occasion was to be 'informal'; this, in effect, meant short or long. Since we knew the Queen was happiest wearing long dresses, I was bold enough to suggest a long evening dress based on the design and colour of the Californian poppy, and Her Majesty was gracious enough to accept. The outfit we presented consisted of a simple, sweater-like bodice embroidered all over with the Californian poppy; the effect was intended to be that of a print. White, it was decided, would be the best background to this embroidery. The skirt was plain and long. We considered the outfit a success and we all waited eagerly to see where and when the Queen would wear it.

While the Queen and the royal party progressed on their tour through Jamaica and Mexico on their way to California, I was in New York at the start of a month-long visit to the United States. Not only did I have by now an invitation to the party to be given for the Queen at the British Consulate in San Francisco, but I had also a ticket to the evening party to be given in Hollywood. This second invitation had been arranged by an old friend of mine, Jerry Zipkin. He has been a long-standing friend of Mrs Reagan, and when the Reagans had made a goodwill visit to London, in the days before Mr Reagan had become the President, Jerry had asked me to entertain Mrs Reagan at luncheon one afternoon, which I did with pleasure. This gesture had not been forgotten and Jerry told me that Mrs Reagan had seen to it personally that I was to be invited to the party. Although the Reagans were not strictly speaking the hosts, they were nevertheless very much involved in supervising the occasion.

With these two invitations in my pocket and an impending sense of excitement that the opportunity of mixing business with pleasure was too good to miss, I left my flat in New York at the end of the week and flew to Los Angeles, California. I packed my tennis racket with the intention of treating the first four days of my visit as a holiday. I had even taken the trouble to book a room at the Beverly Hills Hotel in a ground floor apartment which led into its own private garden. Here one is supposed to take breakfast under the endless sunshine for which California is normally so famous. But as the world now knows, that month proved to be the worst period of bad weather experienced in California for over twenty years. The rain never ceased. The guttering above my room was blocked with leaves and the overflow of rain-water fell like a constant waterfall on to the box containing the air conditioning. This created a sound like the noise of six bass drums, and it kept up for two days and nights.

But of far greater consequence than any discomfort I may have suffered was the effect of this unseasonal weather on the Queen and the royal party. I am sure that the Queen had planned in advance which of her outfits she intended to wear on each particular occasion. Any such plans were now at the mercy of the weather, which if anything got worse as the days passed. This was dreadful bad luck on the Queen who, as a result, had to improvise her wardrobe, and it put her at a disadvantage with certain elements of the fashion press. Some ill-informed and ill-mannered journalists criticized at great length the hat worn by the Queen when she disembarked from the *Britannia* at San Diego. They never stopped to think that the Queen chose this hat, and the outfit that matched it, because it was the only one which would not blow off in what was almost a gale force wind. What mattered, and what these critics should have appreciated, was that the Queen looked relaxed and confident throughout the entire engagement.

To be fair to the American press, though, not all their reporters were so philistine in their attitude, and when the occasional breaks in the weather did allow the Queen to be seen wearing a charming and appropriate outfit the reaction was favourable more often than not. One press lady, at a later stage of the visit, even went so far as to telephone me at my hotel to express her admiration. 'I've been watching the Queen all day,' she said, 'and in spite of her busy routine I notice that there is not one wrinkle in her outfit. What's your secret? Is it simply the material you use?' I replied, 'First, the Queen is not what I call a "wriggler" in her clothes; secondly, the material is very good wool; and thirdly, I employ the best tailors and cutters that I can.' 'So it's just as simple as that,' replied the bemused reporter before ringing off.

The Hollywood party, as we all called it, in Los Angeles a few days later was a truly extraordinary spectacle. The great hostesses of Beverly Hills are notorious for the lavishness of their hospitality; for the visitor like myself it is not at all an unpleasant experience. Hollywood treasures its famous stars of yesteryear and enjoys the almost incestuous celebration of itself whenever there is an opportunity. If success has brought some of them riches and fame they are treated like dowager empresses, if they have not been too clever with their investments over the years they are often discreetly helped by people like the widows of the great moguls of the film industry. Everywhere I looked I was able to see famous faces from the world of show business and it was great fun trying to put names to all these faces. The party was for five hundred guests and to arrange a sit-down dinner for that number of people requires careful organization. We were bidden for seven o'clock to ensure that there was no confusion. My partner for the evening was Edana Romney, a distinguished actress now working in the United States. The Queen was not due to arrive until an hour later and during this interlude cocktails were served. This gave me the opportunity of meeting many old friends and also the chance of making new ones.

When the Queen arrived the enormous crowd of guests parted to allow her to pass through unhindered. A journalist had already come up to me and told me excitedly that the Queen was wearing one of my dresses. Suddenly, there it was: the happy, glistening white and youthful-looking party dress that I had always hoped the Queen would choose to wear. I swallowed a lump in the throat and heaved a sigh of pride and relief. The crowd around her, though big, was very polite. It would have been unseemly of me to have been anywhere other than in the background, so I did not have the pleasure of the

Queen's unblinking wink that I have cherished on other occasions.

The food offered us was consciously simple, as befitted a Sunday night supper party. The Queen took her place as the guest of honour at a table at the farthest end of the room with a line either side of her of famous actors and actresses. I was at the far end of the room but *bien placé*; that is to say, at a table bang in front of the stage placed for the after-dinner entertainments. Whenever I glanced in the Queen's direction I saw that she was either smiling or laughing. My main memory of the evening was in taking so much pleasure in seeing the Queen so obviously enjoying herself.

The dress I had designed for this evening had been a great success. It was also the first dress of ours worn by the Queen on this visit. But I have to say here, in all fairness, that we were lucky that it was an evening function indoors and that the weather had no chance to affect the look of the dress. My colleagues Ian Thomas and the staff of the House of Norman Hartnell were not so lucky, however, because their carefully planned day dresses were often smothered in unglamorous mackintoshes and spoiled by the presence of umbrellas.

If I take pleasure in mentioning the success we had with this dress in Los Angeles, I have to report now on the near-disaster of the dress worn by the Queen at the state dinner a few days later in San Francisco. I had no idea what dress the Queen intended to wear on this occasion and I only discovered which dress was chosen when I saw pictures of the dinner on the television screen. It was a dress of ours, but not the one I had hoped would be worn. Secretly, I hoped that the Queen would have worn a full-skirted dress in soft green silk with a neat bodice entirely embroidered in sequins of soft pink and blue. I did not know then that the Queen had worn this dress at a dinner party on board the royal yacht *Britannia* in Mexico. The dress the Queen did wear was a very pretty dress in champagne-coloured taffeta with puff sleeves decorated with 'ruched' bands of lace edged with gold. It was certainly suitable for the occasion, but with over thirty years of experience behind us we should not have offered the Queen a neckline which, from a photographic point of view, interfered with the magnificent jewellery she chose to wear. The effect on the audience present, however, was nothing short of dazzling. As always the Queen had given herself to the occasion and not to the camera. The dress was subsequently worn, without the bows, at the state banquet in Sweden.

It has to be pointed out that at this stage of the visit the exceptionally high waves offshore, whipped up by the increasingly stormy weather, had forced Her Majesty to abandon temporarily her base on the royal yacht *Britannia* and move instead to a suite of rooms in the Hotel St Francis. The removal of the Queen's wardrobe of clothes and jewellery into rooms at the hotel, from which guests had generously removed themselves, must have been a miracle of organization. Throughout this upheaval the Queen carried out, punctual to the minute, her very busy programme.

The following day the Queen and the royal suite flew to Sacramento, the capital of California, to attend a civic luncheon. She was due back in San Francisco later the same afternoon to attend a tea party at the British Consulate. At four o'clock that afternoon the Queen appeared at the Consulate in Pacific Heights looking unruffled and as immaculate as ever. This was the day Her Majesty wore Ken Fleetwood's olive green outfit. The weather, for once, was clement and, as planned, the Queen gave the coat to her lady-in-waiting, Lady Susan Hussey, and made her tour wearing only the dress and Freddie Fox's smart green straw hat. Two hundred British residents had assembled for the occasion and the Queen and Prince Philip between them had a conversation with all of them. I was present and therefore able to witness this extraordinary act of generosity and patience, for this was, after all, late in the day of a very crowded schedule and during a tour which was already into its third week. The Queen's words to me were few and kind. 'Hello,' said the Queen, 'everything is all right. We're only about fifteen minutes behind schedule.'

The Queen moved out into the front garden where were assembled a large group of children and their parents. The street facing the British Consulate is similar to any one in the better parts of Hampstead and was completely sealed off from traffic. The children swarmed around the Queen offering her bouquets of flowers. This went on for several minutes, with the Queen smiling and laughing throughout while passing on the bouquets to the Duchess of Grafton, Mistress of the Robes, and to Lady Susan Hussey. I stood on a low brick pillar in the adjoining garden watching these tributes from another generation and able to marvel at how they had been effortlessly won over by the natural charm and friendliness of the Queen. The lasting image I have of that scene when the Queen eventually got into her car to drive off was that of the Duchess of Grafton and Lady Susan Hussey so burdened with the weight of flowers in their arms that they could hardly walk to their car.

The next day I returned with my manservant, James, to New York where a round of appointments awaited me. The Queen's tour, meanwhile, continued up the Californian coast to Seattle and into Canada. I was only able to follow her progress through glimpses of the television. I was amused to see the Queen wearing a yellow outfit of ours in Vancouver which we had originally intended for wear on a sunny day in Los Angeles. The Queen has often remarked in the past on the unpredictability of the weather, but I think that never has it played such a disruptive part on a royal visit as it did on this tour. Again it is a tribute to Her Majesty that she literally weathered the storms so admirably and with so little fuss.

It does not need me, a mere dressmaker, to evaluate the success of the Queen's visit to California. I had taken part only as a spectator who was lucky enough to have had the privilege of seeing the Queen 'working', as Her Majesty likes to put it. But to have seen once again the royal suite, the careful planning of her secretaries, and the crew of *Britannia* all coping with the worst weather conditions in California for twenty years and, above all, to have seen the generosity of the Queen and Prince Philip in giving so much pleasure to others, was such an overwhelming experience that I feel I have to record it. I will not let anyone be so frivolous as to criticize the cost of such a visit, for who can measure the result of what is achieved? At the very least it is a movement towards the binding together of two nations with a common language and a common ancestry. Politics may keep us apart materially, but the Queen showed us that when the heart speaks, as she made it, we are one.

The Queen returned to England and after a weekend's respite Her Majesty was once again launched into the busy palace routine of investitures, the greeting of King Hussein of Jordan and the other members of the Arab League, and a state banquet in honour of President Kaunda of Zambia, but a few of the duties that awaited her on her return. Even then Her Majesty's courtiers and advisers were busy planning the final details of the next royal tour which was to be the state visit to Sweden. We at Savile Row were of the opinion that the Queen would not call on us for clothes for this visit. The Queen had taken a number of clothes to California which were never worn.

This must have been true of my colleagues who had also contributed to Her Majesty's wardrobe. We concluded that the Queen must have had enough clothes to see her through the London season as well as other occasions, such as Ascot.

It is perhaps impertinent of me ever to attempt to express what I think the Queen's feelings are about any matter, but I feel I may risk suggesting that on her return from California the Queen must have been relieved at the thought that for the rest of the year 1983 she would not have her privacy invaded by a gaggle of dressmakers.

5

Living Label

The flat in New York is on the twenty-fourth floor of an apartment building put up in 1968. It has been my home in the New World for nearly fourteen years. From it there is a splendid view looking northwards out on to Central Park, where the tops of trees spread like an eiderdown; grey-brown and with a coating of snow in winter, and billowing green in the summer. To the right is the long line of Fifth Avenue stretching into the distance with a perspective that makes the buildings look tall and narrow. When the sun shines they turn into a pearly pastel hue. To the north of them are the buildings of Harlem and, beyond them still, like a faint shadow on the horizon, the Bronx. It is an exhilarating view, and from the central room of the apartment, with two of its interior walls covered from floor to ceiling in mirrors, I can sit almost anywhere and see reflected one of the great sights of New York. I cannot imagine living in New York and not being near Central Park. I try to have nearly an hour's walk every day amongst the trees and grass, and every time I am there I give thanks to the city fathers for preserving this huge piece of land and protecting it from the fierce hands of the developers.

There is something symbolic about the location of this flat. On Fifth Avenue on the right is the famous fashion shop of Bergdorf Goodman, which is situated at the beginning of a long street housing some of the best-known names in the world of fashion. While to the left, on Sixth Avenue, I am near to the equally famous 'Twelve-Ninety' building. It is officially called the Sperry Building but is more coloquially known as the 'Twelve-Ninety' because of its location at 1290 Avenue of the Americas. It is a phenomenon. In this one building are housed 360 firms dealing in men's clothes, principally suits but including other accessories and cloth. The volume of business generated by these firms collectively must be in the billions of dollars range. It is to the offices of the Greif Companies on the nineteenth floor of this building that I go as soon as I can after my arrival.

The flat then is situated in an area I can only describe as my spiritual home. It is not an office but a place to meet people and talk business. I like to have business interviews over meals and it is somewhere where I can feel that I am on home ground and in control. New York is the greatest fashion market place in the world, and I can learn more about the current state to the fashion business there in a few days than anywhere else. It is the solidity of my work in America that allows me to enjoy the fun I have there with a clear conscience. It is also a wonderful jumping-off ground for visits to Canada and, further afield, to Japan, Australia and New Zealand. The flat, therefore, is not a luxury but a necessity, for the licensee operations in these countries provide the revenue to keep the business of Hardy Amies Ltd in Savile Row alive and flourishing. For this reason I seldom go to New York less than four times a year, and sometimes six. The more often we appear in New York the better it is for us. We are always made to feel welcome, but experience has told us that you can be quickly forgotten unless you show yourself from time to time.

It is a good thing that Manhattan Island is made of rock and that the buildings on it are very tall skyscrapers securely built. For New York is a quivering mass of insecurity. There are masses of people struggling to get there, and those that are there cling to their position for dear life. I speak of course of the fashion world, the one I know best. It is full of insecure people and their sense of insecurity is fed by the fashion newspapers. The arch stirrer-up of this feeling is John Fairchild, the president of *Women's Wear Daily* and *W*. Are you in or out?: John Fairchild is the arbiter. Of course, the whole industry will always owe him a tremendous debt. His enthusiasm and drive and the sheer efficiency of the reporting of his staff is of enormous value to the fashion industry as a whole and cannot be rated too highly.

In 1946 my work in America consisted largely of selling *haute couture* clothes from our shop in Savile Row to retail outlets in New York, Chicago and San Francisco. This connection had been inspired by the work I had done for the Board of Trade during the war. Representatives of American clothing firms had come over after the war eager to arrange sales of English and European stock. It was a time of heady buying sprees, and it was through this desire to establish once again a proper trading basis with British firms that I had been invited to visit

America to show our clothes. In those days we dealt with such firms as Marshall Field of Chicago and I. Magnin in California. Although it was but a modest beginning, I remember returning from that first visit with an order for several thousand pounds' worth of clothes.

All of my work in the United States during the early years dealt exclusively with women's clothing. I didn't become involved in the designing of menswear until 1959 when I formed my association with Hepworths. Hepworths' annual show of our menswear gradually attracted interest from abroad, and at one of the early showings there was present the managing director of the large American corporation of Genesco, a man called Ben Willingham. He was so excited by what he had seen that we were invited by him to go to the United States to show our collection. Our first show, given in a large private room at the Plaza Hotel, was a great success, and Genesco duly offered me a contract to work for them for the then enormous salary of $100,000 a year.

Genesco had under its wing several large New York stores, a chain of retail menswear shops and several menswear factories. The founder and head of the company was a man called Maxi Jarman. He decided to set up a company called Hardy Amies USA Ltd, which operated from quite expensive offices in New York. The role of this subsidiary firm was to interpret the designs we sent from London by getting them manufactured in plants owned by Genesco and then distributing them throughout chains of menswear stores also owned by Genesco. Within the Genesco organization there were extremely skilled tailors and, as a result, we made some very handsome suits. The business proved to be very profitable and my contract with Genesco, originally only for three years, was extended indefinitely.

We were asked during this early period to make a tour of the stores that were selling these suits. The Genesco executive jet was put at our disposal. One night we set off to fly across America. There were nine seats on the plane and one sofa. As guest of honour I was given the sofa. I soon fell asleep, only to be awakened in the middle of the night, by the sound of loud voices. 'What's going on?' I said. 'We've landed in Colorado to take on gas,' they said. 'The noise you can hear is the cabin crew arguing amongst themselves about who is going to get the Green Shield stamps for the fuel!' We went to San Diego, where we were told there was a store which had a special Hardy Amies section. This section turned out to be a wardrobe painted bright red in imitation Queen Anne. On the cornice there was in gold letters the name Hardy Amies. As we stood and looked at it the 'y' fell off, and then the 's'. The stock in the wardrobe consisted of six suits and a hat.

One of the jobs that had been assigned to us was to improve the standard and efficiency of taste in the chain of Roger Kent stores owned by Genesco. Eric Crabtree, who was an expert in retailing, suggested certain alterations to the structure of some of the stores in New York. On each visit to New York we would run around to the nearest Roger Kent store to see if there was a handsome window display full of our clothes. We were always disappointed. 'Why aren't there more of our clothes?' I would ask. The answer came – 'The buyer doesn't like them.' This was an absurd situation. We were being paid to design clothes, the most important part of which were suits, which we knew were very excellent reproductions of a Savile Row suit, skilfully graded as to size, and offered at very reasonable prices. The whole organization had been created around this scheme. No one had explained the situation to the man who wrote out the orders. He was probably offended that his taste was being disputed.

In spite of these early muddles our partnership continued, and today I am still working with Genesco. The relationship is a happy one. Today, though, my work in the United States is of a different order and centres almost entirely around our licensing arrangements with firms dealing with all branches of the menswear business. This licensee arrangement allows American retail firms to sell clothes bearing the Hardy Amies label. In 1982 in excess of 15 million dollars of men's clothes carrying our label were sold.

This sum, particularly in American terms, may not seem a great deal of money, but it must be remembered that I am in competition with all the great names in the world: Saint Laurent, Cardin, Givenchy and Lanvin from Paris; Valentino, Cerutti and Brioni from Italy; Aquascutum, Burberry and Jaeger from England; and last but not least, for they are playing on home ground, Bill Blass, Oscar de la Renta and Ralph Lauren in the USA. Sometimes I feel like a minor county tennis player struggling to make a success at Wimbledon.

How have I done it? I think I know a great deal about the design of suits and have passed on the fruits of my knowledge to my American colleagues. One of the striking things I have learned since working in America – and, indeed, some other parts of the world – is that it is dangerous for a menswear designer to have too much power. Suits should never look as though they have been designed: only that they have happened. At the same time I must never stop designing and I do not do so. I never stop bringing new designs with me to America, showing them to the firms with whom I work and, if I have the chance, showing them also to the press. I must never be unable to answer the question 'What's next, and why?' I must be able to furnish a kaleidoscope of colours. All of this has to be done at least a year, and sometimes two, ahead of time. I make these predictions in an orderly fashion. My six years' experience as an intelligence officer in the Army has been of value in this respect. I have had for a long time the satisfaction of knowing that I was respected by the *cognoscenti*. Also, I am now pleased to note in my travels around America that I am not unknown to ordinary human beings.

Most of this has been achieved simply by my being in New York as often as possible. We have spent very little money on direct advertising and have instead relied on public relations. Whenever possible I make myself available for interviews with the press, television and radio. Anne Taylor Davis, my public relations agent in New York, has worked tirelessly in this area and has done much to help promote our name in America. I try to make these interviews as interesting as I can and the hope is that, like seeds on a farm, my words will float out into the air and perhaps come to earth and flower somewhere.

It is known that I am a person with a clear point of view about clothes. As we get better known for our taste and imagination so our name becomes more widespread on a label and, for the moment, I am a living label. If the label is nurtured by intelligent commercial practices and genuinely reflects this taste and imagination then it will, in time, become a brand. I have already achieved this in Great Britain with Hardy Amies ties through my happy association with Michelsons.

Our main outlet in the United States was through a Genesco-owned firm called Phoenix. Eric Crabtree, excited by the possibilities opened up by the American market, had tried to encourage David Greif, whose clothing factory was also owned by Genesco, to make our suits under the same licensing arrangement. At the time David Greif believed categorically that there was no use for the name of designers in the men's clothing trade and, accordingly, he turned down our offer. But eventually the use of a designer's name became an established method of business, and on this principle Phoenix flourished while David Greif did not. The resulting lack of business forced David Greif to leave the firm of his forebears and in his place an extremely intelligent and forceful man called Jim Wilson was put in charge. His arrival and the work he did proved so successful that Genesco amalgamated Phoenix with Greif. The name Phoenix was dropped and the business became known as the Greif Companies. Today this company controls no less than twelve designers' names. This is a typical example of how the use of designer names in the men's clothing trade has developed over the years.

For the past three years we have been greatly helped in the expansion of our business in the United States by the work of Mrs John Manton, who is responsible for seeking new licensees and also keeping us in touch with the firms with whom we have dealt up till now. Ruth Manton works tirelessly in bridging the gap during our many absences from New York. Selling so many suits throughout the United States makes it reasonable that we should seek to branch out into the field of men's shirts and ties. As we get better known for our taste and imagination we hope also to start work on other garments.

Because we started work with all of them at the same time there is a feeling of camaraderie between the managers and the owners of the firms with whom we work in men's clothing in New York.

One of the pleasures of working with firms under licence is that there is a great chance of building a friendship with one's opposite number. This applies particularly in the men's shirt business which is using our name in the United States. This firm, called Berkley Shirts, is a family business run by its founder, Carl Stapf, and his son-in-law Doug Waterman. They wanted to expand their operation by using my name and what taste and knowledge I could bring to them from London. During the preliminary discussions we sensed the usual fear that comes with a commitment to a contract for a period of three years; the minimum time needed to establish a new business.

Polite conversation revealed that I was interested in tennis and I was invited to join Doug Waterman, his wife and Carl Stapf in a game. The atmosphere was relaxed and friendly; the contract was signed the next day.

Equally warm is our relationship with a company called Pebble Beach, who have been making sweaters for us since the beginning of

1981. Although the New York representative (installed, of course, in the Twelve-Ninety building) is enthusiastic and encouraging and, above all, informative – he has had many years' experience in the knitting industry – the company is based in California, outside San Francisco. Here there is a designer of great talent. He has so much more knowledge than I have. My help is confined to mostly giving advice and guidance on colour.

Hardy Amies ties in the United States are made by the Hudson Neckwear Company, with whom we have been working since January 1981. The head of this company is a quiet but charming man called Irving Berger. Michelsons started manufacturing Hardy Amies ties in England twenty years ago. By working with Irving Berger I can have Hardy Amies ties in the United States made in the same silks as those made in England by Michelsons but at a more reasonable price. Michelsons give me every assistance.

The full realization of all the possibilities may well not be achieved in my lifetime. But I hope I live long enough to see the establishment of a women's licensing business as strong as that which we have built up in the men's field. The decline of the popularity of London-designed ladies' clothes with American women, particularly in the area of women's suits, made it unrealistic for us to explore the market possibilities in women's fashion. Now, however, with the advent of the popularity of women's casual wear, the market seems right for exploitation. There has always been much more of an affinity between men's and women's casual wear than between men's and women's suits. I am proud to be alive and working in New York after twenty years of what I can only describe as a pleasant but tough struggle. In the words of the old song, 'I am still there'!

We started our work in Canada almost at the same time as in the United States. A successful licensing operation is a marriage between a design house and the manufacturing firm, and we were very lucky to find ourselves working with a firm called Coppley, Noyes & Randall. This very distinguished Canadian firm was dominated by the Enkin family at the head of which is Max Enkin, probably the kindest and most honourable man that I've ever known. His high standards of integrity still permeate the company today. The fact that I was British and that my work was patronized by the Queen meant that we were able to sell more clothes in Canada than in the United States. Also, because of the high standards set by Max Enkin, we became known very quickly for the quality of our products, and I think it fair to say that we have a bigger slice of the better-priced end of the market than anybody else.

Our success and happiness with the Enkin family led us quickly into a useful relationship with a firm called T. Lipson & Son Ltd. This firm was a greatly admired shirt business and our dealings with them also proved to be a success. Jack Lipson, the owner and son of the original founder of the company, is a big, bearded, burly man whose rather brusque manner manages to hide what, underneath, is the proverbial heart of gold. He and his father, Ted, both have flawless and imaginative taste and our relationship with them has given great pleasure and satisfaction all round. With Lipson looking after the shirt side of the business and Coppley, Noyes & Randall taking care of the clothes side, I can say that the Hardy Amies label in Canada couldn't be in safer hands.

My first visit to Australia was in 1959 and I stayed at the old Australia Hotel, Sydney. Friends in England had been very kind and thoughtful enough to warn the Australians in advance of my arrival, and as a result I had many invitations from people who were, to begin with, complete strangers. But since I was best known for my work as the Queen's dress designer I was warned to expect a difficult time from the Australian press, who are not often the most tactful of people. An example of the sort of question that greeted me on my arrival was: 'Mr Amies, I reckon that you must get closer to the Queen's body than anybody but her husband. How close do you get?' To which I replied after careful thought: 'Sir, I get as close as any professional man in whom the Queen has confidence.'

The 'Queen' of Sydney at the time was Lady Lloyd-Jones, the widow of the son of the founder of the great department store David Jones. The story of this department store is the story of Sydney itself. It had the vitality and range of products of any great shop which dominates a city. They were so meticulous about keeping up to date with their products that they had offices in all the major European cities so that nothing of quality was ever missed.

I have been returning to Sydney on business for over twenty years now and I have seen immense changes, but Sydney Harbour still remains one of the most beautiful sights in the world and it is always a pleasure to go there. Although in the beginning I stayed at the old Australia Hotel, I later moved to the Menzies Hotel and then, when it was built, to the Wentworth Hotel. But about ten years ago I discovered The Sebel Town House, situated ten minutes' walk from the centre of the city, and it is here that I stay when I go to Sydney now. This residence is situated high up and fringing the area known as King's Cross, a location best known today for its rather sexy and sleazy atmosphere. To walk down the street here is to see a market of vice; never really squalid, often funny, and always pulsating with life. This street of iniquity suddenly ends in a respectably laid-out gardens beyond which is concealed my hotel.

If I mention this here it is because a walk in this area can give one a glimpse of the clothes and the fashions followed by the youth of today that are always stimulating and exciting if, at times, downright anarchic. There has sprung up a new school of fashion designers in Australia who are gradually making their voices heard.

I have always hated leaving Sydney for Melbourne, where I miss the soothing sight of its beautiful harbour and where I have fewer friends on whom I can call. But for the last six years we have had a successful licensing arrangement there with the brothers David and Kenneth Turnbull. Together they run the highly respected Australian Tie Company. Not only do they make and sell handsome Hardy Amies ties, but they also keep a very careful watch on the health of all our operations throughout Australia.

Melbourne is also the home of a very lively lady called Diana Bell. She sells Hardy Amies women's dresses which are faithful reproductions of those we have in the boutique at Savile Row. They are not cheap and are only sold in the best shops in Australia. The designing of these dresses and the thought of them proliferating in the very new world down-under gives the boys and girls in the studio and the workrooms back home particular pleasure and enjoyment.

The David Jones department store was keen to continue selling men's suits bearing the Hardy Amies label since we had managed to build up a healthy list of customers. It was decided to export the business to New Zealand and to have the suits actually made there where labour was slightly cheaper. Also, there was a significant difference between the value of the Australian and New Zealand dollar which made the venture even more attractive. Very quickly we entered into a period of happy prosperity. We also started a licensee business for men's shirts with a charming and energetic expatriate Hungarian called Tibor Fabian, also a tennis lover.

When you get off the plane at Auckland you are immediately struck by the smell of newmown hay. Auckland is not a particularly handsome city, though it is interesting and romantic as all ports are. There live the Macky family, who run the Cambridge Clothing Company, with whom we have had a licensee arrangement since 1966. Dane Macky, head of the family, inherited his business, and but for this accident of fortune I doubt whether he would have given much thought to clothes or the clothing business. But he was an immensely conscientious manager and guardian of his factory and we had a very satisfactory business arrangement with him. He copied our method of presenting collections in the way we had done originally for Hepworths and it was a great success. The suits were sold all over New Zealand and at one time it was said that we dressed fifty per cent of the male population. Some of the cloth came from England but most of the material used in these suits came from the local wool which makes a very sturdy cloth. These suits we re-exported and sold in Australia.

It was marvellous to be welcomed there, to find people grateful for news of fashion, for explaining fashion in such a way as for them not to fear it any more. The Macky family repaid this a thousandfold by allowing me to spend on their yacht, the *Leda*, as much time as could be spared. Elizabeth Macky was a marvellous organizer – she had to feed five hungry men for three weeks without seeing a shop. The northern coasts of New Zealand appear untouched since the time of Captain Cook. Beaches in the Bay of Islands yielded crops of oranges which Elizabeth, as a thrifty New Zealand housewife, could not ignore. I must be the only male dressmaker who has made marmalade in a Force Eight gale.

The licensee arrangement with New Zealand shirt manufacturers has flourished alongside that of the suit business, and over the years we have managed to introduce a bit of adventure and colour into the market. I remember on my first visit to New Zealand Dane Macky asking me to go to lunch at the Rotary Club. There were at least a hundred other businessmen at the lunch and all of them in shirtsleeves. Every shirt was dead white; the kind of dead white you see in the drip–dry variety. New Zealanders are a notoriously conservative race and were even more so twenty years ago. We tried over the years very gradually to introduce stripes into some of the shirts. The going was tough, but I am glad to be able to report that on subsequent visits I noticed the odd pale blue shirt creeping into the wardrobe and even the occasional discreet check or stripe. Today plain white shirts are in the minority.

Although we have had nearly twenty years in which to establish ourselves, there has always been an overriding desire to bring women's clothes to New Zealand, and three years ago we had the good luck to be introduced to a charming couple, Maurice and Maria Mihotich. They had a flourishing business making women's clothes. But because the population is a small one (only three million inhabitants) the quantities they produced were small. Where they were clever, though, was in realizing that the average New Zealand lady would require at least one dress which could be kept in store as a 'best dress' for special occasions. Accordingly, they produced clothes in cloths cleverly chosen and in styles suitable for such special occasions. We entered into a fruitful relationship with them and today the arrangement is still a happy and harmonious one. They visit us at least once a year to examine our collection at Savile Row where, naturally, they choose the designs that are made in only the lightest of materials.

Our licensee arrangement in Japan, started in 1981, was peculiar in that from the beginning it covered both the men's and the women's field. This arrangement was, and still is today, with a firm called Diatobo. It is important to remember that a successful licensee operation abroad must be with a company of some substance. You must be sure that the firm with whom you are dealing is big enough and efficient enough to cope with a large volume of orders if the need arises. We were very lucky to find ourselves working with a firm like Diatobo because they are closely associated with one of the most powerful businesses in Japan, Mitsui & Co.

It is more usual to find such a firm in the men's clothing industry than in the women's. Factories producing women's clothes are usually small family affairs. We were therefore lucky that Diatobo is essentially a cloth manufacturing concern, and therefore with an interest in both the men's and women's field. So it was natural, although it did not appear so to us at the outset, for Diatobo to have exacted from us a comprehensive licence covering all types of men's and women's clothing. 'If we invest in you', the heads of Mitsui and Diatobo told us at the outset, 'we will advertise. We will turn you into a household name throughout Japan.' They have done just that, and for the past fourteen years our business has continued to flourish perhaps more successfully than anywhere else. It was extraordinary to find such an interest in western women's clothes, although we quickly saw that full traditional dress was only seriously worn by ladies for formal occasions.

I think we have all enjoyed the years working with our Japanese colleagues. They are so intelligent when it comes to design and the choice of colours. On one occasion we had as many as thirty-five members of Diatobo in the house at Savile Row who had come just to see what it stood for. What they saw was a business that was classic but not old-fashioned and modern but not aggressive. Such a calm attitude to the business of clothes designing appeals very much to the Japanese. Modern Japanese designers are among the most progressive in Europe. Unlike the anarchic designs produced in art schools, the new Japanese designers have found a way of using traditional shapes, often bulky, in an acceptable, even sexy way. One is conscious of a gracefully moving body beneath the bulk.

When we started working in Japan fourteen years ago you rarely saw a man wearing a suit in any other colour than black. This was invariably accompanied by a white shirt and a narrow black tie. Sometimes, worn over this, would be a very plain black mackintosh which was straight and shapeless. Gradually we were allowed to introduce discreet patterns into the cloth of the suits and muted colours into the ties. This process was, to begin with, a slow one, but we have managed to make great inroads over the years. Japanese men adopt traditional dress only on very rare occasions, preferring to be seen in obviously expensive European outfits, and today there is a great interest in suits made of fine English tweeds.

We have had a fashion show staged every two years since we first started working in Japan. From the day of the first show I knew that we need have no fears that our name was going to be associated with anything shoddy or ugly. We never cease to wonder at the Japanese and their immensely sure and quick perceptions.

I must also pay tribute to their hospitality. It is in our contract with them that we visit Japan as their guests. This we do every eighteen months. From the outset this meant first-class air fares and a suite at the Okura, an hotel remarkable for the taste of the decorations of its rooms, the efficiency of its service and, above all, for the quiet of its position in the middle of a large garden; all of this set in the heart of Tokyo where the land is some of the most expensive in the world. Not content with offering us all this, our Japanese colleagues insisted that we see some of the most beautiful sights in Japan. No sooner were our visits concluded to the factories and workrooms where our clothes were being made than we were shipped off to Kyoto and Nara to spend a weekend at the temples there.

We have enjoyed the kindness of no less than three British ambassadors in Tokyo over the years. Through the good offices of the embassy we were able to get permission to visit the famous temple and gardens of Katsura Palace, on the Katsura River just outside Kyoto. Visitors to Japan will know how difficult it is to get permission to visit this beautiful palace. There were many other temples we visited of which we have pleasant recollections, but to name them all would be too discursive.

I realized very quickly that I could become fascinated by Japan. I find its people beautiful and the refinement of taste in living and clothes exceptional. Their fastidiousness of grooming is remarkable.

I cannot leave Tokyo without commenting on the pulsating life of its department stores. The visitor realizes very quickly how densely populated is a city like Tokyo. The seething mass of purchasers in the stores on a Saturday is nothing short of overwhelming. A designer is allocated to a particular department store. You are their pet and they promote you. Our store is Matsuya, although Hardy Amies goods can be seen in other stores as well.

I have mentioned our gratitude for the hospitality shown to us by our hosts in arranging stimulating and exciting visits to particular shrines; another pleasure offered us is that of eating. Roger Whiteman and Ken Fleetwood are as devoted as I am to Japanese cooking. We were all intrigued by their food from the outset. The best example of Japanese elegance in decor and refinement in eating is to be found at Kitcho, a Tokyo restaurant where personal introduction to the proprietors is necessary. This is not for reasons of snobbery but rather as a guarantee that you will arrive on time and the immense preparations will not be in vain.

A family of standing in Japan today will see to it that their daughter is married in the traditional costume for the Shintu ceremony. This costume is very beautiful and very expensive; there is no shame, therefore, if the costume is merely hired for the occasion. Afterwards there is a party, including dancing, at which the bride will wear a western-style wedding dress. The House of Hardy Amies prides itself on its wedding dresses. All the talents of the house go into the making of a dress which is as near perfect as is possible. We were very happy, therefore, when Diatobo included wedding dresses in our contract with them. It was with some surprise, though, that we learned that our dresses were being hired and not sold.

Over the years I have become known for my uniform designs. In 1970 I was asked to design the uniforms for the staff of the London Hilton, Park Lane. The management wanted something grand and distinctly British. We suggested the Eton jacket, made in beige whipcord, for the pageboys, and frock coats for the doormen with black silk hats and cockades, still worn today. The silk hats for the pageboys had a shorter life. Our suggestion of ankle-length dresses for the waitresses and chambermaids was turned down but would now perhaps stand a better chance of being accepted.

Another project, this time in 1968, was our involvement in the designing of uniforms for the female staff of British European Airways, as it was then known. Our first series was so successful that the uniform lasted for three years, whereupon we were asked to design a second series which was also a great success. There had always been intense rivalry between BEA and its sister branch, British Overseas Airways Corporation, and when the two were merged to form the British Airways Company in 1971 the management decided that my designs for the European division would become the standard uniform for the whole fleet. The BOAC staff, who considered themselves élite, were less than favourably disposed to this idea. They were unwilling to accept the uniform of what they considered to be their lesser sister. Furthermore, we considered that our uniform was by this time old-fashioned. Our request to be allowed to modernize was turned down for reasons of economy.

Further unhappiness was in store. As an enthusiastic air traveller, I had been fascinated to hear in the mid-sixties of the plan to launch Concorde. I was very distressed to hear that there were no plans to make special uniforms for the crew and cabin staff of this plane. My unhappiness increased when I learned that the French had commissioned one of the best Paris houses to design uniforms for the stewardesses on their Concorde staff.

About three weeks before Concorde was due to make its maiden passenger-carrying flight in 1976, Sir Henry Marking, the new chairman of British Airways, accepted with what I am sure was genuine enthusiasm my offer to get some new uniforms designed and made. There was no budget. I did not mind working for nothing and I persuaded several friends of mine in the clothing trade to make twelve uniforms suitable for a journey which started in the cold and could finish in a country with a hot climate; in other words, a complete wardrobe. National pride was my first interest, the second was the hope of gaining a contract.

The basic colour of the clothes we suggested was navy-blue, the original colour of the uniforms worn on Imperial Airways, the grandparent of British Airways. This colour suggested a link with the Royal Navy rather than with the Air Force, something which may have come about through the importance in the early days of the flying-boats. We showed these uniforms to a committee of stewards and stewardesses and the reception they received was mixed. This was my first experience of coming up against trade unions. They had to be consulted from the beginning. I learned subsequently that the trade union officials had told the crews to turn down these new designs at all costs. We had made a point of stressing that our designs were only experiments and that we were willing in the meantime to discuss the outfits with the crews and that we were prepared to make any modifications that might have been required. This was all in vain. Concorde flew into the future with its crew dressed in the past.

Worse was to come: shortly after this it was decided to give a completely new uniform to the whole of the British Airways staff and one which was suitable for the crews of Concorde as well. We were asked by British Airways to resubmit our Concorde uniforms, and foolishly we agreed. These uniforms, originally drawn and manufactured within a three-week period, were, quite frankly, not good enough. I had hoped for some air of goodwill after twelve years of working with British Airways, but in the event a new team of designers was brought in. I am sure that our successors had a better time of it than we did.

I consider myself one of the most experienced travellers in the British fashion industry, and I have to say here that the staff of British

Airways are the best dressed of all the international airlines.

Designing for any corporation is always difficult. First, there is the committee, which is usually multi-voiced and never more so than when it comes to discussing clothing; then there is the person in the background – usually the chairman's wife – whom you never meet in person but whose opinion always seems to carry great weight with the chairman.

An example of how differing opinions could disrupt a project in this way was the time we were commissioned to redesign the uniforms of the Armed Forces of South Africa. We were persuaded to do this by the South African Wool Board, who paid us a fee. We travelled to South Africa as guests of the Government. It transpired that the Chief of General Staff was a soldier, and in his initial interview with me he said that, as in times of war all the three services were united under one command, he considered it desirable that the uniforms of all the services should be redesigned to have a common theme of colour and cut. Insignia could be added later to distinguish one service from the other. But above all the new uniforms were to have as little resemblance as possible to those of the modern British Army. This, then, was my brief.

Two months later we presented our designs. We had made a series of uniforms, the most important of which were those for the lowest rank: the soldier, the sailor and the airman. This was our first mistake. The command we met in Pretoria consisted solely of high-ranking officers from all the services, and it soon became evident that their major interest was in their own uniforms. We had presented no uniforms for a rank higher than major, explaining to the committee that for ranks higher than this the uniforms would have a more elaborate and bejewelled insignia. The basic colour of the new uniforms we showed was a sandy beige, the colour of the parched *veldt*. The shape we chose for the jacket was a zipped blouson such as is worn today by young men all over the world. There were different coloured epaulettes to denote the service: sky-blue for the Air Force, navy-blue for the Navy and scarlet for the Army.

This blouson jacket, while being perfectly suitable for the lower ranks, gave no air of authority if worn by the seniors, something which the committee were quick to point out. One member of the command complained that it wasn't a uniform at all. I had the feeling all the time that what they really wanted was something out of a musical comedy set in Ruritania. To comply with some of this expectation we gave the generals a high-crowned and large-peaked cap which, made in the sinister black and silver instead of our suggested colours, could have been worn quite easily by Field Marshal Goering.

After listening to their complaints and taking note of all the points raised, we went away to make the necessary alterations to the uniforms. In due course the redesigned outfits were accepted not only by the chiefs of staff but by parliament as well. However, we had no time to enjoy the success of this because just then the Government fell. In the reshuffle that followed the new Chief of Staff was an admiral. He wasted no time in quashing our scheme and he made it absolutely clear that no one was going to alter the existing uniform of the Navy. Quite frankly, I didn't blame him.

Today, our studio at Savile Row is still preoccupied with uniforms, this time domestic rather than military. For the past fourteen years we have had a happy relationship with a firm called Alexandra Overalls based in Bristol. This firm, run very successfully by a husband and wife team, makes overalls for hairdressers, shop assistants, caterers and dozens of other service industries. We submit designs for them twice a year. Ken Fleetwood, with his wealth of knowledge of the up-to-date trends in fashion as a whole, is able to bring authority to the styles we submit.

During the past ten years we have also had occasion to make designs for many household articles. I have to say here that had I not been a dress designer I might well have been an interior decorator. Through my close associations with such people as John Fowler and Alexis ffrench I think I could have contributed something to the industries that make goods for the household. However, such schemes as I have been involved in have not really been successful. I say this with no bitterness but with a certain sadness, especially for the people who have worked with me.

One area in particular is the modern idea of having bed linen printed with a design chosen especially by a designer. It was the gigantic capacity of the mills in the United States to weave cotton fabrics that started this boom industry. We managed to persuade a manufacturer of bed linen in the north of England to allow us to work for them in this field. Our contact with them was solely involved with sheets and other bed linens. It has to be said that it was not a rewarding experience, either spiritually or financially.

Our entry into the world of what is called small leather goods has been a happy one. These are wallets, purses and bags. We were lucky to be approached in 1981 by a well-established firm called W. A. Goold Ltd, the head of which is Michael Goold.

When Michael Goold asked me about my feelings on men's wallets, I told him that they must be slim so as to fit comfortably into the inside pocket of a jacket. All modern clothing for men and women tries to produce or show off an athletic-looking figure: you want nothing bulky about you. Michael saw the point, and as a result we make the slimmest wallets on the market.

We make also all sorts of bags for travelling and here my experience in travel has been of immense help. We make a very pretty handbag for women which is soft and youthful-looking. We do not make what I call 'serious' handbags, those with clasps that shut firmly. I hate the sound of such a clasp being shut and at no time more than at the end of an opera. The last strains of many an opera have been ruined for me by the click of a handbag belonging to a lady trying to indicate to her husband that she wants to leave and 'grab a taxi' before anyone else.

Pierre Cardin is said to have over five hundred licensee operations at work around the world. I have no means of knowing whether this is true or not – but the true figure is certainly high. My friend Bill Blass has licensed his name to a brand of chocolate, and has been criticized for it. I would love to have a licence for chocolates. My taste is for bitter chocolate on the outside and covering some very sweet filling on the inside. If I had the chance I would ban all milk chocolate, but as milk chocolate is far more popular with the public than plain chocolate if I were to endorse a particular chocolate it would have to be with a small and specialized concern.

We have today forty-eight licensee operations throughout the world and are constantly adding to this number. I have always tried not to get involved, or to let my House get involved, in the design of articles whose character is unsympathetic to me. A typical case is that of jewellery for men. Vast quantities of such jewellery are sold in the United States. The giving of jewellery is considered as a show of affection or gratitude. I appreciate this, but I know that no gentleman wears any ring other than the one with his crest on it. I don't even believe in cufflinks. I know enough about the history of men's clothes to be aware that cufflinks replaced buttons when shirt cuffs were so stiffly starched as to make it impossible to do up the buttons. Today there are no starched shirts so there is no need for cufflinks. If a man is over forty he looks older if he shows a bejewelled cuff. When you have been young as long as I have you need every help.

I think it was the witty fashion writer Michael Roberts who referred to the mass of chains that it was fashionable to wear a few years ago as 'status clutter'. I do not think it enhances a man's status to wear even one gold chain around his neck. A gold chain does not make an old neck or chest any the more handsome and a young body does not need one.

I should like to be involved in the design of articles for the kitchen but not in things to cook in; there are plenty of these already. I should like to try again with wall tiles and to link up the design of these with tablecloths, napkins and tea-towels. Since I believe in eating in the kitchen there is enormous scope for creating elegance and comfort there. And, finally, I should like to be involved in designing things for the garden. Nearly all garden utensils made of plastic are totally repulsive to the eye and to the touch. I realize that it is necessary to have flowerpots made of plastic but often the colour chosen is an ugly red. It is also difficult to find pots of the right size when you wish to take a potted plant into the house. I feel I could make a contribution in solving some of these problems.

I have to end this chapter by returning to thoughts of designing clothes for men and women which is where my work began. This work is our life-blood and we either rise or fall through our achievements in this field. The standards of taste and good work-manship are obviously more securely fixed in clothes that are expensive rather than in those that are cheap. I see no reason why those standards cannot be more widely spread. Hardy Amies ties, for instance, the launching of which was our first entry into the men's field, were expensive. But shortly after that we started with Hepworths whose prices were modest. Because we did a good, honest job for Hepworths and because of their stylish advertising no damage was done to the tie business. I never for one moment thought that our trade in expensive *haute couture* clothes at Savile Row stood to be endangered by our move into the market of cheap clothes for men, and I have since been proved right. I will continue to design and be associated with the marketing of any product which is cheap in price providing we aim at being the best article on the market at that price.

Apart from dressing a few famous actresses such as Edith Evans when she was given a role of a lady who, in character, dressed as one who would patronize a *couture* house such as ours, and the delicious job given us by Glyndebourne to dress Kirsten Myer in an opera, in which she played the richest woman in the world, we have never done much work in the theatre.

I must record, however, the wonderful time Ken Fleetwood and I had working with Mr Stanley Kubrick on his famous film *2001*. Our role on that film was to design clothes for a period in the future. The film, released in 1968, meant that we were dealing with a period thirty-three years ahead in time. To try and get a perspective on this I looked back over the previous thirty-three years to see what had happened in the world of fashion. I realized to my surprise that there had been less change than one had imagined. I didn't foresee, therefore, that clothing in the year 2001 would be dramatically futuristic. Mr Kubrick accepted this. There came a moment, however, when we had to discuss the clothing of the Russians. These he wished to appear as dowdy and old-fashioned. 'Right,' we said, 'we'll put them in clothes of today.' This, of course, he couldn't accept. Nor could he accept our suggestion that the astronauts should wear disposable underclothes. 'Oh no,' he said, 'I shall have every housewife in the audience wondering if she has made a mistake in ordering a new washing machine.'

I admire Stanley Kubrick enormously and I think his film is still one of the most exciting ever made. He was, however, very bad at explaining what he wanted. I don't think he was always sure of this himself. He certainly made it plain to us when we presented anything to him which he didn't want. I cannot resist telling, rather mischievously, a final story. There were in the film several airlines travelling to the moon, to Mars and to other planets. When I suggested that each airline should have its staff in different uniforms, Mr Kubrick said, 'Oh no, in the year 2001 all airlines will be owned by PanAm!'

In the United States I am called a 'living label'. If I am successful enough in my licensee operations my name will become that of a brand. I hope that this will always be based on the present high level of quality so closely monitored by me and my team at Savile Row.

6

Fifty Years of Fashion

I was always very happy designing tailored clothes. As soon as I started work at Lachasse in 1934 I could see that the suit was what the customers there wanted and the staff could make with the greatest ease. It was smart to talk about a suit: common to call it a costume. Certain ladies – some of them quite grand – still spoke of a tailormade.

I have elsewhere paid tribute to the invention, if not to the genius, of Digby Morton. When he left Lachasse to open his own business, he left behind enough suits to show sharp-eyed-me very clearly the way. Firstly there was the tweed. This the designer chose with great care. It had to be firm enough for the jacket to be moulded into a defined shape: and able to withstand the pressures of a beautiful behind wriggling in a sports car. It had, however, to be soft to the touch and have enough wool at the surface to mute the colours.

All colours came from nature: the best from the earth. The greeny-brown of upturned furrows could have little flecks of green like wheat shoots. This green would be sought to make the blouse – more chicly called a shirt.

The most mannish part of the suit would be the sleeves of the jacket. These were narrow: the armhole was what is called high – you were able to move with a minimum derangement of the line. Shoulders were wide and softly padded. The width gave you a good platform from which to drape the cloth over the bust. Bosoms were only just beginning to be rediscovered. The position of the waistline was vital. Its place could be found by tying a piece of tape which rested neatly in the hollow just above the hipbone. In some ladies this was more difficult to find than in others, but you had to do it. Ladies had to be persuaded not to have their jackets fitted too tightly. A man's torso can move within his jacket. A lady should be able to do the same. Great care was taken with the colouring of the buttons, which were always of plain bone with a classic rim. The colour had to be that of the background of the tweed: never that of decorative flecks or contrasting checks. The most popular skirt was of a straight cut with a concealed pleat in the centre back for easy walking. This was, however, unenterprising. Great ingenuity was shown in the arrangement of blocks of pleats on the back and on the front of the skirt, sometimes enlarged into all-round pleated kilts. Finally came circularly cut skirts, less well received by the timid in spite of the slimness over the hips.

The garment I have described at some length dominated the daytime fashion scene for the whole of the thirties. It fitted well into the schemes for utility clothing instituted by the Government during the war. There was no major change until Christian Dior's New Look of 1947. The ingenuity of designers in London and Paris was used to make an infinite variety of pockets and other details. However, the most simple suits were the most successful.

Overcoats had to be cut generously to be worn comfortably over suits. Sometimes these were cut to only hip length. There resulted a boxy jacket of which the shoulders could be widened to give a touch of aggressive chic – to show off a silk-stockinged leg and well-turned ankle. Skirts in general just covered the knee.

Captain Edward Molyneux was one of the reigning kings of fashion in Paris. London was an important branch. The expensive-looking simplicity of his clothes appealed to the English upper classes, whose way of life he understood perfectly and to which he added a flavour of international verve. When the Germans reached Paris he fled to London and retreated to a suite in Claridges. He used to take me to London picture dealers to help him choose Impressionist paintings to make his walls more homely. His favourite drink was a dry martini. Schiaparelli was also in London – immensely stimulating but just slightly *mauvais genre*.

Elsewhere I have told how I came to work with the House of Worth of London: and the work that I did there in my spare time during my war years in London. Worth was almost next door to Molyneux in Grosvenor Street. Molyneux himself had accepted the role of chairman of the Incorporated Society of London Fashion Designers. He and his sister, who had always managed the London house, were both kind and encouraging to me.

Molyneux was my god. I admired tremendously the cool chic of his clothes. Sometimes they might appear heartless, but then he would tuck into the belt of a most severe navy blue woollen dress a bunch of pristine white lilies of the valley.

In London, Norman Hartnell and Victor Stiebel were making very beautiful romantic evening dresses. In the decoration of houses the all-white rooms of Syrie Maugham were gradually being filled with the Regency draperies and painted furniture of John Fowler. Fashion editresses were doing up their rooms with frilled muslin curtains, *papier-maché* tables and Victorian bric-a-brac. A touch of Victoriana crept into clothes. Victor Stiebel put bustles on cocktail dresses as well as on to evening dresses. Hats became small and saucy. The cut of all clothes emphasized the curves of the bosom more and more each season. Inappropriately as to the *Zeitgeist* but correct in its indication as to the way things would go, I started the Spring Show on 22 March 1939 by sending out all the mannequins in little boned corselets, black georgette bloomers with pink bows, and their hair in ringlets. This exuberance was quickly to dive underground during the war years, only to gush forth as fresh as a hidden mountain stream into the New Look. Sir Stafford Cripps, the President of the Board of Trade, complained that the longer full skirts required an indecently excessive expenditure of cloth; if I didn't write a letter to *The Times* about it, I meant to. Fashion has nothing to do with economics: it is ruled by sex and status.

The New Look was unbridled nostalgia. The first showing of a Dior collection in England took place at Blenheim Palace to raise money for the Red Cross, of which the Duchess of Marlborough was the head. I have seldom been so moved by the sight of clothes as I was when I watched the stream of thirty superbly coiffed and shod mannequins gliding through Vanbrugh's hall and library. In the day clothes, with their smooth and tightly-fitted, long-skirted jackets, their deeply-pleated and always ankle-length skirts, their sweeping hats, the girls strode through the rooms like huntresses; their long, narrow agate handled umbrellas like spears seeking only the richest banker as their prey. By night they were less rapacious. There would be some yielding. The many yards of the soft materials in the skirts were so cut and contrived as to never let you forget that there was a pair of beautiful legs underneath: indeed, the skirt was often raised in front to frame a pretty ankle before it fanned out into full sail behind.

Minute waists, held in by the *guêpière* (of course you all know that *une guêpe* is a wasp) invited the hand of a man to span it. Each dress was a carefully composed picture of texture and colour and was named after a great musician – Mozart, Chopin, Tchaikovsky. At the end of the show a voice came over the loudspeaker: 'The Duchess wishes Mr Hardy Amies to go to her boudoir.' As the footman opened the door, the Duchess moved to greet me. She turned to Christian Dior and said, 'Here, Monsieur Dior, is the only man in the world who can make clothes for me.' The Duchess should be forgiven for this slightly dramatic gesture: she wasn't going to allow the Frogs to get away with everything, any more than did her husband's ancestor, whose victories the Palace commemorates.

It must have been about a year later that I had supper at Claridges with Bettina Ballard, the then editress of American *Vogue*. She was wearing a black taffeta Dior cocktail dress: sleeves, bodice, waistline – all typical of the New Look: but with a gasp I noticed that her skirt only just came over her knees. The ankle-length draperies had all been cut away. Here was a woman – to quote Christian Dior's own phrase – whose spring had left her face but who was triumphantly showing a beautiful pair of legs. It was the long skirts of the New Look which went first, but the tiny waist and full skirt remained for a long time afterwards.

Events came quick and fast. Balenciaga brought out his chemise dresses I think as early as 1948. These were more prophetic in their looseness than were the tight waists of the New Look. Balenciaga showed in his day clothes a bravura of cut which made so much of what we did in England seem governessy. My old friend Cammie never stopped pointing out how beautifully our Mr Ernest's collars were set. Balenciaga, by thrusting the collar away from the neck, made our jackets look like those of a school uniform. It was the end of the export of London-designed suits to the USA. Since the Coronation of George VI in 1937, buyers from all the great stores in New York, and indeed in Montreal and Toronto, had come to us to buy suits which they had had copied back home. There was, of course, another factor: that was the rise of the power of the American clothing industry itself on to which platform were beginning to stride great men like Norman Norrell and, a little later, the still greater Bill Blass. There were already bright stars like Hattie Carnegie and the much undervalued Claire McCardell. The Balenciaga collar is still with us.

In the thirties and forties the Peter Pan collar was popular. It lay flat. Balenciaga raised it onto a band which he shaped carefully around the base of the neck but away from the throat. It gave a cherished look to the head.

The sixties really were a watershed. I was more than peeved when I read that Mary Quant had said that *haute couture* was dead. The implication was that she had killed it. I now see that what she really meant was that the influence on dress design of the *haute couture* was beginning markedly to decline. It is not dead. The House of Yves Saint Laurent has at its core an *haute couture* business and has as powerful an influence as has had any great house in the past. Mary Quant's designs, in my opinion, were essentially a demonstration of an attitude. This would have happened without her. I have to say, however, that I am full of admiration for what she did. She showed that cheap clothes (I despise the gentility of the expression 'reasonably priced') could be designed, manufactured and marketed in their own right. They were clothes for the working and playing young of all ages. They were not copies of clothes of the rich.

As a man of taste, I disliked the vulgarity of the mini-skirt. As a designer, I could find no inspiration or challenge in the cutting required of clothes of such skimpy proportions. Mary Quant was the first London-based designer to move the pulse of world fashion. She was helped, in my opinion, by the appearance in Paris of the work of Courrèges. He was expressing the same feelings about clothes as was Mary Quant, but his clothes were for the rich. They required a precision of cut and fit as only a first-class *atelier* can provide. To aid the dissemination of this new philosophy of dress, the American clothing industry seemed just ready to apply itself to making very competent copies. The very short skirts which suddenly appeared all over the world gave birth to women's tights. Decency was preserved.

From now onwards the body was all-important. Your dress for the whole day had the outline of the gym tunic. Your status symbol was the gold chain on the handbag slung from your shoulder; the elaborateness of your coiffure, which meant for a grand lady a daily visit either to or from her hairdresser; and, of course, an expensive tan. Mrs Jackie Kennedy exemplified this new look.

It was not a happy period for me. My star customer was the Queen, a reigning queen as distinct from the consort of a king. The Queen today still believes in good manners. When visiting her people she feels behoven to crown herself with a hat and to accoutre herself with gloves and handbag. The short skirts of the sixties made no silhouette on which to balance a hat. The Queen, ever anxious to cooperate with her advisers, allowed us to shorten her skirts considerably but insisted that her knees should be covered as much as possible when sitting down.

Our patience was rewarded. I doubt if the young will ever again yearn to look like grown-ups as they did in the thirties. Quite rightly, they want to have their own clothes. Suddenly the girl becomes a woman. There are more women in the world than there are girls. Only a few women look good in mini-skirts. There are an awful lot of women who are knock-kneed. Norman Hartnell said that the back of women's knees look like underdone rock cakes. Skirts had to come down again, and did. Suddenly a Courrèges dress looked like a matchbox with holes for your arms. We rediscovered the charm of softly-draped cloth: that a soft hemline could caress and flatter a calf. Let us not forget that the mini-skirt is still with us. It suits the young for dancing: it suits the not-so-young by the seaside.

Nowadays all is not simple. There are large bolts and bundles of anarchy around. Students in colleges of art and fashion are encouraged to express themselves and produce what used to be called creations made out of rags. Cotton is revered by some designers because of its magnificent creasing qualities. Anything goes. It should be noted, however, that fashion editors and editresses who put illustrations of crumpled clothes into their magazines take care to use models, male and female, of startling beauty (nothing new in that) but who have bodies comparable to those of athletes of world class.

I have books filled with press cuttings covering my work over the last fifty years. Starting with the thirties and carving one's way through to today, it is impossible to avoid the impression that very little has changed. The first outfit of mine to be honoured with a full-page photograph in British *Vogue* was called 'Panic'. It had a jacket of quite large checks in jade green and cerise, worked on a background flecked in the same colours on a base of deep plum. This tweed made the skirt. The suit could be worn in the winter today. I tell this not to vaunt myself as being an avant-garde designer but to show that so many of

28 Dotted tulle evening dress, *Vogue* front cover, March 1950 (*Norman Parkinson*)

29 Circular skirted dress, *Vogue*, March 1952 (*Henry Clarke*)

30 Wenda Parkinson at Hyde Park Corner, 1951 (*Norman Parkinson*)

31 Encrusted evening jacket, *Vogue*, September 1962 (*David Bailey*)

32 Rose pink twill cape-coat, *Vogue*, March 1966 (*Vernier*)

33 Two wool check suits with velvet collars made for the Packer International Collection, 1983
(*Christopher Moore*)

34 Prince and Princess Michael of Kent, the Princess wears a pale lilac, slubbed silk ballgown, 1983
(*Norman Parkinson*)

The Dalkeith Weddings
35 Miss Jane McNeill marries the Earl of Dalkeith, 1953 (*Lenare*)

36 Lady Elizabeth Kerr marries their son, the Earl of Dalkeith, 1981
(*Norman Parkinson*)

the principles of dressing – especially expensive dressing – have changed but little.

Women, of course, wore trousers in the thirties. A stylish model girl at Lachasse made for herself a pair of quite wide trousers – slim over the hips, of course – which she wore with a knee-length wrap-around coat tied at the waist with a sash. The cloth used was very fine, smooth, navy-blue wool. The war established the use by women of trousers cut exactly as those of men. The post-war invasion of jeans completed the job.

An aspect of the history of fashion which is of great interest to me is the watching of the creation of the Dress of the Year. Fashion writers talk of the Dress of the Year. They usually refer to a dress that is fashionable enough to warrant their approval or at least to avoid their boredom. However the real Dress of the Year is probably the one that appears most often on the teaming streets of London, Birmingham and Glasgow. Could it be that the Dress of the Year for 1984 is blue jeans, a cotton shirt and an anorak?

Most dress designers would like to be thought of as innovators. There used to be a romance that some *couturiers* went to great trouble to protect their designs from being copied. Chanel was more realistic. I don't think she encouraged copying but she did say, 'To be copied is to be a success.' Chanel is to be admired for having proposed a way of dress for women: narrow but easy-fitting jackets, collarless to make room for a soft shirt and rows of pearls and chains; and straight skirts cut to flatter the leg; the cloth used for the suit a tweed soft to the touch and of colours becoming to the skin. They have been around during most part of my fifty years.

Of course young designers start out with the desire to design and make something quite new. When well done this is a sure way to get publicity. You would have attracted sales from professional buyers. Private buyers, you would discover very quickly, were less enthusiastic about the very new. They preferred the familiar with a twist so clever as to avoid the banal. A designer soon finds that he has a clientele and that he has *ateliers* which have to be kept fully occupied. The cherishing of a clientele is the most important function of a designer. He must never lower the standards of his advice to the customer but he must always respect her wishes. Experience will bring a knowledge of her life-style. It is the life-style which sparks the desire for the new dress.

Even if I could never be called a creative designer I hope nobody would deprive me of the right to be called a professional. I have never wanted to make a new collection totally different from the previous. I like to look at the successes and develop them evolving something different but not unfamiliar. I believe in the evolution of fashion: never more so than now when I am reviewing pictures of clothes of the last fifty years.

The greatest of my modest gifts has been that of being able, at the sight of quite a small piece of cloth – I would, of course, prefer a large one – to see a dress not only finished and in the collection, but copied and worn by a customer: in the Concorde lounge at Heathrow or in the ballroom at Syon House. I draw badly. I had to make sketches as a guide and a record to the tailors and dressmakers who were going to cut the garments. From my earliest days in *haute couture* until today, I have had the great joy of working with very skilled cutters. I have often wished that I had learned to cut. On reflection, however, I console myself with the thought that I could never have achieved the skill of my own employees. It is very different today. *Haute couture* supplies only a miniscule proportion of the clothes made each year in the world. Young designers today have to have a profound know-ledge of pattern cutting if they are going to achieve any security of position. I want to exhort them to try and decide what kind of clothes they want to make, in what market they want to sell them, and for what life-style they envisage them being used. I like to think of clothes being used rather than worn.

It is now *démodé* to be dressed up: especially by day, and very often at night. The suit, once the most worn garment, is too serious if the jacket and skirt are made of the same material. A grey flannel pleated skirt, with a silk shirt, is united with a jacket of suede or camel-hair. It all looks artlessly chosen. It's only by accident that it looks so expensive. There are fewer dresses worn than there are blouses and skirts.

One of the most pointless occupations is that of railing against current fashion. '*La mode est toujours jolie,*' said Chanel. You may not like certain clothes pictured in a magazine. You can dismiss them as tentative experiments. But when you see twenty girls in the street all wearing the same dress you have to consider this as a serious manifestation.

It must be ten years now since Ken Fleetwood has taken over the organizing and supervision of the design and making of all women's clothes at Savile Row. My *forte* was tailored clothes. I learned a lot from the tailors and tailoresses at Lachasse. There there were no dressmakers for what the French call the '*flou*': the evening dress with flowing skirt and seductively revealing bodice; the cocktail dress in pleated chiffon or draped jersey. More experience in this field was gained during the years at Worth. Ken's work complemented mine. For several years we worked together, buying the cloth for the collection, planning the design, with Ken completing my rough sketches and supplying many of his own. There were other designers in the studio.

By the mid-sixties our work in the men's market had spread overseas. Our contracts had to be nurtured by frequent visits. The making of the *couture* collections, launched immutably in the middle of July and in the middle of January, required the maintenance of a strict timetable. I began to allow Ken to make decisions for me and to buy cloth from visiting merchants. There has always been perfect accord in our tastes.

It is extraordinary how timeless some fashion is. The other day Ken called me into his studio. 'Now I will show you', he said, 'something so typically Amies it will make you laugh.' It did. It was a dress and coat in fine wool. It could have appeared in any collection over the last fifty years.

In spite of his sturdy Lancashire background, Ken Fleetwood is a dreamer. He sometimes forgets to eat. Soon after he came to work for me I noticed that he wasn't well. I sent him to Dr Sharma, my homeopathic doctor. He quickly discovered that the two severe bouts of hepatitis that Ken had had during his years of military service had left serious damage to the liver. Strict diet was essential. I brought him to my house so that my housekeeper could look after him. Shortly afterwards I moved to a larger house in which he was able to have a self-contained flat. When I later moved to a flat he installed himself in one within two minutes' walk of mine. It's an awesome thought that for about twenty-five years we have followed the same routine: that of walking through Kensington Gardens and across Hyde Park to the car waiting at Hyde Park Corner to carry us through Mayfair to Savile Row. The day's business is discussed: plans are made for the future. Rain so heavy as to render umbrellas useless is the only deterrent. My office is next to his at Savile Row. I am interrupted in all but the most important meetings to be shown models when they are being fitted. This happens so often that by the time the collection is ready on show day I really feel that the clothes are mine. I say this not in any way wishing to diminish the skill and devotion which Ken and his team give to their work.

The growth of our business at Savile Row in off-the-peg clothes is mostly seen in the popularity of the casual clothes for day – blouses, skirts, jackets. Tailored suits are less in demand than they were. There are, however, still enough fastidious ladies who like to have their jackets and overcoats made for them to keep the tailoring workrooms busy. What makes the House – from the seamstresses, fitters, *vendeuses* to the designers in the studio – very happy is the large quantity of elaborate wedding dresses we are now being asked to make.

The desire of parents to order a beautiful wedding dress for their daughter was not entirely inspired by the wedding of the Princess of Wales. I have been concerned with the making of many wedding dresses over the past fifty years. Such orders were always treated with loving care, not always matched by the parents' willingness to spend money. 'After all, it's only for one day,' the landowners rich in acres but rather pressed for cash would say. There has now been a marked change in attitude. I suppose the fact that there are now very few *couture* houses in London makes us sought-after and allows us to charge prices which we wouldn't have risked before. I should add that there is no stinting of time, labour and cloth and that it is very difficult to work out the cost of a dress which has never been made before.

Two patronesses who were impeccable in their behaviour as regards money and totally inspiring in their enthusiasm for our designs were the Duchess of Marlborough, the mother of the present Duke, and the Duchess of Buccleuch, who brought all her daughters to us for wedding dresses including Lady Caroline, who married Ian Gilmour. She also brought us her future daughter-in-law and the future Duchess, the very beautiful Miss Jane McNeill whose marriage to the Earl of Dalkeith took place in Scotland in the autumn of 1953. It was the grandest ceremony since the Coronation. We made a dress in silver lace, very plain as to detail, very bold in outline. Skirts of crinoline proportions were very fashionable. We gave one to the bride, and allied it with a very simple bodice and long tight sleeves. The lace was so stitched and appliquéd that there was no break in the

line anywhere. It was magnificently simple and simply magnificent –
helped, of course, by the bride's beauty and elegance of figure. She
was crowned, literally, by one of the sumptuous Buccleuch tiaras.
There were several to choose from.

One of the pleasures of working as a designer for fifty years and
running one's own business for nearly forty is that of seeing the
families of your customers burgeon. Weddings are often involved in
this way. There is a happy sequel to the Buccleuch wedding.

Jane McNeill's groom was Lord Dalkeith. He became Duke of
Buccleuch on the death of his father. In turn their son and heir grew up
to be Lord Dalkeith and became engaged to Lady Elizabeth Kerr,
daughter of the Marquess and Marchioness of Lothian. Lady Lothian
was already a much-loved patroness of my house. It therefore seemed
natural that we should do the wedding dress. This time it was Ken
Fleetwood's turn. His dress for the Lady Elizabeth was as different as
could be from mine for the previous Lady Dalkeith. It was greatly
admired, particularly by Lady Lothian whose Italian blood bubbled
enthusiasm. It was based on a design of about 1880. The dress of white
taffeta had a skirt draped back into a bustle, the draperies held by
bunches of white roses. It admirably suited the bride's small features
and dark hair.

During the wedding service, to which both Ken and I had been
invited, in the small chapel at Dalkeith where two hundred special
guests were seated, Ken said to me, 'We've got very grand seats; we
are just behind the family and, I think, in front of the cousins.' I
replied, 'It's a bit like *Upstairs, Downstairs*.' 'Can't think what we are,'
said Ken. 'We're not upstairs and we're not downstairs; I think we're
entresol.'

When the bride appeared I felt considerable pride that a pupil of
mine had made such a beautiful wedding dress.

A wedding dress of a different sort was the cream silk suit that we
made, in a great hurry, for Princess Michael of Kent. She wore it at the
civil wedding ceremony in Vienna in 1978 and again at the validation
service in London in 1983. Princess Michael is a customer who had
done us many kindnesses and leads the applause at our dress shows at
Savile Row. The Princess has a professional eye for clothes which she
chooses with great care. Not for the first time am I glad that our
clothes last. They have to be of great use to the very busy Princess
Michael who is exceptionally photogenic.

Princess Alice, Countess of Athlone, was a customer during the last ten years of her long life of ninety-seven years which ended in 1980. The Princess would come into the boutique quite unannounced. I am the proud owner of a signed photograph of Princess Alice, taken by Lord Snowdon for the Queen's Jubilee. It was Princess Michael of Kent who asked Princess Alice to sign the photograph for me. I treasure this memento of Queen Victoria's last surviving grand-daughter.

It is much easier to see a pattern in the development of design in men's clothes than it is in that of the women. For one thing, the tremendous variety in women's clothes obscures the picture. For women there is a big difference in style between day and evening; for men the cut of a jacket by day and for evening is almost the same.

There is a pattern in the development of men's clothes which is startlingly clear. Before 1800 there were clearly defined fashions for the rich and fashions for the poor. From 1800 onwards the strength of the distinction weakens and today has disappeared. The pattern is that the clothes used for formal occasions vanish and are replaced by those of a rank lower.

By 1800 the silks and satins of the eighteenth century were reserved for court occasions only. For everyday wear the riding coat was worn universally. It had status – the wearer was a gentleman, possibly with land, certainly owning a horse. It was the beginning of a habit of using a garment designed for sport for every day.

The Industrial Revolution produced a different ideal man. He was more concerned with money making than with social climbing. The riding coat developed into the frock coat, which was essentially a city garment.

There were very complicated rules for dress and these were not relaxed for sport. In the mid-1860s there appeared a short jacket in check tweed. It was for shooting, stalking or just plain walking in the Scottish hills. It was called a Deeside jacket. It is still with us. It's called simply a sports jacket.

The riding jacket of 1800 influenced the shape of evening clothes and the tailcoat is derived from it. This is still used for certain very rare occasions, but has truly been overwhelmingly replaced by the dinner jacket. This in its turn is doomed, its place will be taken by the dark blue suit (the *dunkler Anzug* of the Germans).

We still sometimes talk of a modern suit as a lounge suit. It is an official term for regulations of dress on formally printed invitation cards. It is a term incomprehensible to our friends in America. I agree that it is not a very pretty name. It first appeared about 1900. To talk of a lounge suit then was like talking about casual wear today. It freed you from the terrifying restrictions, both moral and physical, of the morning coat and the frock coat with stiff collar and silk hat. The pattern of social life which formed the stage where these clothes were worn was shattered by the First World War.

When the temporary officer and gentleman returned to civvy street in 1918 he wanted a lounge suit, not to lounge in but to work in. Messrs Moss Bros were ready to supply him with an authentic gentleman's Savile Row suit. Their department, which dealt in misfits (suits which arrogant young customers had refused to accept from their tailors for often the most trifling of reasons) was very popular. The supply was naturally limited. There then sprang into being the multiple tailors.

Multiple tailoring was a phenomenon of the English menswear trade. It so dominated the market that by 1960 – after a decade of heavy buying by the public to replace the shortages of the war years – it is estimated that approximately sixty per cent of the male British population dressed at a multiple tailor. The British have always loved cloth and understood it. It was pleasant to choose good cloth in a bunch supplied by a first-class mill. The multiple tailor offered the customer the right to dictate his personal preference of style. Orders were speedily executed by skilled cutters and efficiently planned machinery. It was bespoke tailoring for the masses.

By the end of the fifties intelligent firms like Hepworths began to suspect that they were not only in the multiple tailoring business but they were in the fashion business too. Fashion was not a word much loved in Leeds. It scared them.

Looking back over the twenty years of my association with Hepworths I can see various things. One is that I showed Hepworths and the manufacturers of shirts, ties, shoes and socks with whom I was later associated, that there was no need to be frightened of fashion. There was a discernible pattern in the past which could point the way to the future. The lounge suit had become simply the suit. For the past twenty years suits have been the most important part of a man's wardrobe. I am prepared to stake a great deal on a statement that it will be an awful long time a-dying.

Because so many formal garments have disappeared from the market, the suit still occupies an enormous part of the traditional men's trade which has shrunk; only the efficient survive. It is always a relief to discard the suit for leisure, hence the tremendous growth in demand for and manufacture of large quantities of casual wear. Jeans, cotton trousers, t-shirts and blousons: this is the everyday wear of millions around the world. However most men still need a suit if they want to get a conventional sort of job.

In the 1950s the men's trade discovered that it needed designers. Hepworths chose me because I was a designer with a reputation for making good, tailored women's clothes. I knew that a suit could be designed so as to show off an athletic body and, where there wasn't one, to suggest one. I knew that the idiom and the practice of conventional dressing was being assailed from below. Jeans would affect the shape of trousers. For ten years I've been trying to feed the interest in the blazer. The Italians, with their innate sense of taste as regards appearance and of display as regards sexual prowess, got the message.

The most distinguished-looking blazer is in navy blue. With trousers of the same material, it can be a man's best suit. The brass buttons add a twinkle of gaiety. On them the crest, phoney or otherwise, indicates that you are a member of a club, i.e. socially acceptable. The original blazer was created to keep an oarsman warm when he came ashore. It is therefore a garment intimately connected with sport. The blazer is still a jacket. Its shoulders, cut wide, can be padded to help the narrow-chested. The whole cut must be loose rather than tight: room for a sweater underneath. When a tie is worn it must be striped and look as though it has something to do with a club. Authenticity is not necessary: gaiety is.

A man wearing a blazer, either with trousers matching the jacket or contrasting, as in grey flannel, would be an admirable companion to the girl in the skirt of pleated grey flannel, silk shirt and casual jacket that I described earlier. It is quite possible that the girl would be wearing a jacket of a cut based on that of a man's blazer.

A review of fifty years of men's fashion would be incomplete if the sweater were not mentioned. I suppose it began with the pullovers worn by the Prince of Wales in the late twenties and early thirties. This started the popularity of the Fairisle sweater. You were bang up-to-date and athletic yet giving more than a nodding tribute to the ritual of the moors. There has been no looking back. Men marched arm-in-arm with the girls: the girls in their cashmere twinsets. The cashmere pullover and cardigan have been part of men's and women's wardrobes for fifty years. The supremacy of the genuine Scottish article has been attacked by imports from the Far East and by the use of lambswool at home. Fine as lambswool often is, it still cannot give the subtle caress of touch of genuine cashmere.

The shape of men's casual jackets – blousons and anoraks and others of that ilk – requires a great breadth of shoulder. Bigger stitching and thicker yarn than those used traditionally by the spinners of Hawick come into the picture. The Italians, sensitive as always to the wind of fashion, use mohair. If cashmere is cream, mohair is whipped cream. But if the designers of traditional cashmere sweaters take note of this desire for more bulk without weight, give an ease of fit which allows the actual stuff – the very substance – to drape and thus show itself off rather than to cling to the body, the spinners of cashmere will be unassailable.

Cashmere is expensive. For the ordinary man there are miles and miles of what is called Shetland – rugged in texture, light in weight and absorbing every nuance of the colours of the countryside.

No man or boy living between now and the year 2000 can have too many sweaters in his wardrobe. To make full use of them he will have to rethink the technique of his dressing. Both man and boy will have to realize that a long-sleeved pullover is uncomfortable when worn under a tailored jacket. He will be happier with a sleeveless pullover. If he doesn't want to wear a tie, his sleeveless pullover should have a round neck rather than a V. His neck will be dressed – particularly necessary when wrinkles appear. If he enjoys the comfort of a long-sleeved sweater at home – a fashionable sweater with rather deep armholes and rather big stitches – he will want a special jacket to put on when he goes out. If he chooses his shirt, sweater, trousers and the aforementioned jacket with care, he will find himself very fashionably dressed for any occasion except for an occasion that requires a tie to be worn.

In the course of my fifty years in fashion there is evidence of the purloining of men's clothes by women. I cannot complain: my good fortune in the men's trade was based on the success I had with women's suits in the thirties. The suit itself is masculine. I find the sight of a girl in a man's jacket beguiling. Her femininity is enhanced: she is a pretty little squirrel protected by a chap. If you see a couple both wearing jeans there is no chance of mistaking identities.

I have greatly enjoyed giving great attention to the design of men's suits over the past twenty years. There have been changes, some of them imperceptible to all but the professional. When I came on the scene in the late fifties jackets were on the whole short and shapeless: the Italians had brought what must be called, frankly, sex into trousers. Virile bottoms were in.

Trousers were narrow (we had an awful job at Hepworths in 1960 to get rid of braces). The influence was that of jeans and of the Beatles and their boots. Teddy boys were showing a sort of pantomime version of Edwardianism. Jackets had to become longer. The authority of Cardin helped. Long jackets meant vents. Cardin's were the longest. Vents were arrows which pointed to a narrow waist. Tommy Nutter brought in revers so wide as to almost reach the shoulder. Ties followed suit and became as wide as a kipper. As athleticism in dress increased, so did the jacket have to become less tight. The ideal answer was to copy the cut of the genuine blazer. It's been just as much a struggle to get the trade to abandon vents (which are part of the waisted look) as it was to get them accepted in the first place. Of course fashion will win. It always does.

I must mention hair. Its importance, I think, goes with the demonstration of a tendency for anyone to be allowed to do their own thing. There is nothing wrong in this. I must point out, however, that it is perfectly possible to satisfy your individual taste whilst remaining obedient (perhaps that's the side of things which offends) to the rules of fashionable dressing. True fashion – that which lasts over a decade – is never eccentric but it can be influenced by eccentricity.

It requires great skill to dress well: you have to be disciplined when buying, particularly if you are poor. But it is possible to be perfectly well-dressed with very little money. The cheapest, but not always the most effective means of self-expression is eccentrically long hair or a beard.

Long hair came in in the sixties. It was part of the 'peacock revolution'. Here was something new, youthful, exciting, freedom-encouraging. 'What is going to be fascinating', I said, 'is to see a grey-haired man with long hair.' I am afraid that today you see all too many of them. I would not dare to tell men that they are wrong not to change in middle age the style of their hair from that to which they were used when young. Their barber will gradually lure them to the shorter hair of today: shorter hair which is demanded by the look of the sportsman which is more and more part of the ideal man. I would not dare to say that Borg might have remained champion if he had cut his hair: but I am sure the application of the scissors to the locks of McEnroe has helped him.

I see very little lessening in the wearing of jeans around the world. They are work clothes sometimes elevated to status dressing when allied with the name of a stylish designer. The pressure in men's fashion is from below. At the top the morning coat, the tailcoat and, of course, the dinner jacket are pushed out of the wardrobe into the cupboards of Messrs Moss Bros.

What of the future? It is pleasant to note that there is no conflict between men and women as demonstrated by their clothes. They show an insistence on a freedom of choice in life: to make love and have children without marriage but with camaraderie; to wear clothes made of natural fibres like wool and silk, of a cut that gives freedom of movement and seduction of outline. It's all eminently sensible without being self-conscious.

There is, however, no shame in making obeisance to the Establishment. England is overwhelmingly royalist. If proof were needed, you have only to remember the sight of the enormous crowds outside the Palace and down the Mall on Jubilee Day and at the wedding of the Prince and Princess of Wales. On the afternoon of the day following the wedding, we were fitting the Queen. The Queen, not usually given to speech not immediately relevant to the matter in hand, remarked with obvious feeling that she had been amazed at the sight.

There is a very clearly defined element in modern dressing which shows an awareness of this love of tradition. Status dressing is still with us. The man needs a suit, the woman some jewellery.

In all cases health is cherished. Shining hair, glowing skin, supple limbs are proudly flaunted by the young and carefully nurtured by those whose youth is not allowed to leave them.

Nudity is already permitted on many beaches. The practice of bathing naked will not be hindered if a careful code of behaviour is established. Bodies, tanned lying down, all white zones banished, can be carefully draped when borne to the water's edge. Only the very young and the very beautiful should be allowed to forget that swinging London is a thing of the past.

Nudity will affect dress, especially of course for women. In the future ladies entertaining at home will wear loose frocks which will clearly indicate that they veil a naked body. The woman who knows her business of being a woman will understand instinctively how to manipulate such a garment to suit her ends: to seduce her man or to keep him.

However, I think that status dressing will remain with us. For men the suit will still be the most important status garment. It will be very plain and expensive-looking. This is essential for status. There will be in a man's wardrobe a mass of 'freedom clothes'. Grandad will still have his jeans: grandsons will probably be wearing tracksuits.

I do not think that a woman's dress by day will differ greatly from that of a man. As I said earlier, at night I believe that she will always want to be dressed like a princess.

7

Moi

I am no longer six foot tall. As the years increase the spine shrinks. This is one of the many things you have to suffer without complaint. I weigh less than 170 lbs: so I am not fat. Pino, the men's tailor at my shop, makes the waistband of my trousers 33 inches. This is tight but bearable: there is a small but ugly roll of fat above it. There was 5 lbs more of it which I have reduced by cutting out sugar in tea and coffee and drinking practically no spirits. I should like to have a waist of 32. It must not be more than 34 inches. With a 40-inch chest, these are the standard measurements of a size 40 suit. If I keep to these measurements I can try on a Hardy Amies man's suit anywhere in the world and judge its fit, finish and quality.

This is just one excuse for spending time and money on keeping my body trim. I want to avoid manifestations of old age: the movement of the torso instead of the neck. I want to avoid all stiffness of the joints for as long as possible. I do about ten minutes of exercises every morning. I walk for threequarters of an hour every day whenever possible. I play tennis for one and a half hours every Saturday and every Sunday. I insist that the motorcar I have in London, as well as the one in the country, have a sunshine roof. Constant contact with fresh air and sunlight keeps the skin of my face youthful. I never use any creams, tanning lotions or sun oils. I no longer lie in the sun: I take exercise in it. Sweat is a good moisturizer.

I am grateful for the way my head is placed on my shoulders. The proportions are right. I keep my hair short and wash it every day under the shower. I never put anything on it. I also have a torso which is over an inch longer than is normal. This is good for wearing jackets. All fashion sketches, of both men and women, show bodies which are long in the torso, with a low waistline and often absurdly long legs.

I am vain in the sense that I take care to look as well as I can. But I do not prink in front of the looking-glass. I dress very quickly indeed. I like to put my clothes out in an orderly fashion. Decision as to choice of suit, shirt, tie and shoes is mady very swiftly. The choice has usually been made at time of ordering or of purchase. I play safe: it's more relaxing. To attempt to make an effect requires extra effort.

I have well-shaped, straight legs and feet with high arches: so high that I have had to have my shoes made for me since I was seventeen. I keep my shoes immaculate, always using trees the moment I take them off. The high instep avoids fatigue. My legs do not get tired at tennis: it is the concentration that exhausts me.

I am always happy to take my clothes off. I like very simple dressing-gowns of wool for the winter and of cotton for the summer. I dislike silk. It often creases and cannot be washed.

I am always aware of the feel of cloth on skin. As a child I disliked more the feel of cheap or badly made clothes than I did the appearance. This makes me have affinity with customers – *couture* customers – who feel they must have their clothes from us, even if it means having fewer.

All good dress designers must be body lovers. I love seeing beautiful bodies and I love touching them and being touched. This is one of the many reasons why I am a bachelor. I am quite certain I was never meant to marry. I am a confirmed bachelor: what the Germans call '*ein eingefleischter Junggeselle*' – born-in-the-flesh bachelor.

This does not mean I am not a family man. I am. I have a clear recollection of a Christmas spent in my grandfather's small Victorian house in Maidstone. He was widowed but very much the patriarch. There were old maiden aunts, one of whom cooked, another did embroidery on church vestments; ten bodies at table; kitchen in the basement; another aunt made peppermint creams. It was 1912. After 1914 nothing was indeed the same.

Our own family life, with my sister six years younger than I, and a much younger brother, a mongol – lodged away from home most of the time – was happy enough. Both parents were young rather than old. But we lived in isolation in an ugly suburb. Boarding school had more attractions and the escape to France and Germany opened up new worlds. There was family life in the Pfarrhaus in Bendorf: but I was an outsider.

The death of my mother, aged fifty-nine, in 1938 put an end to our family reunions at Christmas, and they were not re-established on my father's remarriage.

Shortly after I started to work at Lachasse in February 1934 I began to dislike the daily journey to London from home in Essex, a scramble in the morning; tiring at night. I was very happy to accept the offer of a room in a flat in Kensington owned by a decorator and antique dealer called Alexis ffrench. He and his wife Anne gave me a family life for the next twenty-two years. Alexis had a daughter and Anne three, all by previous marriages. Anne possessed a modest fortune inherited from her forebears, important landowners in New Zealand although she had been brought up in 'county' and hunting circles in England. She had been a customer of Digby Morton's at Lachasse. She was amused to meet Digby Morton's successor, and her strong maternal instincts were aroused. She adopted me into the family. It was useful to have a brother to the girls, especially when the time came to 'give them a season'. It was a wonderful experience for me to go to debutante balls in Belgrave Square and Pont Street.

Alexis belonged to an Irish family of standing and distinction. Possessing only a little income from a marriage settlement, he was anxious to be financially independent from Anne. He had, a few months before I appeared, started an antique shop in South Kensington. Anne and he arranged to have a flat each in London but to reunite at the weekends at a country house in Kent. This plan did not last long. Alexis became more and more absorbed in his shop. Weekends were used to hunt for stock in country towns or the alleyways of Brighton. Anne was very busy with her daughters. They were either having their season or finishing their education at the famous school at Hinterhör, run by the much loved Gräfin Degenfeld.

Alexis loved finding and doing up new houses and flats, especially for himself and, as it turned out, for me. As I progressed at Lachasse and became more sure of myself, so did I yearn for a flat of my own. This Alexis found for me. In the little bit of Pont Street between Sloane Street and Chesham Place there is, on the south side, a single-storied shop, now occupied by a picture dealer. To this Alexis moved his antique business. He made a very smartly decorated flat above – with bedrooms for each of us. I was allowed to buy the contents and soon found myself running the flat, with the help of a manservant. In return for keeping Alexis during the week, I was allowed a room in a cottage in Kent, only two miles away from Anne ffrench's own house.

Happy days! So much to learn. Alexis was very close to his only sister Yvonne. She was an authoress, much respected for her lives of Mrs Siddons, of the novelist Ouida, and of Mrs Gaskell. Yvonne shared a flat with Countess Voss, May to her friends, an Italian who had had two German husbands. May Voss was already middle-aged: tiny and neat of figure and very chic as to dress. She was totally at home in the *monde* of England, France, Italy, and of course Germany. My fluency in German amused her. She, like Anne, and indeed Yvonne, took me under her wing. I was an apt pupil, learning what Kitty Miller in later years was to call *'les usages'*.

Alexis and his brother had spent many years of their childhood in Italy: for their father had left his wife, a member of the distinguished Thursby family, to lead a quiet but self-indulgent life in Rome. He was a Roman Catholic and was eventually given a papal title. Alexis and his brother Conrad were brought up as Catholics; Yvonne, the daughter, as a Protestant.

I appreciated my good fortune in being taken into the heart of an English upper-class family. With Anne as the matriarch, it was essentially conventional. But the close friendship made by the girls with Gräfin Degenfeld opened many foreign vistas. Anne's youngest daughter became a Princess Wittgenstein. Alexis's daughter Jackie speaks fluent German.

Alexis and Yvonne spoke good Italian and were at home in Italy. May Voss hopped around all over Europe in mind and body. Holidays were taken in Germany, Austria, France and Switzerland. Enjoyment was enhanced by my ease in speaking French and German. There was great profit for me in learning the art of living.

Alexis loved good food. He was greedy and always ate too fast. He enjoyed Italian dishes like *gnocchi alla romana*: and French provincial food of all kinds. Feast days at Christmas and Easter were kept with style.

I gave up the Pont Street flat to go into the Army. When I was posted to the War Office I took another in Chesham Place. This was a *pied-à-terre* for Alexis. He bought a fine house in Essex with a hundred acres of parkland. Here his daughter Jackie was installed as *châtelaine*. Then Anne did up some rooms for herself. I had my own room for weekends whenever I wanted to leave London. It was a family life, with the members all having a great deal of independence.

I got much more than I deserved from the ffrench family. I helped a little financially when Alexis had to educate Jackie's son by a neglectful husband. But it was Anne ffrench who bore the brunt of the responsibility of nursing Alexis when he developed cancer of the marrowbone in his leg. He died in 1956. I was able to take him and Anne on a last holiday to Italy.

Alexis taught me a lot about food: more, of course, about antiques and decoration. A great friend was John Fowler with whom Alexis had worked at Peter Jones, together with Margaret Kunzer, the founder of the decorative furniture department. Margaret is my oldest living friend. Her father and my father were friends. Another member of the 'clan' was Bridget Gilligan, later to become Countess Bernstorff. She is still very much part of my life.

Much has been written about John Fowler: very sensitively so by John Cornforth in articles in *Country Life*. John was a more important influence eventually, but his attitude to Alexis was in 1934, when we first met, one of admiration and respect from the humble countryman to a well-born man of the world with a well-to-do wife. John did not seek comfort in those days: only beautiful objects in harmonious surroundings. Alexis had grander furniture in his shop and in his rooms than did John. Alexis was fascinated by the more bizarre demonstrations of the the the tastes of the Regency: the Brighton Pavilion and Sezincote; Strawberry Hill Gothic; and by the Egyptian furniture of his friend Eddie Knobloch. All this intrigued John Fowler, too. But he loved and sought above all the simple painted furniture – painted in soft faded pastels of French and English furniture of the late eighteenth century. His rooms at 292 King's Road were a piece of the country brought to London. It all seemed at ease there: he made one very aware that London is made up of groups of villages: Chelsea, Battersea, Fulham, Highgate, Islington. Fifty years ago 292 King's Road was in a row of houses straight out of a country town.

When I was working at Lachasse, John was with Sybil Colefax in Bruton Street. We met most days for lunch at a pub in Hill Street, The Running Footman. We would compare notes on our progress and discuss our customers, some of whom we shared. We talked of fashion but without knowing it. We chatted about customers' foibles – these are the elements which harden into serious trends.

My knowledge of the world was, I knew, very slight. But I had travelled more than had John. It made me feel almost sophisticated compared with his simple country upbringing. But I was always the pupil.

Alexis taught me how to arrange rooms so as to be comfortable to live in – where to put the sofas and armchairs and where to place the lights and where the table for the ashtrays and cocktails; what to eat and how to prepare it. He also taught me how a gentleman should dress and where he should order his clothes. Anne ffrench never failed to command respect: her well-carved features and height helped. Above all, she had an air of wisdom and humour. She guided me out of the styles and habits of my middle-class upbringing into the idiom of English upper-class life. 'You must not, dear Hardy, call the lady who prepared your meals Cook. She should be Mrs Whatever her name is.' Anne loved reading English history and passed on this interest to me. 'Get the Plantagenets right. The rest is easy.'

I have loved books and collected them since I was five. When moving house, it has been the books which were most protected and their future housing most carefully planned. The house in Hill Street where Yvonne ffrench and May Voss lived was full of books – many in French, German and Italian. I felt at home there. I could discuss *Bleak House* with Yvonne; with May the *Buddenbrooks*. She was the first grand European lady who showed interest in me. When in later years I was to visit Florence often and admire the standards of taste and workmanship reigning in the workshops and *ateliers* there, I remembered her saying that the Florentine housewives were the best shoppers in the world. They knew how to select the best linens for their beds and tables and appreciated the fineness of the embroidery of the monograms and crests.

John Fowler's dicta on taste were, however, to be a most indelible memory. His views on furniture and decoration were only little different from those of Alexis, Anne and Yvonne ffrench. Alexis sometimes allowed himself to be beguiled by the opulence of some Empire furniture: tolerant as he often was, John required more 'humble' elegance, a philosophy easily understood.

It was in the choice and in the evaluation of beauty in flowers that John literally shocked me into readjusting my standards. All flowers were beautiful in the suburban garden of my parents. The bigger and brighter they were, the more were they admired. Alexis and I read Bunyard's book on old garden roses and planted many bushes in the garden in Kent. Alexis was still anxious to have the herbaceous borders of his Edwardian parents. John Fowler built himself passages and rooms of pleached limes and box hedges at the Hunting Lodge, his country house in Odiham. Flowers were treasured for their design of petal and leaf rather than for the effect of a mass of colour. Choice for annual planting, not so much of annuals themselves – these were always (but necessarily justly) suspect – but for bulbs, was more dangerous. I was proud of my tulips – 'Very effective, dear boy, but can't you see that they are a little big and vulgar' – and I was taken down to see his *clusiana* tulips, the Lady Tulip. Heads only two inches tall, pale greeny white striped with pink, on slender stems and modest leaves, they were truly of humble elegance and of a touching charm. The great pleasure I get today from the clumps of old-fashioned pinks and species violas in my own garden today is full of grateful memories of John and of Alexis.

Good taste springs so strongly from good education: from experience. You learn most easily from seeing. If you've never seen a Lady Tulip or a bush of *Rosa Mundi*, you will be content with Pride of Haarlem and Whisky Mac.

We were, of course, all terribly pleased with ourselves. 'Quite nice people,' Alexis would say, 'but I'm afraid no taste.' That meant that they did not like Regency furniture and thought that bowls of white lilies were funereal. 'They've got quite a nice place in the country,' he would add, 'but I'm afraid rather a lot of oak.'

John Cornforth describes John Fowler's dislike of what he called 'brown' furniture: mahogany, walnut and, of course, oak. I shared the feeling until about ten years ago. French provincial furniture was permitted. It was elegant and yet rustic.

John Fowler decorated a room for me at 14 Savile Row which was my office. He understood perfectly the correctness of the proportions of the George II mouldings – and gave me a serious bookcase and carved armchairs, olive green velvet curtains, fringed and draped for the windows, an open coal fire in a brass and iron fire basket, a beautifully pierced steel fender. Alas! such splendour was to be short-lived. The price of the rent per square foot was decreed by the accountants to be too high. It could only be sustained by becoming the potentially profitable boutique, which it still is.

My first house was at 22 Eldon Road, a remarkably quiet street in Kensington. Each floor had a pair of small rooms, piled on each other from a basement to a fourth floor. Sunlight poured in. There was a narrow garden with green grass, two acacia trees and, after experiments of various sorts, surrounding beds of white hydrangeas. The decoration and furniture were all by Alexis – I had several bolts of heavy satin, hand woven by Warners of Braintree. I had hoped to make ball dresses of it, ordered in the days of serious shortages in the forties. It was too heavy and warm for dresses, but superb in its true role of curtains. This opulence pushed us to use as much French furniture as I could afford. Alexis and I each had a floor: a bedroom and a bath/dressing room. In the basement there was a dining room, with room for eight at a marble-topped table. Marble-topped dining tables do not add to the warmth of one's hospitality: they chill the knees and the elbows.

All the rooms were small. The house was in truth overdecorated. It was uncomfortable to entertain in. I was becoming known overseas and visitors were frequent. In the meantime Alexis had sold his house in Essex and had bought, with Anne, a house in Kent. As he became more and more ill, so were his visits to London less frequent. There followed the unfolding of the last act: the ray treatments, the amputation of a leg; the measuring for and fitting of a false one; delivery of it cancelled by his sudden and merciful death in the Marsden Hospital.

Alexis ffrench gave me a tiny store of knowledge of the arts, familiarity with *les douceurs de la vie* in England, France and Italy. He gave me a family life for twenty-two years. He left me a little bit of money, some pretty furniture, and the right to consider that I had some responsibility for the well-being of his sister Yvonne. We became closer after the death of May Voss. We live very near to each other in Kensington. Many years ago Yvonne began to deal in Old Master drawings, in which she has always been interested. The same quick eye as Alexis, the same taste – but supported by knowledge and study of an application of which he was not capable – have brought her recognition in the world of private and museum collectors. Very independent by nature and beloved by a network of friends, my responsibility has been one of pleasure, and only justified by my being a man ten years younger than she.

Alexis ffrench loved French music. As a young man he had written popular songs – his most famous was called 'Hawaiian Moon' – and he had for a few years a contract with Chappells. He studied in Paris. He had a great feeling for the songs of Fauré and Duparc. He was not really interested in opera, with one important exception. He was nothing short of enchanted by the opera *Pelléas and Mélisande*. This was the first complete opera I heard on the gramophone. He played it all day long. I know almost every note and certainly every word.

At 22 Eldon Road I was able to instal a proper gramophone. There I discovered the pleasure of doing my homework before hearing an opera: or after hearing one and becoming intrigued and frustrated by my ignorance of music.

My father had an above average beautiful baritone voice: lack of money and of true ambition stopped the study of music which he started as a young man. Family responsibilities forced him to be content with singing in the choir of St Mark's, Hamilton Terrace. I was a terrible disappointment to him. I simply couldn't sing in tune: in fact I can't sing at all. The notes just don't come out. This gave me an inferiority complex: until I discovered the gramophone. Then I remembered how much I had enjoyed the opera in Coblenz in the twenties, and the singing of Schlusnuss in the Festhalle there; the songs of Duparc sung by Maggie Teyte and Oggie Lynn (both friends of Alexis).

During the war, whilst visiting Liverpool on a mission to recruit parachutists amongst the Belgian seamen there, I met and became a close friend of David Webster and Jim Cleveland Belle. Our bond was the business of fashion: for both David and Jim were working at the great shop the Bon Marché at Liverpool. We talked unendingly of the future: the future which was to bring David away from the prospect of the editorship of *Vogue* to the direction of Covent Garden, Jim to the Cotton Board, and me to Savile Row. With them I lived through the re-establishment of Covent Garden. Musically I was fascinated but annoyed at my ignorance.

When did the magic start? With the first night of *Peter Grimes* at Covent Garden when the fog outside seemed to blow in across the seashore on the stage; with Vinay as Othello and Gré Brouwnstein as Desdemona; with the first night of real Grand Opera, that of *Don Carlos*, again with Gré Brouwnstein and, of course, Boris Christoff; with Gerda Lammers, an overnight and unexpected replacement, singing Electra; with the very much, and totally justified, heralded appearance of Joan Sutherland, who burst into eternal fame as the

Philistine woman in *Samson*, who was shortly to turn into a Scottish lady called Lucia.

Glyndebourne wedded me forever to *Falstaff*; Bayreuth to *Fidelio* (although there was a good production at Covent Garden under Klemperer) and to the *Mastersingers*; Salzburg to *Parsifal* and *Lohengrin*. At Salzburg I had a silver wedding with the *Rosenkavalier*. And what can you do with *The Ring* but seize it whenever you have the chance?

1953 was, of course, an exceptionally exciting year. The Coronation alone assured that. I had moved into my first complete house. Enjoyment of this was marred by Alexis ffrench's fatal illness.

Alexis ffrench was always concerned about his health. He went to see Dr Chandra Sharma, an Indian doctor who was beginning to build in the early fifties a large and loyal practice.

The doctor prescribed a course of powders, elegantly packaged into minute daily doses. Six weeks later a rash appeared all over Alexis's torso. It was more than an irritation: it was painful. Dr Sharma was delighted. 'It's a miracle,' he said. 'The poisons are being expelled.' 'But I can't stand it,' said Alexis. 'You must stop it.' Anne ffrench, only too anxious to bring Alexis back into orthodoxy, called in the family doctor. He immediately ordered compresses and washes of soothing ointments. Comfort was restored. Dr Sharma retired, more sad than hurt. He asked to see me.

'Alexis must be prepared to suffer some inconvenience, even pain. His doctor is repressing an illness. I find Alexis a patient who might be cancer-prone.' He was indeed: for two years later Alexis was killed by cancer of the marrowbone.

I liked Chandra Sharma from the outset. He takes unending trouble with his patients. He has converted me to homeopathy. He taught me to avoid palliative medicine like aspirin: to seek the causes of discomfort and pain rather than removing them by patent medicines. He taught me to starve for a day if I had any tummy upset (so utterly reasonable: so very hard to carry out) and he showed me how a headache can be cured instantly by manipulation of the neck. I'm blessed with a healthy body, a body which reacts very quickly to the smallest doses of medicine.

Sharma makes new patients fill in a questionnaire of several pages. 'Are you sensitive to draughts?' 'Do you like being massaged?' Patients are interviewed totally naked.

The drugs used are very often taken from herbs. In 1953 I began to be interested in gardening and, of course, in herbs. Chandra told me which herbs were most helpful to me: what were my constitutional remedies. They are bryony – I'm not sure whether it's black or white bryony. I hope the white: I think it such a beautiful plant. Beautiful too is *pulsatilla* – the Pasque flower – this has great restorative powers: the reawakening at Easter. Most useful of all is *chelidonium* – the major celandine. This beautiful plant, with its well- designed leaves and simple yellow flowers, is everywhere in my garden in Oxfordshire. It does not seem offended when I ruthlessly tear it up to prevent it smothering its neighbours. It cheerfully reappears.

Chandra prescribed *chelidonium* to take on journeys round the world as I have, or had, a weak liver. I am a hepatic subject: emotional upsets affect my liver. Thirty drops of liquid extract of *chelidonium* before breakfast each day is my rule. Readers should note that one of Chandra Sharma's rules is that every patient is different. *Chelidonium* may be poison to you.

I tried to grow herbs in the garden at 22 Eldon Road. Quite hopeless: not much better at the larger 17b. Peter Coats was right. Herbs do not flourish in modern central London. There is not enough space and too much shadow from trees and walls of neighbouring houses. There is too much talk of herbs in pots, in window boxes and tiny beds. Herbs need a lot of space and sunlight.

I have never wanted to grow herbs for medical purposes. Those that are good for me, like *chelidonium* and bryony, I liked to keep somewhere, in some odd spot. *Pulsatilla* is so pretty and, as sometimes happens, it's the common variety which is the most satisfying – *pulsatilla vulgaris*, the common Pasque flower, is the prettiest mauve.

Herbs for cooking are very important to me. The taste of tarragon never ceases to beguile me. Is it pepper? Is it cloves? Is it aniseed? It is all three, and much more. You can never have enough of it. I try to grow a row of tarragon plants in my village allotment which is my kitchen garden. I have plants amongst the flowers in several beds in the garden proper. Tarragon requires the siting you would give a precious plant: full sun and good drainage. And you must cut and use it frequently. Neglect is fatal: it grows tall and tasteless.

It was the history of homeopathy which led me to drug jars and on to Delftware. I decorated 17b Eldon Road in a style different from that of

Alexis ffrench and John Fowler. Alexis, of course, never saw it: but John did. In his usual generous way he approved. He saw that much that was good in the house obeyed his rules of understatement and of good proportions. The furniture of small No 22 was easily absorbed into 17b. The plain walls and the modern steel windows made an excellent neutral background to a good old muddle of periods. I worked on the house with Micky Raymond. We rocked with laughter at ourselves talking about 'brutal' effects, but it was under his influence that I began to prefer the style of the seventeenth century as distinct from the eighteenth.

Readers who have followed me so far will have seen how much my taste was influenced by my friendship with Alexis ffrench and John Fowler. This enriched my life enormously. It coloured my choice of reading. Horace Walpole, Beckford, Princess Lieven, the Regent himself, Fanny Burney – I mention a jumble of names who were to appear as living people. John Fowler's favourite historic character was without doubt Marie Antoinette, her '*Hameau*' the epitome of humble elegance.

Versailles itself was of unending fascination. Here Felix Harbord looms up. Felix, a decorator and arranger of houses of immense taste and knowledge, but with no office or shop from which to work. A magician living in some flat or house, lent him by some friend, sumptuously decorated and furnished (he did deal in beautiful objects, stored in warehouses), with a little court of devoted courtiers and artisans – painters and cabinet makers, brilliant artists in *trompe l'oeil* and gilding.

When Felix Harbord died in Paris the funeral was arranged and paid for by Prince Ernst August of Hanover. His whole family came to the ceremony to pay tribute to a man of great integrity, who never lowered his standards of quality and style, who put art before commerce. This excused the lack of professionalism which often infuriated many customers and patrons. At Père Lachaise I sat next to two young Frenchman, who wept. 'He was teaching us about *vernis Martin*,' they said. To the young I explain that *vernis Martin* is a complicated method of varnishing much used at Versailles. Felix loved Versailles, for which he was the most entertaining and rewarding guide. John Fowler's Versailles was that of Marie Antoinette at the end of the eighteenth century: Felix Harbord was happier with Le Grand Monarque.

From such grandeur to my little dwelling in Oxfordshire is a big leap. But it is so much part of Moi now that I must introduce it very soon. Its development is the development of my taste and the influences which formed it.

If I take you to Langford you have to meet my sister. I have told earlier how much I value family life. A bachelor has to nurture it: it does not have the cast of characters, the mum and dad and the kiddies, of the average domestic scene.

My sister Rosemary was christened Rosemary Peggy. Rosemary was chosen because my maternal grandmother was called Rose, my mother Mary. My father insisted that he wanted a girl to call Peggy. He called her Peg, as did the family. To the world however she is Rosemary.

As I was six years older and a male, as I escaped to school, to France and Germany to work, then to London into the world of fashion and the arts, I became very much the leader. I was thirty, my sister twenty-four when our mother died. My father's second wife made him comfortable: but she always seemed restless and unsettled.

There were many things that united my sister and me. We complement each other. There is a small good side of me which could be called intellectual: with a little more application I could become a scholar. Peg would never be that. Great commonsense is her main attribute, and good application to practical problems. My father loved her deeply and she him. It was the classic pattern: mother likes son, father likes daughter.

I knew that it would be good for my sister to get away from a dull suburban life into the wider intellectual world of Berlin and encouraged her to follow in my footsteps to the Pfarrhaus in Bendorf. From there she went to Berlin where she lived with a family who did much to broaden her outlook and intellect. Our knowledge of Germany, its culture and history, has been a great bond between us. Seeking to carve a way of life on her return from her year's stay in Berlin, Peg helped Alexis in his shop. This again was an education.

Immediately after the war my sister joined the overseas section of the Women's Voluntary Services whose members were running mobile canteens, and clubs for the 'other ranks' of His Majesty's Forces. She served in Italy, Greece, Austria, Hong Kong, Malaya and finally in Germany. In Malaya and Germany her talents in administration and the ability to handle people were used to the full and this experience was to be of great benefit to my business in Savile Row,. By 1960 I needed help with the running of Hardy Amies Ltd where the number on the staff was over 100 – ninety per cent of which were women. I was therefore delighted to have Rosemary as my personnel and administrative manager. She worked very closely with Stanley Cox, my Company Secretary whom she greatly admired. I was lucky to have him on my staff – a man of practical Christian standards and integrity coupled with a respect for business procedures in general and a knowledge of the often slightly dotty trading habits of the *haute couture*. Stanley Cox remained with me at Savile Row until he reached retirement age in 1976. I shall always be indebted to him for his loyalty and help from the earliest days. London life held little enchantment for my sister whose heart has always been in the country. When I sold part of my business to Hepworths I was able to give Rosemary a little capital. With this she bought a cottage in an Oxfordshire village on the fringe of the Cotswolds to which she hastened every weekend. I had originally hoped my sister would buy a small flat or house in London so that she would continue to help in Savile Row and oversee the running of my household in London.

I was living in the five-storey house at 17b Eldon Road, happy with my garden and my tennis at Queen's Club at the weekends. Ken Fleetwood had his own flat in the basement. A loyal and decent Italian couple looked after us. There was a guest bedroom and bathroom. The rooms were planned for modest entertaining: dinners for ten were part of the routine of the house, which was not disturbed by a party for twenty. I was free to accept invitations for the weekend in the country if I wished for a change. I had experienced the strain of the journey to one's own place during the years with Alexis and Anne in Kent and Essex.

I was sure that I would never let myself be trapped into the burden of the responsibility of a place in the country. But I fell: I fell for a very modest but well-proportioned schoolhouse in my sister's village; built of Cotswold stone in 1840. It was Victorian, but the stone transoms of the latticed windows were of the style of the seventeenth century in true Cotswold tradition.

The reasons for my being trapped into owning a new home were several. The house, 17b Eldon Road, belonged to Hardy Amies Ltd.

When I sold part and later the whole of my business, I knew that however friendly were my relations with the new proprietors, I did not have a dwelling which was entirely mine. I was also aware that I was no longer young. My sister and I, always close friends, began to feel very dependent on each other. What pleasanter than to be in the same village and to have one's favourite oak furniture and stone floors kept polished by Mrs Lafford and Mrs Jones? Another reason – by no means the least important – was the charm of the building. It had not been used as a school since 1934. Nothing had been done to spoil it. The price asked by the owner was ridiculously small. Its siting was such that there was sunshine all day long. A narrow garden protected the front from the quiet village street: behind, grey walls enclosed a small plot, originally the school playground, now an untidy village garden alive with enough flowers and vegetables to proclaim excellent soil.

There were two schoolrooms joined at an angle. Attached but not connected was the minute cottage of the schoolmistress. A steep staircase led up to a tiny room, the only bedroom. It was the size of the main schoolroom which literally beguiled me. Nearly thirty feet long and half as wide, it was so high-ceilinged as to give the room almost the elegance of a double cube.

This book has a chance of living if it is considered seriously a record of taste and fashion over the past fifty years. My redesigning and furnishing of a modest property in an out-of-the-way Oxfordshire village (two miles outside the Cotswolds proper) was an act of importance to me. It was a statement of personal taste.

I have been close friends with many interior decorators: Alexis ffrench, John Fowler, Felix Harbord, Micky Raymond (part of the John Fowler team), Tom Parr, who guided the John Fowler business tactfully and successfully through the last years of John Fowler's illness, David Hicks, a designer independent enough to turn away from the John Fowler school without losing some of its best qualities, and Billy Baldwin, the distinguished American decorator of whom I once said in reply to a remark about how well we seemed to get on, 'You see, Billy was born a gentleman and became a decorator, I was born a dressmaker and became a gentleman.' They all have helped me. I do not think that anyone is clever enough to do without the professional advice of a decorator. Cost is important to almost everyone and a good decorator can help you avoid wasting money on mistakes.

Alexis was at my side for the flats in Pont Street, Chesham Place, and for the tiny house at 22 Eldon Road. Micky Raymond and I worked in happy harmony at 17b Eldon Road. We converted a magnificently well-built house of 1880 into a sunlit background for modern pictures and eighteenth-century furniture (as early as I could afford) of strong design. We restored with loving care the window frames and doorcases, the staircase, the folding doors made of Columbian pine and teak. I was leaving Marie Antoinette and the Regent for William and Mary.

I sold my business to Debenhams just before I bought the schoolhouse at Langford. I gave a little of the sum I received to my sister and to Ken Fleetwood. The rest I took to Warburgs, the bankers. 'Give us only a third,' they said. 'Spend a third on property, and the last third on furniture.' I did just that. I changed the tiles of the schoolhouse from Victorian slate to Cotswold stone. I built two bedrooms and three bathrooms. Ken Fleetwood, with his usual modesty took the schoolmistress's tiny room for himself.

The conversion of the Old School was carried out by local labour – men who understood how to build in stone – but a great deal of co-ordination was required and there was need for someone to be on the spot who could interpret my taste and ideas. Once again I was lucky to have my sister close at hand. Her cottage is almost next door to me. Here she lives with a friend from the wvs days (they have shared a home for over twenty-five years) and continues to help with the day to day running of my house and garden and often helps me to entertain the many friends and business acquaintances who come to see me here.

The Old School allowed me, at last, to have furniture made of oak. It was a long way from Alexis's disparaging remarks about it. The colour entrances me. It is a mixture of black, dark brown, olive green and honey. The thought that quite modestly-priced pieces of furniture have been in family use for over three hundred years moves me deeply.

I see the seventeenth century as a time when cultural life was not yet dominated by the city. I am still fascinated by cities. I love London. I am exicted by New York, and always betwitched by Paris: but I am really only at rest in my heart in the country. I must, however, in fairness add that life in the country would be dull indeed if I couldn't enjoy in peace the town-made pleasures of printed books, chats on the telephone, endless gramophone playing, Radio Three and occasionally that old box.

Anne ffrench's encouragement to read English history in general, Mollie Buccleuch's pointing the way to the Stuarts, the Winter Queen's connections with Germany, the home of so much youthful experience, all contributed to Langford. A portrait of a lady, bought quickly one lunchtime at Christie's, turned out to be that of Catherine of Braganza. Another piece of luck was finding Mary of Modena, quite clearly an authentic copy of the picture by Rigaud at Sizergh Castle.

My garden is of considerable importance to me. I believe that we are just coming out of an epoch in which the herbaceous border dominated the scene. I don't think anybody would want to make a new garden today featuring an herbaceous border. Something on a smaller scale would be desirable.

The most elegant small gardens are those which form parts of the estate of a manor house at the end of the seventeenth century. The grander the garden, the more such 'compartments' you had. I think there is today a very great interest in individual flowers moving away from the old fashioned mass of colour! To achieve style in a small space you need very careful planning. I see a return to formality in gardening. Rosemary Verey, who since I became a neighbour in the country, and since she has so generously offered her advice with my own little garden, has become a great friend, says categorically that she believes in the reintroduction of formality into garden design so strongly that she is stocking the shop in her garden with as many box shrubs, clipped into shapes, as she can obtain.

My home – my base – is now in Oxfordshire. The village where I live contains many enthusiastic gardeners and a strong bond is therefore forged between us. From her house at Bampton, until her death in 1982, Peggy Münster, whose taste in flowers was as impeccable as should be that of a patroness of John Fowler, gave constant encouragement. My sister has quite simply very green fingers. I just do my best.

When I go to New York I travel by Concorde. It takes exactly six hours from my flat in New York to my house in Oxfordshire. I love going to New York: it's the greatest tonic. The effect of tonics, however, wears off, and after two or three weeks I am very happy indeed to be met at Heathrow by my chauffeur, who drives me back to my Oxfordshire village. There I find my sister, who has seen that the central heating is working, and Helen, my housekeeper, who has arranged for the deep freeze to be filled. Snatched away from her village on the German-Polish borders at the age of nineteen, she never returned and it has taken many years of working in England to restore a tiny grain of faith in humanity into Helen's battered soul. I have managed to buy a cottage for her (dated 1774, it was challenge to restore it). So splendid is the display of flowers in her garden that she earns more compliments than I do for mine. She is a compulsive and natural cook.

I have managed to buy a hard tennis court. It was placed on a plot of land which was originally a farmyard. There was a barn attached to which were some stables. After living at The Old School for a few years, I had the idea that it would be pleasant to convert the barn into a guest house. I was able to make two bedrooms, two bathrooms and a tiny kitchen. The latter was for guests to make their breakfasts independently. The barn itself became a really rather elegantly-proportioned living room. There was room for many books. A gramophone had a beautiful tone and it could be played very loudly without disturbing the neighbours. A large log fire was not only cosy in winter but provided comfort after a hard game of tennis. It is a super pav.

I have played tennis seriously for thirty years – that is to say since I was forty. I have had many lessons. I have a very accurate eye. For nearly five years Steve Newman, who is a young professional coach, comes every Saturday and often on Sunday as well. He is a born teacher with perfect manners. I don't have many lessons now. It's nearly too late to learn any more. Steve partners me in doubles. I still have a very weak backhand, but he has enormously improved my volleying. He has made me so accurate in serving that I can land a ball on three tennis ball boxes placed by Steve in either the forehand or the backhand corner. I record all this not to show off but to encourage anyone either to take up a sport or not to neglect one already started. It's impossible to record the fun I've had from tennis. The automatic functioning of brain control over the direction of the ball to the spot you can only see in your mind's eye has an eternal appeal.

Lest it should be felt that I am being unduly hearty, I have to mention that there is a similar satisfaction in placing a needle in the correct square on a canvas of needlepoint. I often smile at myself getting on a plane to Tokyo or Sydney with two tennis rackets under one arm and with a travel bag containing a piece of needlepoint on the other.

In London I now have a flat in Cornwall Gardens. It is within spitting distance of my previous two houses in Eldon Road. I love the area because it has many trees and because I suppose I am used to it. The flat has one well-proportioned, south facing living room. Here I can relax of an evening and entertain three friends: the dining table is uncomfortable for more than four. It is only seldom a hardship to be selective. There is a bedroom and bathroom for me and another for James. James is a rarity: a totally professional manservant. Chosen six years ago by a secretary, we discovered that he had been trained at Buckingham Palace. Mr Gulbenkian once said that at an ideal dinner he only wanted one other person present – a good *maître d'hôtel*. I am happy to share a flat with James. Naturally he packs and polishes to perfection. He has learnt to be very interested in food and cooks it extremely well. We part company after lunch on Friday and are happy to see each other again on Monday morning. James comes with us when we go to New York. So I am able to entertain our licensee friends and members of the press in style at the flat.

The maintenance of a flat in New York and the bringing over of one's own manservant may sound awfully grand. We believe in the long run that it's cheaper than hotels. I am also pleased to be independent of restaurants. With very rare exceptions, mostly in France, I have found it excessively fatiguing to eat in restaurants. It is the part I dislike most in travelling. It is a rare hostess who can understand that one would much prefer a poached egg in her kitchen.

The description of my way of life I have tried to give in this book would perhaps indicate that I have had a certain amount of success. I do not fool myself that it is anything but modest; I have not amassed a fortune. I have achieved a way of life that is comfortable and civilized: comfortable enough to avoid unnecessary fatigue (when I travel it's *en prince*, and at home I don't have to wash up), civilized in the sense that I can buy what books and records I want and can go to the opera. I note this with gratitude but also with the hope of inspiring the young.

It is time to mention one's mistakes. If I had my time again I would like to have become thoroughly proficient in the techniques of my trade. I would like to have learnt to cut and sew to perfection. Starting as I did at twenty-four, I ought to have stopped after a year or so and left Lachasse and gone to a trade school or college of art. The quality of my needlepoint convinces me that I would have been a good tailor.

Secondly, as soon as I achieved independence I ought to have worked to gain premises on either a very long lease or freehold in which to have my business. The excuse that the house at 14 Savile Row must always be on lease because of the family trust to which it belongs is not good enough. The charm of the eighteenth century house has been of enormous help: as was the Savile Row address when I started to work in the men's trade. Tolerant and courteous as are my landlords, I have been at the mercy of huge increases in rent and rates. The houses at 22 and 17b Eldon Road were both freehold properties. They were bought by the firm for me to live in. We ought to have spent the money on business premises.

On the other hand, these houses were backgrounds against which I developed myself. There are several stories in this book. One is that of a boy from a suburban family who climbed out of a nondescript background into a place in *Who's Who*. I've seen a great deal of the world: so much that it's easier to enumerate where I haven't been – South America, China, Russia and India. I am quite at home in any major city in Europe. I have not paid enough attention to painting. I am attracted by colour and design and I can appreciate good drawing: but my mind is too superficial to penetrate into the heart of a good picture. Perhaps it's just a question of time. One needs time to study a picture, just as I need time to study an opera.

There hasn't been enough time. There have been new countries, new cities, new buildings and new landscapes to see. There has been a new stratum of society into which I have risen quite automatically and unself-consciously. It has been fun. The best people aren't always the nicest people, but they're often the most interesting. 17b Eldon Road was a good house for entertaining. I enjoyed organizing dinner parties. I was only a moderately enthusiastic social climber. The true social alpinist is a dedicated person. He's hopeless if he has a place of his own in the country: he should always be free to take part in

37 The classic man's blazer, 1983 (*Christopher Moore*)

38 The Queen wearing the yellow coat and spotted dress that we made for her Mexican tour in 1975 and which she later wore for the Jubilee firework display

39 Mrs Ronald Reagan and the Queen in the Californian poppy dress at the party given in her honour at Twentieth Century Fox, Hollywood, February 1983 (*Anwar Hussein*)

40 Two trouser suits made for the Packer International Collection, 1983 (*Christopher Moore*)

41 Double breasted white silk coat from the Hardy Amies Ready-to-Wear Collection, 1983
(*Christopher Moore*)

My first three London residences, designed by Alexis ffrench:
42 Pont Street, SW1, 1934, 43 22 Eldon Road, W8, 1953, 44 Chesham Place, SW1, 1941

45 The garden at Langford (*Georges Lévêque*)

46 The famous drawing-room in my house at 17b Eldon Road, w8, designed by Michael
Raymond of Colefax & Fowler in 1969

47 My house at Langford (*Alex Starkey*)

fascinating weekends anywhere in the world. My greatest drawback is
that I am a *couche-tôt*, I am at my best in the early morning. I believe the
world to be divided into *matinales* and night birds, just as it is into
smearers and polishers. I am a polisher.

After 11 o'clock I start to think of my bed and book. I have enjoyed
the dinner party: I have admired the decorations of the ball: I have
cased the joint with my dinner partner on my arm: I have danced with
her and with the lady who was on my left at dinner: I have danced with
my dinner hostess. I have chatted with some old friends. I have had a
good look at the dresses, so that I can report back to Ken the next
morning – who was looking nice in our dresses – or who was just
looking nice. That's it.

This is of course quite wrong. I ought to stay and try to contribute
something to the party: dance and talk and above all laugh until at least
1 a.m. Peter Coats says that most of the really interesting things
happen at about 2 a.m. Peter Coats has been a good guide to me on the
upper slopes of the social hills; we share an interest in gardening and in
history. We are both fascinated by the way people behave. Peter is
most generous in giving introductions to people he thinks will turn
into friends. His biggest success was with Rosemary and David
Verey.

Angus Menzies, who ran the decorating department of The General
Trading Company very successfully until his pathetically early death
in a road accident, lived in Chesham Place, where I had a flat during
the war. Angus introduced me to Loelia, Duchess of Westminster
later to become Lady Lindsay, who was as keen on canasta as she now
is on gardening, opera and friendship. A superb needlewoman, she
encouraged my needlepoint. She persuaded me to interest myself in
the affairs of the Royal School of Needlework. Alas! I am ashamed
that I have given so little time to that much underrated institution.

Loelia was then and still is, a figure of today. For me she was an
unquenchable source of information on the manners of the past. She
told me, when considering the manners of the Bright Young Things
of the twenties, not to forget that although the skirts of ball dresses
only came to the knees that you still never went out in the evening
without elbow length white gloves of the finest kid, which fastened
with twenty four buttons. It was Leolia who introduced me to Kitty
Miller.

Kitty was a great hostess of the new school. She had establishments in London and New York: a house in the country in England: a house in Majorca: and each winter rented a house in Palm Springs or Palm Beach, which would accommodate comfortably a staff of butler, chef, chauffeur and lady's maid: and of course a handful of guests to keep them busy.

Kitty was exceptionally well brought up. She spoke perfect French and was as much at home in Paris as she was in London or New York. There was nothing in her houses or her wardrobe that was not in perfect taste: just a little too perfect to be really stylish. Kitty and her husband Gilbert enjoyed their social success enormously. 'Do you know what the Duke of Kent calls Kitty?' asked Gilbert of a group of guests, 'no' we said breathless with expectation. 'Kitty' replied Gilbert. During one of my early visits to New York, Gilbert died. I had a call from Kitty asking me to go with her to the funeral. I was produced as an old English friend. It was my social début in New York.

Although I had just acquired my New York flat I had no James in those days and it was pleasant to join what was always an interesting party at Kitty's. Diana Vreeland, surely one of the most famous fashion journalists of all time, lived in the same building, and was often there. As was Bill Blass, the nicest man by far in the American fashion industry; also Josephine Hughes, the doyenne of the New York *vendeuses*.

Kitty Miller was a gloriously self-centred woman. But she was a great hostess of the new international school. As she had not the security of position given to those born of good blood, being a Jewish banking heiress, she made up for it by real hard work. She carried herself well and wore clothes with a rare grace; she could discuss furs with the most skilled and knowledgeable furriers, and chose her clothes from the Paris collections with a professional eye.

To watch her organize a party was to see a general at work. I greatly treasured her friendship for the insight it gave me into the workings of the mind of a chic woman. She helped me to establish myself in the *monde* which gravitates between London and New York.

I am nearly finished with the portrait of myself. I present it and my life to you because I think it might be amusing to show what can be done with a boy from the suburbs with a little bit of talent. I must show some of the results. I think that very often much too much fuss is made about dress designers and their lives. We are tradespeople, shop-keepers and artisans and should be respected as such. Yet we are designers: we have to sense the tastes of today and foresee those of the future. We are mirrors of the age.

I love seeing and being in fashionable life. But I won't be its slave – out of business hours. My life with my sister among the grey stone roofs and the pink roses in Oxfordshire is more important than anything, except my business which gives me the means of keeping my house there.

I love going back to Germany. I treasure my friendship with Bridget Bernstorff who in the 1930s worked with John Fowler and remained his and my friend. Now the widowed Countess Bernstorff, still the *châtelaine* of a charming small country estate near Hamburg, she lived, an Englishwoman, all through the war in Germany. On her first visit to London after the war, she brought to luncheon with me a charming Englishwoman and her very endearing German husband. They were the Prince and Princess of Hesse. Peg Hesse, born the daughter of Lord Geddes – formerly Sir Auckland Geddes – had also gone through the war in Germany and had thus formed a close friendship with Bridget.

Also widowed, Peg now has still more of her time for giving pleasure to her friends and the supporting of all the charities and institutions for which she is responsible. After forty years of friendship, I am still realizing how grand she is. Before the war she would have been a Grand Duchess. She still is a Royal Highness. Her husband Louis was a great grandson of Queen Victoria, his grand-mother being Princess Alice, Queen Victoria's favourite daughter. The wedding was planned for November 1937. The aeroplane bringing the members of the Hesse family to the wedding crashed at Ostend. There were killed the widowed Dowager Grand Duchess, the new Grand Duke (Peg's brother-in-law), his wife and two children. In one fatal moment Peg and her fiancé became hereditary Grand Duke and Duchess of Hesse and by Rhine.

I tell this story in the barest terms. I would have liked to follow Peg's example in never speaking of it. But Peg Hesse's triumph over the tragedy of this terrible accident and the shadow it cast, particularly in view of the family's previous devastation at Ekaterinburg in 1918, add so immeasurably to the scale of the nobility of her character that I have to record it. Today there is not, in my opinion, one cloud of tragedy in the sunny sky of her being. She has a truly great heart. The nicest words said to me this year were those of Peg Hesse: 'I feel as though you, your sister Rosemary and Ken were part of my family.' It was after a happy holiday spent together in a beautiful castle in Switzerland owned by Peg. Bridget Bernstorff was, of course, there too.

I have just finished reading, for the fourth time, Proust's *A La Recherche du Temps Perdu*.

My *temps* is almost *retrouvé*. Bridget Bernstorff is a friend because I admire her courage and the orderliness and sense of style. (I wish I could remember exactly what Edith Wharton said when asked what she admired most in life. It was something like 'Order, justice and the love of dogs'.) But what makes her friendship treasured is that we not only feel happy together today but because she is so much part of my past of forty years ago: when I was learning about life with Alexis ffrench and John Fowler.

The years 1928–1930, which I spent in the Pfarrhaus in Bendorf-am-Rhine and which ended with my twenty-first birthday, were like the years spent at a university. I can forgive old Herr Pfarrer von Claer his snobbery and the hurts he inflicted on me, when I remember how pleased he was when I liked my first opera, *The Magic Flute*.

How interested Jonny Witte and Herr Pfarrer would be to know that through Peg Hesse I have glimpsed the independence of a great art-loving Grand Duke – Peg's father-in-law: and that I am aware of childless Peg Hesse's plans to make Prince Moritz of Hessen-Cassel her heir, thus uniting Hessen-Darmstadt with Hessen-Cassel after a break since 1567.

I cannot help it if I am thought a snob to recount all this. I have to repeat that I felt an outsider in Germany in 1930: that in 1984, over fifty years afterwards, I feel I am inside. The closed door figures sometimes in my rare nightmares. Love locked out is the saddest thing I know.

Now I stand before you, dear reader, sometimes stripped down to my underpants, sometimes a little too carefully dressed to achieve true style: trusting that if I record achievements with pride it is not with a lack of modesty but with a sense of gratitude for minor gifts carefully used. This is for those of my generation.

The young I want to encourage to work so that they can have the means to enjoy 'an intense savour of the quality of all that you come across in literature and drama and music and life'.★

There is still much for me to do. Between the writing and the publication of this book I shall have gone to Tokyo, Seoul (where there are Koreans hot with desire for Hardy Amies ties), Hong Kong, Auckland, Sydney, Melbourne, San Antonio in Texas and home to New York. I shall have to discuss the colours and shapes of all kinds of men's and women's clothes.

In London we have just launched a collection of women's night-dresses and dressing gowns: in a month's time there will burst on an expectant world our first collection of women's day clothes made in Italy. Everybody in 14 Savile Row is busy. I have the feeling that I'm very much STILL HERE.

★ From a letter from George Lyttleton to James Agate on p. 298 of *Ego I*.

Index

Abyssinia, 29
Aden, 97
Agate, James, 185n
Aldershot, 31
Alice, Princess, Countess of Athlone, 153–4, 183
Allen, Violet, 37, 39, 49, 52–3, 84
Alperton, 2–4
America *see* USA
America, South *see* South America
Amies, Edwin (HA's grandfather), 1–2, 162
Amies, Hardy: starts at Lachasse, xiii, 22; born, 1–3; childhood visits to Miss Gray Ltd., 3–4; at school, 5–7; and his mother, 8–10; in France, 10–12; in Germany, 13–17; career choice, 16–17; works for Avery, 17–20; beginnings as a designer, 22–7; and House of Worth, 26, 37–9, 49; in Army, 30–48; leaves Lachasse, 33–4; recognised as designer by Board of Trade, 33–4, 40; first uses own label, 34–5; sets up on his own, 49–57; early successes, 58–60; staff difficulties, 61–3; establishes Boutique, 64–5; designs men's ready-to-wear, 67–9; in association with Debenhams, 70–75; honoured by Queen, 74; and sole ownership of Hardy Amies Ltd., 74–83; dressmaker to Queen, 84–122; flat in New York, 123; and foreign outlets, 124–36; designs uniforms, 136–9; and new areas of design, 139–42; on fashion, 143–60; personal life, 161–85; *Just So Far*, xiii
Amies, Herbert William (HA's father), 1–9, 11–12, 16, 27–8, 50–51, 163, 173
Amies, Mary (*née* Hardy; HA's mother), xiii, 1–12, 27–8, 51, 58, 88, 95, 162, 173
Amies, Mary, (HA's stepmother), 50
Amies, Rosemary Peggy (HA's sister), 4–5, 9, 28, 100, 173–6, 184
Ann (at Lachasse), 22
Anne (Henderson), (telephonist at Hardy Amies Ltd.), 80
Antibes, France, 8, 10–11, 29
Aquascutum, 126
Arisaig, 40
Aston, 17
Auckland, New Zealand, 132, 185
austerity measures: effects on design, 39–40, 85, 144
Australia, 73, 87, 89, 97, 111–3, 124, 130–31
Austria, 28, 164, 173
Avery, W & T., 17–20
Avignon, France, 11
Aykroyd, Sir Alfred Hammond, 66
Aykroyd, Sir William Miles, 66

Baden-Baden, Germany, 16
Baldwin, Billy, 175
Balenciaga, Cristóbal, 146–7
Ballard, Bettina, 146
Balmain, Pierre, 105
Barker (1920s correspondent of *Sunday Times*), 12
Barking, 5
Barrington, Fitz, 32
Bayreuth, Germany, 170
Beard, Mabel, 57–8
Beard, Maud, 4, 57–8, 95
Beaulieu Abbey, 35–6, 39

Becontree, 5, 7–8
bedlinen: HA designs, 139–40
Beethoven, Ludwig van, 16
Belgium, 7, 17, 40–41
Bell, Diana, 131
Belle, Jim Cleveland, 169
Bendel, Henri, 34–5
Bendorf-am-Rhein, Germany, 13–14, 28, 101, 173, 184
Bergdorf, Goodman, 123
Berger, Irving, 129
Berkley Shirts, 128
Berlin, Germany, 14, 16, 173
Bernstorff, Bridget, Countess (formerly Bridget Gilligan), 165, 183–4
Binder Hamlyn Ltd., 70
Birmingham, 17, 149
Blass, Bill, 126, 140, 182
blazers, 156; see also jackets
Blumenfeld, R. D., 7–8, 16
Board of Trade, the, 33–4, 40, 124
Bohan, Marc, 104–5
Bonn, Germany, 13, 100
Bonser, Harry, 65
Borg, Björn, 159
Boston, USA, 58
Brioni, (Italian designer), 126
Brisbane, Australia, 113
Bristol, 78
Britannia (yacht), 97, 116–7, 119–21
British Airways, 136–7
British European Airways, 136; see also British Airways
Britten, Benjamin, Gloriana, 88
Brouwnstein, Gré, 169
Brühl, Schloss, 100
Brunhoff, Michel de, 64
Brussels, Belgium, 14, 44–6, 49, 53
Bourne & Hollingsworth, 34, 36–7
Brentwood School, 5–7
Brockenhurst, 35
Buccleuch, Jane, Duchess of (formerly the Countess of Dalkeith; née McNeill), 152–3
Buccleuch, Mary (Mollie), Duchess of, 152, 177
Buckingham Palace, 87–90, 93, 113, 179
Burberry, 126

Burney, Lady (formerly Mrs Parr), 69–70
Burney, Sir Anthony, 70, 72

California, USA, 54, 116, 120–22, 125
Cambridge, 6–7
Cambridge Clothing Co., 132
'Cammie' see Campbell, Miss
Campbell, Miss ('Cammie'), 37–9, 49, 51–3, 56, 59, 61–3, 84, 146
Campbell Nelson, Mr (accountant), 66
Canada, 58–9, 63, 65–6, 73, 84, 124, 129–30; see also individual towns
Canberra, Australia, 113
Cannes, France, 56
Cardin, Pierre, 65, 105, 126, 140, 158
Carnegie, Hattie, 146
Cattel, Derek, 80
Cayman Islands, 113
Cerutti, (Italian designer), 126
Chanel, 50, 149–50
'chapeaux de la Résistance', 46–7
Chaplin, Charlie, City Lights, 49
Chappells (music publishers), 168
Chapple, Elsie, 2
Charles, Prince of Wales, 112, 159
Chelsea, Viscount, 73
Cherrill, Virginia see Jersey, Countess of (Mrs Florek Martini)
Chicago, USA, 54, 58–9, 124–5
China, 180
Chopin, Frederic, 146
Christoff, Boris, 169
City of London Yeomanry, 4
Claer, Ernst von, 13, 28, 162, 173, 184
Claer, Frau Ernst von, 13, 28, 162, 173
Clarence House, 85, 89
Clemenz August, Prince, 100
coats: for Princess Elizabeth, 85–6
Coats, Peter, 171, 181
Coblenz, Germany, 13, 15–16, 102, 169
Colefax, Sibyl, 165
Cologne, Germany, 14–16, 65
Colorado, USA, 125
Como, Italy, 65, 82
Cook, Miss, 4
Cook, Captain James, 132
Cooper, Gary, 110
Coppley, Noyes & Randall, 129–30
Corfe, 32

Cornforth, John, 165, 167
Costa Rica, 2
Country Life (magazine), 165
Courrèges, André, 147–8
Covent Garden, 169–70
Cox, Stanley, 58, 174
Crabtree, Eric, 66–7, 69, 72, 126–7
Cresta Ltd., 69
Cripps, Sir Stafford, 145
Cumberland, 48, 50

Daily Express (newspaper), 7, 101
Dalkeith, Richard, Earl of, 152–3
Dalkeith, Countess of *see* Buccleuch, Duchess of
Dalkeith, Countess of (*née* Lady Elizabeth Kerr), 153
Dartmouth, Countess of *see* Spencer, Countess
David Jones, 130–31
David, Mollie, 11
Davis, Anne Taylor, 127
Day, Kate, 91
Debenhams, 66, 69–76, 176
Debenham & Freebody Ltd., 70
Degenfeld, Gräfin, 163–4
Detroit, USA, 59
Diana, Princess of Wales (*formerly* Lady Diana Spencer), 112, 152, 159
Diatobo, 107, 133, 136
Dickens, Charles, *Bleak House*, 166
Dietrich, Marlene, 110
Dior, Christian, 60, 85, 91, 144–6
Dior, House of, 60, 81, 85, 105
Don Carlos (opera), 169
Dora (Hoare) (stock-keeper at Hardy Amies Ltd.), 81
Dorking, 2
Douglas, Norman, xiii–xiv
Dullin, Charles, 12
Dunkirk, France, 31–2
Duparc, Henri, 169
Durrant, Madame, 2–3, 10
Düsseldorf, Germany, 14–15

Egerton, Lady Alice, 84
Egerton, Lady Susan (later Askew), 84
Ehrenbreitstein (fortress), 102
Elizabeth, Princess *see* Elizabeth II, Queen of England

Elizabeth the Queen Mother, 105
Elizabeth II, Queen of England, xiii, 63, 66, 80, 84–122, 129, 147–8, 159
Ellesmere, Countess of, 84
England, 7, 12–13, 46, 97, 113–4, 139, 145, 159, 164, 182
Enkin, Max, 129–30
Ernest, Mr (tailor), 24, 52, 60–62, 81, 94, 146
Ernst August of Hanover, Prince, 172
Essex, 5, 163, 168
Evans, Dame Edith, 142

Fabian, Tibor, 132
Fairchild, John, 124
Fashion Group, 37
Fath, Jacques, 65
Fauré, Gabriel, 168
ffrench, Mrs (*née* Thursby; Alexis' mother), 164
ffrench, Alexis, 28, 50–1, 55–6, 139, 163–70, 172, 174–6, 184
ffrench, Anne, 163–6, 168, 170, 174
ffrench, Conrad, 164
ffrench, Yvonne, 164, 166
Fidelio (opera), 170
Fiji, 97
Finnie, Sergeant, 31
First World War *see* World War I
Fleetwood, Ken, 71, 77–83, 96, 103–4, 113–6, 120, 135, 150–3, 174, 176, 184
Florence, Italy, 166
Floris, Madame, 59
'*flou*': nature of design, 26, 151
Fothergill, Ted, 53, 56
Fowler, John, 55, 139, 165–7, 172, 175, 177, 183–4
Fowler, Miss, 4, 58
Fox, Freddie, 91, 104, 107–8, 112
France, 7–8, 10–12, 17, 21, 27, 56, 72, 76, 81, 98–9, 102–6, 162, 164; *see also* individual areas and towns
Frankfurt, Germany, 14

Galitzine, Prince Yurka, 67–8
Garland, Madge, 34
Gaskell, Mrs Elizabeth, 164
Geddes, Sir Auckland, 183
General Trading Company, the, 181
Genesco Ltd., 68, 125–7

George VI, King of England, 86, 97, 146
Germany, xiii, 7–8, 13–17, 21, 27, 47, 81, 99–102, 162, 164, 174, 177, 183–4; *see also* individual towns
Gilligan, Bridget *see* Bernstorff, Bridget, Countess
Gillson, Mrs Dickie, 50
Gilmour, Lady Caroline (*formerly* Lady Caroline Montagu-Douglas-Scott), 152
Gilmour, Sir Ian, 152
Givenchy, Hubert de, 126
Glasgow, 149
Glyndebourne, 142, 170
Goethe, J. W. von, 15
Goold, Michael, 140
Grafton Duchess of, 120
Graham, Sarah, 80
Grant, Cary, 49
Gray, Miss *see* Shingleton, Mrs Fred
Greece, 173
Greif, David, 127–8
Greif Companies, 124, 128
Grodin's, 114
Gulbenkian, Nubar, 179

H. & M. Rayne Ltd., 70
Haggard, Rider, 6
Hallam, Henry, 6
Hamburg, Germany, 14, 16
Hampshire, 35
Harbord, Felix, 172, 175
Hardy, Mary (HA's grandmother), 2, 173
Hardy Amies Ltd.: established, 49–57; early successes, 58–60; and ready-to-wear, 64–5, 67–9; given Royal Warrant, 66, 87, 93; in association with Debenhams, 70–75; solely owned by HA, 74–83; foreign outlets, 124–42; wedding dresses, 136; Rosemary Amies helps run, 174; *see also* Amies, Hardy
Harpers (magazine), 24
Harrods, 71
Hartnell, Norman, 87–8, 93, 99, 102, 105, 116, 145, 148
Harvey Nichols, 71–2, 74
Havinden, Margaret, 37

Hayden, Howard, 6–8
Heine, Heinrich, 15
Henry Morgan, 59
Hepworths Ltd., 66–9, 73, 125, 132, 141, 155–6
Hesse family, 183
Hesse, Louis, Prince of, 183
Hesse, Princess Margaret (Peg), (*née* Geddes), 183–4
Hicks, David, 175
Hinds-Howell, Dick, 51
Hinterhör, Germany, 163
Hollywood, USA, 114, 116, 118–9
Hong Kong, 173, 185
Houghton-Brown, Geoffrey, 51
Hudson Neckwear Co., 129
Hughes, Josephine, 182
Hussein, King of Jordan, 121
Hussey, Lady Susan, 120

I. Magnin, 54, 125
Incorporated Society of London Fashion Designers, 37, 39, 144
India, 180
Israel, 69
Italy, 17, 72, 76, 81, 110, 164–5, 173; *see also* individual towns

jackets: HA lengthens, 25; *see also* blazers; suits
Jaeger, 126
Jamaica, 113, 115–6
James (Donahue), (manservant), 179, 182
Japan, 73, 106–7, 124, 133–6
Jardin des Modes, le (magazine), 64
jeans: and development of fashion, 156–7, 160; *see also* trousers
Jersey, Earl of, 50
Jersey, Virginia, Countess of (Virginia Cherrill), 49–51
Johns, Commander Philip, 43–4
Jones, Mrs, 175
Jonny *see* Witte, Johann
Juan-les-Pins, France, 11

Karlsruhe, Germany, 17
Katsura (river), 135
Katsura Palace, 135
Kaunda, Kenneth, 121

Kennedy, Mrs Jackie, 104, 147
Kent, 1, 4, 163, 167–8
Kent, Duke of, 182
Kenya, 86, 97
Kerr, Lady Elizabeth see Dalkeith, Countess of
Kim (McManus) (in charge of sales ledger at Hardy Amies Ltd.), 80
Kingston, 2
Kipling, Rudyard, 6
King, Viva, xiii
Klemperer, Otto von, 170
Knobloch, Eddie, 165
Knox, Betty see Reeves, Betty
Knox, Teddy, 95
Kubrick, Stanley, 142
Kunzer, Margaret, (Mrs Derbe Berry), 165
Kyoto, Japan, 135

Lachasse: HA works at, xiii, 22, 84, 143, 163, 165, 180; establishment of, 21; HA and, 22–7, 30–1, 33–4; HA misses workrooms, 35; Cammie runs, 37; Violet Allen at, 37–8, 57; shared management, 38; sobriety of wartime designs, 46; conditions for HA at, 49; customers at, 50, 70; Ernest at, 52, 81, 94; Victor leaves, 53
Lafford, Mrs, 175
Lammers, Gerda, 169
Langford, 173–7
Lanvin, (French designer), 126
Lauren, Ralph, 126
Le Cannet du Luc, France, 11
Leatherhead, 32
Leclerq, Nina, 28, 59–60, 64
Leda (yacht), 132
Leeds, 67
Legge, Mrs Gerald see Spencer, Countess
Leonard, Mr (tailor), 38–9, 53, 57, 94
Lewisham, Lady see Spencer, Countess
Lilian, Miss (Burfield), (dressmaker), 80, 95, 111
Lindsay, Lady see Westminster, Loelia, Duchess of
Linton, Mr, 50
Linton, Angus, 50

Linton Tweed Mills, 50
Lipson, Jack, 130
Liverpool, 169
Lloyd-Jones, Lady Hannah, 130
Lock, Mr (embroiderer), 77
Lohengrin (opera), 170
London: HA's grandfather visits, 1; HA's mother works in; 2; visits to, 4; and Becontree, 9; trade with Paris, 12; suburbs, 17–18; during 1937 Coronation, 25; bombed, 33; Paquin in, 38, 49; Belgians return from, 45; couture in, 58, 64, 144, 149; Cammie outstanding saleswoman, in, 62; HA in, 78, 176, 185; Rudi Newton in, 81; 'swinging', 160; growing herbs in, 171; Kitty Miller and, 182
London County Council, 4–5, 7, 9
London Hilton, 136
Loose, 1
Los Angeles, USA, 113, 117–9
Lothian, Marchioness of, 153
Lothian, Marquess of, 153
Louie, Aunt see Probet-Piolat, Louise
Louis XV, King of France, 98
Lumley, Kathleen (née Molyneux), 58–9
Lumley, Peter Hope, 59, 100–1, 103–4, 111
Lynn, Oggie, 169
Lyons, France, 75
Lyttelton, George, 185n

Macaulay, Thomas Babington, Lord, 7
McCardell, Claire, 146
MacDonald, Miss (Queen's dresser), 87, 90
McEnroe, John, 159
Machinka's, 3, 10
Macky, Dane, 132
Macky, Elizabeth, 132
McNaughton, General, 32–3
McNeill, Jane see Buccleuch, Jane, Duchess of
Maida Vale, 1–2, 10
Maidstone, 1, 162
Majorca, 182
Malaya, 173–4
Manchester, 41
Mann, Thomas, Buddenbrooks, 166

Manton, Ruth, 128
Margaret, Princess, 84–5
Marie Antoinette, Queen of France, 98, 172
Marlborough, Mary, Duchess of, 145–6, 152
Marlborough, 10th Duke of, 152
Marseilles, France, 11
Marshall Field, 54, 58, 125
Marthe (*vendeuse*), 56–8, 63, 65
Mary, Queen of England, 90, 92
Masterman, J. C., 32
Mastersingers, the (opera), 170
Matsuya, 135
Maugham, Syrie, 145
Maupassant, Guy de, 11
Mauretania (ship), 58
Melbourne, Australia, 131, 185
menswear: HA designs, 125–9; developments in, 154–60; see also Hepworths Ltd.; trousers
Menzies, Angus, 181
Mexico, 106, 113, 116, 119
Meyer, Mrs Montague, 50
Michael, of Carlos Place (previously of Lachasse), 81, 94
Michael, Mr (tailor), 81, 94
Michael, Princess, of Kent, 153–4
Michelsons, 65, 73, 127, 129
Middlesex, 2
Middlesex Hospital, 20
Mihotich, Maria, 133
Mihotich, Maurice, 133
Miller, Gilbert, 182
Miller, Kitty, 164, 181–2
Mintz, Louis, 69
Miss Gray Ltd., 20, 37, 51, 58
Mitla, Mexico, 106
Mitsui & Co., 133
Molyneux, Captain Edward, 58–9, 144–5
Molyneux, House of, 58–9
Molyneux, Kathleen see Lumley, Kathleen
Montreal, Canada, 58–9, 109, 146
Moon, Lilian, 58
Moore, Jon, 78–9
Morar, 40
Moritz, Prince, of Hessen-Cassel, 184

Morley, Austin, 18
Mortimer, Mrs Charlotte, 38, 53
Morton, Digby, 20–24, 37, 143
Moselle (river), 16, 102
Moss Bros, 155, 159
Mozart, Wolfgang Amadeus, 15–16, 146; *The Magic Flute*, 16, 184
Munich, Germany, 28, 102
Münster, Countess Peggy, 177
Myer, Kirsten, 142

Neumann, Balthazar, 101
New Look, the, 47, 85, 144–5
New York, USA; Henri Bendel in, 34; Board of Trade projects sending collection to, 36; wholesale houses in, 54; HA in, 58–9, 77, 111, 113, 116–7, 123–9, 176, 178–9, 185; Queen's visits to, 108–9; buyers from, 146; Kitty Miller and, 182
New Zealand, 73, 111, 124, 131–3
Newman, Steve, 178
Newton, Rudi, 81
Nice, France, 10–11, 56
Norman Hartnell, House of, 119
Norrell, Norman, 146
Norton, the Hon. Kay, 51–2
Nutter, Tommy, 158

Odette, Mlle (fitter), 38–9, 53, 56–7, 63
Odiham, 167
Officiel, l' (newspaper), 65
Ogden, Mrs Sheila, 91, 95, 109, 111
Ouïda, 164
overcoats: designs in '40s, 144; see also coats; tailoring; textiles
Oxford, 7, 19
Oxfordshire, 173–8

Paquin, 38, 49
Paris, France: HA in, xiii, 11–14, 60, 176; *couture* in, 20, 25, 64, 77, 82; Paquin in, 38, 49; Molyneux in, 58, 144; Queen visits, 99; Felix Harbord buried in, 172
Paris Match (magazine), 105–6
Parr, Mrs see Burney, Lady
Parr, Tom, 69, 175
Parsifal (opera), 170
Paulette, House of, 20–23, 38, 52, 57

Pay, Col. (director of Worth), 38, 49, 53, 57
Pebble Beach, 128–9
Pelléas and Mélisande (opera), 169
Peter Grimes (opera), 169; *see also* Britten, Benjamin
Peter Jones, 165
Pfarrhaus *see* Claer, Ernst von; Claer, Frau Ernst von
Philadelphia, USA, 108
Philby, Kim, 35
Philip, Prince, Duke of Edinburgh, 105, 107, 120–21
Phillips, Mrs, 21
Phoenix, 127–8
Pino (Pugliese) (tailor), 81
Pompidou, Mme Jacques, 105
Portsmouth, 97
Probet-Piolat, Louise (Aunt Louie), 10–11, 20, 56
Proust, Marcel, *A La Recherche du Temps Perdu*, 184
Puglia, Italy, 81

Quant, Mary, 147
Queen Elizabeth (ship), 60

Rameau, Jean Philippe, *Les Indes Galantes*, 99
Raymond, Michael, 172, 175–6
Raymonde, Madame (Dunster), (at Hardy Amies Ltd.), 81
Reading, 19
ready-to-wear clothing: HA markets, 64–5; men's, 67–9; and casual clothes, 152
Reagan, Mrs Ronald, 116–7
Reeves, Betty (*later* Mrs Betty Knox), 57, 84–5, 87–8, 91, 95
Renta, Oscar de la, 126
Reville (designer), 38
Rhine (river), 13, 16, 102
Ring, the (opera), 170 *see also* Wagner, Richard
Rita, (Triggs) (dressmaker), 81
Riviera, the French, xiii, 22
Robb (artist on *Daily Express*), 101
Roberts, Michael, 141
Roger, 'Bunny', 66
Roger Kent (chainstores), 126

Rome, Italy, 82, 164
Romney, Edana, 118
Rosenkavalier, the (opera), 170; *see also* Strauss, Richard
Rothschild, Lillian de, 104
Roy (tailor), 80–81
Russell & Allen, 52
Russia, 180

Sacramento, USA, 120
Saint Laurent, Yves, 126; *see also* Yves Saint Laurent, House of
Salzburg, Austria, 170
Samson (opera), 170
San Antonio, USA, 185
San Diego, USA, 113, 117
San Francisco, USA, 114, 116, 119–20, 124
Sandringham, 115
Saudi Arabia, 110
Savile Row: HA sets up house in, 49–84, 124, 180; Queen's visits to, 90, 94; HA's staff in 96, 121, 142, 174, 185; shows in, 115; boutique dresses reproduced, 131; Japanese visit, 134; Ken Fleetwood and, 151–3; suits from, 155; John Fowler decorates room in, 167
Schiaparelli, Elsa, 50, 144
Schlusnus, Heinrich (singer), 169
Schubert, Franz, 15
Second World War *see* World War II
Selincourt Ltd., 69
Seoul, South Korea, 185
Shakespeare, William, *Henry IV (Part II)*, 5; *The Merchant of Venice*, 5; *A Midsummer Night's Dream*, 5; *Twelfth Night*, 6
Sharma, Dr Chandra, 151, 170–71
Sheridan, Richard Brinsley, *The Rivals*, 5
Shingleton, Fred, 4, 20–23, 26, 28–31, 33–4, 37, 94
Shingleton, Mrs Fred (*née* Gray), 3–4, 10–11, 20, 26; *see also* Miss Gray Ltd.
Siddons, Mrs, 164
skirts: length, 47, 144; mini, 104, 147–8; New Look, 145–6
sleeves: fullness characteristic of '80s fashion, 93; Queen's preference for, 103

Smethwick, 17
Soames, Lady, 105
South Africa, 86, 138–9
South America, 33, 36, 180
Southampton, 32
Spain, 17
Special Operations Executive, 35–6, 40–7, 53
Spencer, Lady Diana see Diana, Princess of Wales
Spencer, Countess (formerly Mrs Gerald Legge; Lady Lewisham; Countess of Dartmouth), 80
Sri Lanka, 111–2
Stapf, Carl, 128
Stiebel, Victor, 81, 145
Stockwell, Mr (in Paris), 12
Strauss, Richard, 15
suits: Morton's transformation of, 21, 24; HA lowers waistline, 25; nature of design, 26, 143–4; HA concentrates on, 38; Zazou, 47; HA designs men's ready-to-wear, 67–9; HA design in Vogue, 148; developments in men's, 155, 158–9
Sutherland, Miss (fitter), 53
Sutherland, Joan, 169–70
Swanage, 32
sweaters: in menswear, 156–7
Sweden, 119, 121
Switzerland, 16, 164
Sydney, Australia, 112, 130–31, 179, 185
Szell, Michael, 103

T. Lipson & Son Ltd., 130; see also Lipson, Jack
tailoring: and HA's innovations, 55; and HA's first Royal collection, 85–6; HA's forte, 151; and menswear, 155; see also jackets; suits
Tchaikovsky, Peter, 146
Tennyson, Alfred, Lord, 6
Texas, USA, 185
textiles, 97–9, 103, 108–9, 112, 143, 148, 154, 157
Teyte, Maggie, 169
Thaarup, Aage, 91
Thomas, Ian, 106–7, 111, 116, 119

Thornton, Bob, 72–3
Threlfall, Henry, 42
Thursby, Miss see ffrench, Mrs
ties: HA designs and sells, 65, 127, 141, 185
Times, The (newspaper), 30, 61
Todd, Mr (tailor), 24
Tokyo, Japan, 107, 135, 179, 185
Tonga, 97
Torcy, (Mahoney), 81
Toronto, Canada, 59, 146
Touraine, France, 7
trousers: women wear, 149; changes in design of men's, 158; see also jeans
Turnbull, David, 131
Turnbull, Kenneth, 131
tweeds: Lintons design, 50; see also textiles
Tweedsmuir, John, 32–3

USA: HA sells to, 25–6, 65–6, 73, 139; Board of Trade projects sending collection to, 36–7, 39; HA in, 56, 58, 60, 123–9, 142; customers from, 76; press in, 104; Queen visits, 108, 113, 116; Edana Romney in, 118; sales of jewellery in, 140; exports of designs to, 146; see also individual states and towns
utility clothing see austerity measures

Vanbrugh, Sir John, 145
Venice, Italy, 62
Verey, David, 181
Verey, Rosemary, 177, 181
Vernet, Mme see Vernet-Barbarroux, Mme
Vernet-Barbarroux, Mme, 11
Vernier, Rose, 91
Versailles, France, 98–100, 102–5, 110, 172
Victor, Mr (tailor), 52–3, 55, 57, 60–61
Victoria, Queen of England, 88, 154, 183
Vieux Cannet, Le, France, 11
Vinay, Ramón (singer), 169
Vionnet, Mme, 81
Viyella Ltd., 34
Vogel, Lucien, 64
Vogue (magazine), 24, 34, 64, 146, 148, 169

Voss, Countess (May), 164, 166, 168
Vreeland, Diana, 182

W (magazine), 124
W. A. Goold Ltd., 140
Wagner, Richard, 15
Wain Shiell, 52
waistlines: lowered, 25; importance,
    143; *see also* suits
Wallach, Hans, 65
Warburg, S. G. & Co Ltd (bankers),
    176
Waterman, Doug, 128
Webster, David, 88, 169
Webster, John, *The Duchess of Malfi*, 6
wedding dresses: House of Hardy
    Amies makes, 152–3
Wembley, 5
Wentworth Woodhouse, 48
Westminster, Loelia, Duchess of (*later*
    Lady Lindsay), 181
Wharton, Edith, 184
Whiteman, Roger, 79–80, 83, 135
Whitstable, 4

Who's Who, 180
Willingham, Ben, 125
Wilson, Jim, 128
Wimbledon, 126
Windsor, 2
Windsor Castle, 115
Witte, Johann (Jonny), 14–16, 28, 184
World War I, 3–4, 7
World War II, 30–48
Women's Wear Daily (newspaper), 124
Worth, House of, 26, 37–9, 46, 49–50,
    53, 56–9, 81, 94, 144
Worth, of Paris, 38
Wyser & Bryant Ltd., 68
Wyser, Mr (tailor) 68

Yorkshire, 48
Yves Saint Laurent, House of, 147

Zambia, 121
Zazou suits, 47
Ziegler, Alys, 34–5
Zipkin, Jerry, 116–7